Dinah Maria Mulock Craik

The Woman's Kingdom

A Love Story

Dinah Maria Mulock Craik

The Woman's Kingdom
A Love Story

ISBN/EAN: 9783744709316

Printed in Europe, USA, Canada, Australia, Japan

Cover: Foto ©Thomas Meinert / pixelio.de

More available books at **www.hansebooks.com**

BY THE AUTHOR OF "JOHN HALIFAX."

From the North British Review.

She attempts to show how the trials, perplexities, joys, sorrows, labors, and successes of life deepen or wither the character according to its inward bent.

She cares to teach, *not* how dishonesty is always plunging men into infinitely more complicated external difficulties than it would in real life, but how any continued insincerity gradually darkens and corrupts the very life-springs of the mind; *not* how all events conspire to crush an unreal being who is to be the "example" of the story, but how every event, adverse or fortunate, tends to strengthen and expand a high mind, and to break the springs of a selfish or merely weak and self-indulgent nature.

She does not limit herself to domestic conversations, and the mere shock of character on character; she includes a large range of events—the influence of worldly successes and failures—the risks of commercial enterprises—the power of social position—in short, the various elements of a wider economy than that generally admitted into a tale.

She has a true respect for her work, and never permits herself to "make books," and yet she has evidently very great facility in making them.

There are few writers who have exhibited a more marked progress, whether in freedom of touch or in depth of purpose, than the authoress of " The Ogilvies " and " John Halifax."

HANNAH.   8vo, Paper, 50 cents ; 12mo, Cloth, $1 50.

MOTHERLESS ; or, A Parisian Family.   Translated from the French of Madame De Witt, *née* Guizot.   For Girls in their Teens.   Illustrated.   12mo, Cloth, $1 50.

FAIR FRANCE.   Impressions of a Traveller.   12mo, Cloth, $1 50.

A BRAVE LADY.   With Illustrations.   8vo, Paper, $1 00; Cloth, $1 50; 12mo, Cloth, $1 50.

A FRENCH COUNTRY FAMILY.   Translated from the French of Madame De Witt, *née* Guizot.   Illustrated. 12mo, Cloth, $1 50.

A HERO, AND OTHER TALES.   12mo, Cloth, $1 25.

A LIFE FOR A LIFE. 8vo, Paper, 50 cents; 12mo, Cloth, $1 50.

AGATHA'S HUSBAND. 8vo, Paper, 50 cents; 12mo, Cloth, $1 50.

A NOBLE LIFE. 12mo, Cloth, $1 50.

AVILLION, AND OTHER TALES. 8vo, Paper, $1 25.

CHRISTIAN'S MISTAKE. 12mo, Cloth, $1 50.

FAIRY BOOK. Illustrated. 12mo, Cloth, $1 50.

HEAD OF THE FAMILY. 8vo, Paper, 75 cents; 12mo, Cloth, $1 50.

JOHN HALIFAX, GENTLEMAN. 8vo, Paper, 75 cents; 12mo, Cloth, $1 50.

MISTRESS AND MAID. 8vo, Paper, 50 cents; 12mo, Cloth, $1 50.

NOTHING NEW. 8vo, Paper, 50 cents.

OGILVIES. 8vo, Paper, 50 cents; 12mo, Cloth, $1 50.

OLIVE. 8vo, Paper, 50 cents; 12mo, Cloth, $1 50.

OUR YEAR. Illustrated. 16mo, Cloth, Gilt Edges, $1 00.

STUDIES FROM LIFE. 12mo, Cloth, $1 25.

THE TWO MARRIAGES. 12mo, Cloth, $1 50.

THE UNKIND WORD, AND OTHER STORIES. 12mo, Cloth, $1 50.

THE WOMAN'S KINGDOM. Illustrated. 8vo, Paper, $1 00; Cloth, $1 50; 12mo, Cloth, $1 50.

BOOKS FOR GIRLS. Written or Edited by the Author of " John Halifax." Illustrated. 16mo, Cloth, 90 cents each. Now ready :

 LITTLE SUNSHINE'S HOLIDAY.
 THE COUSIN FROM INDIA.
 TWENTY YEARS AGO.

☞ HARPER & BROTHERS *will send either of the above works by mail, postage prepaid, to any part of the United States, on receipt of the price.*

THESEUS AND ARIADNE.

WOMAN'S KINGDOM.

A LOVE STORY.

BY THE AUTHOR OF

"JOHN HALIFAX, GENTLEMAN," "HANNAH," "A BRAVE LADY,"
"MISTRESS AND MAID," "OLIVE," "THE OGILVIES,"
"THE HEAD OF THE FAMILY," &c., &c.

"Queens you must always be: queens to your lovers; queens to your husbands and your sons; queens of higher mystery to the world beyond. . . . But, alas! you are too often idle and careless queens, grasping at majesty in the least things, while you abdicate it in the greatest!"—JOHN RUSKIN.

NEW YORK:

HARPER & BROTHERS, PUBLISHERS,

FRANKLIN SQUARE.

1872.

Dedication:

TO

MONA MARGARET PATON.

My little girl! sweet uncrowned queen
    Of a fair kingdom, dim and far;
Whose budding life 'neath rosy screen
Scarce recognizes yet, I ween,
    What lives of other women are;

Child, when the burden we lay down,
    Thy tender hands must lift and bear;
The household sceptre and love-crown,
Green-wreathed, or hung with dead leaves brown—
    Take courage. Both are holy wear.

Better to love than to be loved:
    Better to serve, and serving guide,
Than wait, with idle oars unproved,
And flapping sail by each breath moved,
    The turning of life's solemn tide.

Live, work, and love; as Heaven assign
    For heaven, or man, thy sacred part;
Ancestress of a noble line,
Or calm in maidenly decline;—
    But keep till death the woman's heart.

THE WOMAN'S KINGDOM.

"Queens you must always be: Queens to your lovers: Queens to your husbands and your sons: Queens of higher mystery to the world beyond. ......But, alas! You are too often idle and careless Queens, grasping at majesty in the least things, while you abdicate it in the greatest."—JOHN RUSKIN.

THE TWO SISTERS.

CHAPTER I.

"OH, Edna, I am so tired! And this is the very dullest place in all the world!"

"Do you think so, dear? And yet it was the place you specially wanted to go to."

A 2

Edna spoke in the soothing yet cheerful tone which all people—that is, people like Edna Kenderdine—instinctively use towards an invalid; and, laying down her work—she rarely was without some sort of work in her tiny hands—looked tenderly and anxiously at her sister. For they were twin-sisters; though, as sometimes happens with twins, so excessively unlike that they would scarcely have been supposed akin at all.

"You know, Letty dear, that as soon as you began to get better the Isle of Wight was the place you fancied for a change."

"Yes; but we might have found many a nicer spot in the Isle of Wight than this—Ryde, for instance, where there are plenty of houses, and a good pier, and probably an esplanade. Oh, how I used to enjoy the Brighton esplanade in the days when I was a little girl, and we were rich and happy!"

"Were we happy then? I don't remember. But I know I have been quite as happy since."

"You always are happy," returned the invalid, with a vexed air. "I think nothing in the world would make you miserable."

Edna winced a little, but she was sitting in the shadow of the window-curtain, and was not seen. "Come, come," she said, "it is of no use quarrelling with me because I will not see the black side of things; time enough for that when we go home to Kensington. Here we are, out on a holiday, with beautiful weather, comfortable lodgings, no school to teach, and nothing in the wide world to do but to amuse ourselves."

"Amuse ourselves! How can we? We don't know a soul here. In-doors there is nothing to do, and nobody to come and see us; and out-of-doors there is not a creature to look at or to speak to."

"I thought we wanted to get out of the way of our fellow-creatures. Besides, they would not care for us just now. It is not every lodging-house, even, that would have taken us in, and we lately out of scarlet-fever."

"We need not have told that."

"Oh, Letty! we must have told."

"Edna, you are so ridiculously conscientious! I have no patience with you!"

Edna made no reply; indeed, it was useless replying to the poor convalescent, whose thin face betrayed that she was at the precise stage of recovery when every thing jars against the irritable nerves, and the sickly, morbid fancy changes its moods twenty times a day. Otherwise, to people in the somewhat dreary position of these two young school-mistresses—driven from their labors in the midst of the half-year by a dangerous fever which had compelled the shutting up of the school, brought the one sister nearly to death's-door, and the other not far from it by the fatigue of sick-nursing—even to them the parlor they sat in was not uncheerful. It was very neat and clean, and it had a large bay-window looking out on a verandah; beyond that a little garden; farther, a narrow strip of bright, green, grassy cliff, fringed with a low hedge, where the "white-blossomed sloe" was in full glory, and a pair of robin-redbreasts were building and singing all the day long. Below, at the cliff's foot, the unseen sea was heard to tumble and roll with a noisy murmur; but far away in the distance it spread itself out in sleepy stillness, shimmering and glancing in the sunshine of early spring. The sight of it might well have gladdened many a dull heart; and the breath of it, which came in salt and fresh, though not cold, through the half-open window, might have given health to many a sick soul, as well as body—granting that soul to be one of those whom Nature can comfort. It is not every one whom she can.

Poor Letty was not of those thus comforted. Her eyes looked as sad as ever, and there was a sharp, metallic ring in her voice as she said:

"I can't imagine, Edna, why you make so much fuss about the fever. You would drive every body away from us as if we had had the plague. This morning I overheard you insisting that the gentleman who wants the opposite parlor should be told distinctly what had been the matter with me. It is very foolish, when I am quite well now."

"Yes, dear, quite well, thank God!" returned Edna, soothingly. "And the gentleman said he was not in the least afraid; besides, he was a doctor."

"Was he, indeed? A real gentleman, then!"

"Supposing that a doctor is—and he certainly ought to be—a real gentleman."

"Nonsense! I mean a professional man; not one of those horrid shop-keepers whose children we have to teach —how I hate them all! And we must go back and begin again after midsummer. Oh, Edna, I wish I were dead!"

"I don't, and I doubt if you do—not just this very minute. For there is your dinner coming in—and you like fish, and you declared you were so frightfully hungry."

"You are always making fun of me," said the sick sister, half plaintively. Nevertheless she yielded to the influence of that soft, caressing, and yet encouraging tone; her gloomy looks relaxed into a faint smile, and she fell to her simple invalid meal of fried sole and rice-pudding with an appetite that proved she was really getting well, in spite of her despondency and fretfulness. Edna sat by her and ate her own cold mutton with an equal relish; and then the sisters began to talk again.

"So, after to-day, we shall not be the only lodgers in the house. How very annoying!"

"I don't think the new-comers will harm us much. They are likely to be as quiet as ourselves. Besides, they will have a fellow-feeling for us. One of them is also an invalid, and a great deal worse than you, Letty."

"The doctor?"

"No; his brother, whom he has brought here for change of air."

"Did you see them? Really, you might have told me all this before. I should have been so glad of any thing to interest me. And you seem to have inquired all about them."

"Of course I did. It was very important to us whom we had in the next parlor, and probably to them also, in the young man's sickly state. I dare say the brother took as much pains as I did to find out all about his opposite neighbors."

"Did you see him?"

"No; except his back, which was rather round, and the coat very shabby at the shoulders."

"He isn't a gentleman, then?"

"I can't tell. If he happened to be a poor gentleman, why should not his coat be shabby at the shoulders?"

"I don't like poverty," said Letty, with a slight shrug; and drawing round her the soft, rich shawl, relic of the "happy" days she regretted, when the little twins were expected to be co-heiresses, and not school-mistresses. Those days were dim enough now. The orphans had been brought up for governesses, and had gone out as governesses, until difficulties arising, from Letty's extreme beauty on the one hand, and Edna's fond clinging to her sister on the other, they had resolved to make themselves a home by setting up one of those middle-class day-schools which are so plentiful in the immediate suburbs of London. It had done well, on the whole; at least it had sufficed to maintain them. They were still young women — only twenty-six—though both, Edna especially, had a certain air of formality and authority which all school-mistresses seem gradually to acquire. But they were, as could be seen at a glance, well-bred, well-educated women; and, besides, Letitia was one of those remarkably handsome persons of whom one scarcely sees half a dozen in a lifetime, and about whose beauty there can not be two opinions. You might not fancy her style; you might have some ideal of your own quite contrary to it; but if you had eyes in your head you must acknowledge that she was beautiful, and would remain so, more or less, to the last day of her life. Hers was a combination very rarely to be met with; of form and color, figure and face—enough completely to satisfy the artist-eye, and indicate to the poetical imagination plenty of loveliness spiritual beneath the loveliness external. Even her illness had scarcely clouded it; and with her tall figure shrouded in shawls, her magnificent brown hair cut short under a cap, and her graceful hands, white and wasted, lying on her lap, she was "interesting" to the last degree.

Indeed, to tell the truth, Letty Kenderdine's beauty had been the real hindrance to her governess-ship. Wherever she went every body fell in love with her. Mothers dreaded her for their grown-up sons; weak-minded wives were uneasy concerning their husbands. Not that Letty was the least to blame; she was so used to admiration that she took it all quite calmly. Too cold for passion, too practical for philandering, there was no fear of her exciting any unlawful jealousies; and as for regular love-affairs, though she generally had one or more on hand, it was a very mild form of the article. She never "committed" herself. She might have married twenty times over—poor tutors, country clergymen, and struggling men of business; even a few younger sons of good families: but she had, as she said, a dislike to poverty, especially matrimonial poverty.

> "Will the flame that you're so rich in
> Light a fire in the kitchen,
> Or the little god of love turn the spit, spit, spit?"

was the burden of her sweet, smiling refusals, which sent her lovers away twice as mad as they came. But, though she smiled, Letty never relented.

So, though she had been once or twice on the brink of an engagement, she had never fallen over the precipice; and as she confided all her difficulties to Edna, and Edna (who had never any of her own) helped her out of them, they came to nothing worse than "difficulties." True, they had lost her a situation or two, and, indeed, had determined Edna to the point which she carried out—as she did most of her determinations, in her own quiet way—the setting up of a school; but they never weighed seriously upon either sister's mind. Only sometimes, when the school duties were hard, Letty would sigh over the comparatively easy days when she was residing in "high" families, well-treated, as somehow she always had been, for there was a grace and dignity in her which compelled re-

spectful treatment. She would regret the lost luxuries—
a carriage to drive in and a park to walk in with her pupils, large rooms, plenty of servants, and dainty feeding—
recapitulating all the good things she used to have, balancing them against the ill things she had now, until she
fancied she had made a change for the worse; complained
that her present life was not half so pleasant as that of
a resident governess, and lamented pathetically over the
cause of all—what she called "my unfortunate appearance."

Still the fact was patent—neither to be sighed down nor
laughed down—and it had a laughable side—Letty was
much too handsome for a governess. Too handsome, indeed, for most of the useful purposes of life. She could
not pass anywhere unnoticed; to send her out shopping
was a thing difficult enough, and as for her taking a walk
alone in pleasant Kensington Gardens, or the lonely Brompton Road, it was a thing quite impossible. Edna often said,
with a queer mixture of perplexity and pride, that her beautiful sister was as much trouble to her as any baby. And,
invalid as Letty now was, it must be confessed that not
without a secret alarm had Edna heard of and made inquiries about the impending lodgers.

Letty half guessed this, though she was not very vain;
for she had long become used to her "unfortunate appearance;" and, besides, your superlatively handsome people
generally take their universally-acknowledged honors as
composedly as a millionaire takes his money, or a poet-
laureate his crown. When, after Edna's communication
respecting the gentleman's shabby shoulders, the two sisters' eyes met, Letty broke into an actual smile.

"How old is he? Are you afraid that something will
happen?"

"Perhaps. Something of that sort always is happening,
you know," said Edna, dolefully; and then both sisters burst
out laughing, which quite restored Letty's good-humor.

"Come, dear, don't be alarmed. He will not fall in love
with me—I'm getting too ugly and too old. And as for
myself, no harm will come to me. I don't like shabbiness,

and of all people alive, the person I should least like to
marry would be a doctor. Only fancy having one's husband at every body's beck and call—out at all hours, day
and night; never able to take me to a party—or give me
a party at home without being fetched away in the middle
of it; going to all sorts of nasty places and nasty people;
bringing home fevers, and small-pox, and the like—oh!
what a dreadful life!"

"Do you think so?" said Edna. "Why, when I was a
girl I used to fancy that had I been a boy, and could
choose my profession, of all professions I should choose a
doctor's. There is something in it so grand, and yet so
useful. He has so much power in his hands. Such unlimited influence over souls as well as bodies. Of course it
would be a hard life—nothing smooth or pleasant about it
—but it would be a life full of interest, with endless opportunities of usefulness. I don't mean merely of saving people's lives, but of putting their lives right, both mentally
and physically, as nobody but a doctor can do. Hardly
even a clergyman could come so near my ideal of the perfect existence—' he went about doing good.'"

Edna spoke earnestly, as sometimes, though not often,
she was roused to speak, and then her plain little face
lighted up, and her tiny form took an unwonted grace and
dignity. Plain as she was—as noticeably so as her sister
was handsome—there was a certain character about her
in her small firm mouth, and babyish yet determined little chin—in her quick motions and active ways, and especially in her hands, the only decided beauty she possessed—which, though they flitted hither and thither, light
as snow-flakes and pretty as rose-leaves, had an air of
strength, purpose, and practicability which indicated fully
what she was—this merry, busy-bee-like little woman—
who

> "Gathered honey all the day
> From every opening flower;"

but yet, on occasions, could be the very soul of the household—the referee, and judge, and decisive voice in all matters, great or small.

"Edna, you are preaching me quite a sermon," said Letty, yawning. "And I really don't deserve it. Did I ever say I wouldn't marry a doctor?—even this very doctor of yours, if he wishes it particularly. I am sure," she added, plaintively, with an anxious glance towards the mirror, "it is time I should make up my mind to marry somebody. Another illness like the last would altogether destroy my appearance."

"What nonsense you talk!"

"No, it isn't nonsense," said Letty, with a queer humility. "It is all very well for you, who are clever and can talk, and do things prettily and practically, and make yourself happy in your own way, so that, indeed, it is little matter whether you are ever married or not. But if any body marries me, it will be only for my appearance. I must make my hay while the sun shines. Heigh-ho! I wish something would happen—something to amuse us in this dull place. Do tell me a little more about the new lodgers."

"I have nothing to tell; and besides—there they are!"

At that moment, coming round the corner of the house (the Misses Kenderdine's parlor-window had to be passed in reaching the front door), appeared a porter and two portmanteaus, and immediately afterwards a Bath chair. Therein sat a figure so muffled up, in spite of the sunshiny day, as to awaken a feeling of compassion in any beholder.

"Do come away, Letty. It is the sick brother. He may not like to be looked at."

"But I must look at him. I have not had the least thing to interest me all day. Don't be cross. He shall not see me. I will hide behind the window-curtains."

And curiosity quite overcoming her languor, she left her easy-chair, and crouched down in a very uncomfortable attitude to watch the proceedings outside.

"Do come and look too, Edna. I wonder—is he a man or a boy? He has got no whiskers, and he is so very thin. He looks a walking skeleton beside his stout brother. Do say if that big, awkward man is the brother, the doctor,

I mean, whom you are so extremely anxious for me to marry."

"Letty, what foolishness!"

"Well, I'll promise to think about him if he ever gives me the chance. He does look like a gentleman, in spite of his shabby coat. But, as for the other, you need not be alarmed about him. He seems to have one foot in the grave already. Just come and peep at him. No one can see you, I am sure."

Edna looked—she hardly knew why, unless out of pure compassion. It was a face that any woman's heart, old or young, would have melted over—white, wan, with heavy circles under the large eyes, and a drawn look of permanent pain round the mouth. One of those faces, so delicately outlined, so almost feminine in contour, as to make one say, instinctively, "He must be very like his mother," and to wish likewise that he might always have his mother or his wife close at hand to take care of him. For it was undoubtedly one of those sensitive yet passionate faces which indicate a temperament that requires incessant taking care of—the care that only a woman can take. Though the big brother seemed tender enough. He wrapped him, and lifted him, and talked to him gently, as if he had been a child. Something touchingly child-like—the poetic nature is always young—was in the poor fellow's looks, as he wearily obeyed; doing all he was told to do, though every movement seemed a pain.

"I wonder what his illness has been," said Edna, won into a sympathy that deadened even her sense of propriety. "Not consumption, I fancy. I should rather say he was just recovering from rheumatic fever."

"Never mind his illness. What do you think of himself?"

"I think it is one of the most interesting faces I ever saw. But if ever I saw death written in a face— Poor fellow—and so young, too!"

"Not much above twenty, certainly."

"There, he has turned, and is looking right in at our window. Come away—you must come, or he will certainly see you, Letty!"

It was too late. He had seen her; for the poor sensitive youth started violently, and a sudden flush came over his wan cheek. He drew back hastily, and pulled his fur cap closer down over his face.

Edna rose quickly and shut the Venetian blind. "It is cruel — absolutely cruel—to stare at a person who is in that sickly, nervous state. How angry I should have been if any body had done it to you when you were ill! and I am certain he saw you."

"POOR FELLOW—AND SO YOUNG, TOO!"

"Never mind: the sight is not so very dreadful; it won't kill him, probably," laughed Letty, whose spirits had quite risen under this unwonted excitement. "Perhaps it will even do him good, if he wants amusement as much as I do; and he need not excite your sisterly fears: he won't fall in love with me. He is too ill to think of any body but himself."

"Poor fellow!" again said Edna, with a sigh.

She was too well accustomed to her sister's light talk to take it seriously, or indeed to heed it at all. People cease to notice the idiosyncrasies of those they have been accus-

tomed to all their life. Probably, if any other young
woman had talked as Letty did, Edna would have disliked
it extremely; but she did not mind Letty—it was her
way. Besides, she was her sister—her own flesh and
blood, and the two loved one another dearly.

Shortly the slight bustle in the hall subsided, the Bath
chair was wheeled empty away, and a confusion of footsteps outside indicated that the sick man was being carried up stairs by the brother; then the house sank into
silence.

Edna drew up the blind, and stood gazing out meditatively upon the sunshiny sea.

"What are you thinking of?" Letty asked.

"Of that poor fellow, and whether this place will do
him any good—whether he will live or die."

"The latter seems most likely."

"Yes; and it seems to me so sad, especially—" and her
voice sank a little — "especially since, thank God! we
have passed through our time of terror and are safe again.
So very sad, with every thing outside bright and happy;
trees budding, birds singing, the sky smiling all over, and
the sea smiling back at it again, as if there was no such
thing as death in the world. How the brother's heart
must ache through it all!"

"The big brother—the doctor you mean?"

"Yes; and, being a doctor, he must know the truth—
that is, if it is to be—if the young man is not likely to
recover."

"Yet the doctor seems cheerful enough. As it sounded
outside in the hall, I thought I never heard a more cheerful voice."

"People often speak cheerfully—they are obliged to
learn to do it—when—" Here Edna suddenly stopped.
It was not wise to enlighten Letty, still an invalid, upon
her own sad sick-room experience. "But things may be
more hopeful than we suppose. Nevertheless, I am very
sorry for our new neighbors—for them both."

"So am I. We must ask the landlady all about them
when she brings in tea."

But though, in her extreme dearth of outside interests, Letty's curiosity became so irresistible that she hurried on the tea by half an hour, her inquiries resulted in very little.

Mrs. Williams knew no more of her new inmates than most sea-side landladies do of their lodgers. The gentlemen had come from the inn; they were named Stedman —Dr. and Mr. Stedman—and she rather thought they were from London. "As the ladies also lived in London, perhaps they might know something about them," suggested the simple island woman, who was quite as eager to get as to give information, for she owned to being rather sorry she had taken them in.

"Why?" asked Edna.

"I do believe the young gentleman is only brought here to die; and death is such a bad thing to happen in any lodgings."

"Nay, we will hope for the best. This fine, pure air may restore him. See how strong my sister is getting."

"Yes, indeed, miss; and so I told his brother. I wished he could have seen how wonderfully the young lady had picked up since she came. And he said, 'Yes, she didn't look a bit like an invalid now.'"

"Had he seen me?" asked Letty, half smiling.

"I don't know, miss; but he has got sharp, noticeable eyes—real doctor's eyes."

"Oh!" said Letty, and subsided into silence.

"Does he seem very anxious about his sick brother?" Edna inquired.

"Ay, sometimes, to judge by his look. But he talks quite cheerful-like. Just hark! you can hear 'em a-laughing together now."

"How I wish we had any thing to make us laugh!" sighed Letty, when the door closed; and the important event of tea being over, she relapsed into her former dullness, leaned back again in her easy-chair, letting her hands fall drearily on her lap—such soft, handsome, idle, helpless hands.

"Shall I read?" said Edna, with an anxious glance at

A DAUGHTER OF THE GODS.

the clock. It was too late to go out, and it was many—oh! so many hours till bed-time.

"You know I never cared for reading, especially poetry books, which are all you brought with us."

"Shall I try to get a novel from the library?"

"Threepence a volume, and you'll grumble at the extravagance, and I shall be sure to go to sleep over it too. Well, I think I will lie down and sleep a little, for I am so tired I don't know what to do."

She rose, walked once or twice across the room, looking most majestic in her long, soft, flowing draperies—for it was twenty years ago, and women's draperies were both graceful and majestic then: with her large lovely form and classical face she was the personification of Tennyson's line—

"A daughter of the gods: divinely tall,
And most divinely fair."

And when she lay down, she idealized the common horse-hair lodging-house sofa by an outline most artistically beautiful—fit for a sleeping Dido or dying Cleopatra. Such women nature makes rarely, very rarely; queens of beauty, crowned or uncrowned, who instinctively take their places in the tournament of life, and "rain influ-

ence," whether consciously or not, to an almost fearful extent upon us weak mortals, especially men mortals, who,
even the best of them, are always prone to reconstrue the
dogma that the good is necessarily the beautiful, and to
presuppose the highest beauty to be the highest good.

But this is wandering into metaphysics, of which, however she might be the cause of them in others, there certainly was no trace in Letty Kenderdine. She lay down
and made herself comfortable, or rather was made comfortable by her sister, with shawls and pillows; then she
fell sound asleep, like any other mortal woman, breathing
so peacefully and deeply that, if it would not utterly destroy the romance about her, I feel bound to confess she
almost snored.

Edna sat beside her till certain of her repose, and then
crept softly away. Not for idleness, and not for pleasure,
though the sweet evening tempted her sorely, with its
sunset of rose and gray, its fresh sea-breeze, and, as is
found along most of the south coast of England, and, especially the Isle of Wight, its delicious mingling of sea
and country pleasures. Above the lapping of the tide on
the beach below was heard the good-night warble of the
robins and the deep note of the thrush; and besides the
salt sea smell there was an atmosphere of trees budding
and flowers blossoming, giving a sense of vague delight,
and tender foreboding of some unknown joy.

It touched Edna; she could not tell why, except that
she loved the spring, and this was the first April she had
spent out of London for several years; scarcely since
those dimly-remembered years of their country house in
Hampshire, which, to her, balanced Letty's memories of
the Brighton esplanade. One had been the summer, the
other the winter residence of the rich merchant, who, absorbed in money-making, and losing fortune and life together, had left no remembrances to his motherless twin-
girls but these.

They recurred at times, each in their turn, and to each
sister according to her nature. To Edna at this moment
came a rush of the old child-life—the pony she rode—a

pretty little gentle thing, loved like a human companion;
a certain stream, which danced through a primrose wood,
and over which dragon-flies used to skim, and where endless handfuls of king-cups grew; an upland meadow, yellow with cowslips—Edna could smell the odor of it yet.

"How I should like to make another cowslip-ball! I
believe I could do it as well as ever. I wonder if cowslips grow anywhere about here!"

And then she smiled at the silliness of a school-mistress
wanting to make cowslip-balls, and wondered at the foolish feeling which came over her in her monotonous life;
and why it was that, just rising up out of the long strain
of anxiety, her heart was conscious of a sudden rebound—
a wild longing after happiness: not merely the busy content of her level life, but actual happiness. In picturing
it, though it was very vague too and formless, she, however, did not picture the usual sort of happiness which
comes most natural at her age. Unlike her sister, no lovers had ever troubled Edna's repose. In the dull city
family where she had been governess ever since leaving
school no such things were ever thought of; besides, Edna
was plain, and knew it—felt it too—perhaps all the keener
for her sister's beauty and her own intense admiration of
the same. No; Edna Kenderdine was not a marrying
woman. She herself was convinced she would be an old
maid, and had laid her plans accordingly; and mapped
out her future life with a quiet acquiescence in, and yet a
full recognition of—alas! what woman was ever without
that?—its sad imperfectness.

Thus her ideal of happiness was not love, or, at least, not
consciously, and certainly not love on her own account.
This golden dream — this seeming height of complete
felicity — was thought of with reference to Letty alone.
For herself, she hardly knew what she wanted; perhaps
a better school, more pupils, and these of a higher class,
for it was hard and thankless work trying to make lit-
'tle common girls into little gentlewomen. Or possibly—
though to that El Dorado Edna scarcely dared to lift her
eyes—some extraordinary windfall of fortune—a legacy,

or the like—which would forever lift her out of the necessity of keeping school at all, and enable her to set up a
cottage in the country—ever so small, she did not care, so
that it was only in the country, and had a garden to it,
and fields around it, where she might do as she liked all
day long, without being haunted by the necessity of
school-teaching, or by that dread of the future, of breaking down helpless in the midst of her career, which, since
the fever time, had often painfully pursued her. She herself, though not exactly ill, had been very much enfee-
bled; and probably it was this weak condition of body
which made the little woman mentally less brave than
usual; caused her to long, with a sore yearning, not merely to be sheltered from evil, but to have her dull life turned into brightness by some absolute tangible good.

So, while Letty slept—the sound, healthy sleep of which
her easy temperament never made any difficulty—Edna
stood looking out on the twilight sea, still thinking—
thinking—till the tears came into her eyes, and rolled
slowly down.

They were soon wiped away—not dashed off, but quietly wiped away with a resolute hand. She could not
have repressed them, they would have choked her; but
she could help indulging in them, taking a sentimental
pleasure over them, or exalting them into a real grief.
Alas! she knew what real grief was when Letty was at
the crisis of scarlet-fever.

"No! I'll not cry—it's wicked! What have I to cry
about? when my sister is nearly well, and we shall be
able to gather the school together very soon, and meantime we have enough money to last us, and no other
cares. There is much more to be thankful for than afraid
of. And now, before she wakes, let me see exactly how
we stand."

She took her little writing-desk to the window, that she
might catch the utmost of the fading light, and with one
anxious glance at the sofa, set herself to a piece of work
which always fidgeted Letty—the balancing of her weekly accounts. Nominally the sisters kept these week and

B

week about; but Letty's week was always behindhand,
and caused her such distress that gradually Edna took
the whole upon herself—a very small whole; a ledger
that a man and a millionaire, or even a petty merchant,
would have laughed at, and wondered how it could possibly make the womanish head ache and the womanish
heart beat, as it did many a time. For Edna was no
genius at arithmetic; besides, hers was not the amateur
masculine arithmetic, worked upon paper, in thousands
and tens of thousands, though the total, be it loss or gain,
affects little the current expenses of daily life—since in
this strange commercial world of ours a man may risk or
lose a quarter of a million, or go through a bankruptcy or
two, yet still keep his carriage, and eat his diurnal dinner
—just as handsome a dinner as ever—though oftentimes
the appetite brought to it must be small.

But Edna's arithmetic was a different thing. To her a
balance on the one side or other of that tiny page implied
an easy mind and a gay heart, or else—well, it implied
want of needful clothes, of household comforts, perhaps
even of sufficient food. Only want—the sacrifice of
things pleasant and desirable. That other alternative,
debt, in all its agonies, humiliation, and terrors, these
poor school-mistresses knew not: never would be likely
to know, since, opposite as their characters were, the two
Misses Kenderdine had one grand point in common—they
would have starved rather than have owed any man a
half-penny.

So poor little Edna sat at her task; and it was a task,
for she did not like it any more than she liked school-
teaching; but Letty liked it still less than she, and since
it had inevitably to be done, of course Edna had to do it.
This was the law of their life together, and always had
been.

She sat, her head propped on her two hands, quite absorbed. Pathetically so, for she could not make her accounts meet; there was a half-crown gone a-missing somewhere; and a half-crown was an important sum to her,
poor thing! Not for itself, but for what it represented—

a fortnight's butter, or a pair of gloves for Letty, or something else that otherwise would require to be done without. She racked her brains to remember how she had spent it, added up the conflicting columns of figures again and again, and counted and re-counted the contents of her two purses—one for current coin, the other the grand receptacle of the family income.

Vain, vain! Poor Edna could not make matters right. Her head burned, her brow throbbed — she pushed her hair back from it with trembling fingers—she was very nearly crying.

It was a small thing—a silly thing almost; but then she had been weakened by anxiety and fatigue, and do what she could, the future rose up before her darker, and reasonably darker than it had ever done before. What if the pupils, scared by fever, should not readily return? What if she and her sister were to be left with a house on their hands, the rent to be paid, the servant to be kept, and nothing to do it with? That morbid dread of the future—that bitter sense of helplessness and forlornness which all working-women have at times, came upon Edna, and made her think with a strange momentary envy of the women who did not work, who had brothers and fathers to work for them, or at least to help them with the help that a man, and only a man, can give.

And then looking up, for the first time for many minutes, Edna became aware of two eyes watching her, resting on her with such an expression of kindliness and pity, the sort of half-amused pity that a man would show to a troubled and perplexed child, that this poor child—she was strangely young still in many ways—looked fearlessly back into them, almost with a sort of appeal, as if the observer had been an authorized friend, who could have helped her did he choose. But the moment after she drew back, exceedingly annoyed; and the gazer also drew back, made a slight apologetic half-bow, then blushed violently all over his face, as if conscious that he had been doing a most unwarrantable and ungentlemanly thing, rose from his bench by the window, and walked hastily away.

As he turned, by the broad stooping shoulders and well-worn coat rather than by the face, which she had not seen until now, being so attracted by the face of the invalid brother, Edna recognized the doctor, Dr. Stedman.

CHAPTER II.

THIS will be a thorough "love" story. I do not pretend to make it any thing else. There are other things in life besides love; but every body who has lived at all knows that love is the very heart of life, the pivot upon which its whole machinery turns; without which no human existence can be complete, and with which, however broken and worn in part, it can still go on working somehow, and working to a comparative useful and cheerful end.

An author once wrote a book of which the heroine was supposed to be painted from a real living woman, whose relations were rather pleased than not at the accidental resemblance. "Only," said they, with dignified decorum, "in one point the likeness fails; our Anastasia was never in love with any body." "Then," replied the amused author, "I certainly can not have painted her, for she would have been of no use to me; such an abnormal specimen of humanity is not a woman at all."

No. A life without love in it must of necessity be an imperfect, an unnatural life. The love may be happy or unhappy, noble or ignoble, requited or unrequited; but it must be, or have been, there. Love absolute. Not merely the tie of blood, the bond of friendship, the many close affections which make existence sweet; but the one, closest of all, the love between man and woman—which is the root of the family life, and the family life is the key to half the mysteries of the universe.

And so, without disguise of purpose, and rather glorying in the folly, if folly it be, I confess this to be a mere love-tale, nothing more. No grand "purpose" in it, no dramatic effects—scarcely even a "story;" but a few pages out of the book of daily life, the outside of which looks often so common and plain; and the inside—but One only reads that.

Under Mrs. Williams's commonplace unconscious roof were gathered these four young people, strangers to one another, and ignorant of their mutual and individual destinies, afterwards to become so inextricably mingled, tangled, and crossed. The like continually happens; in fact it must, in most cases, necessarily happen. The first chance-meeting, or what appears chance; the first indifferent word or hap-hazard incident—from these things do almost all love-stories date. For in all true marriages now, as in Eden, the man and woman do not deliberately seek, but are brought to one another; happy those who afterwards can recognize that the hand which led his Eve to Adam was that of an invisible God!

But this only comes afterwards. No sentimental premonitions weighed on the hearts of any of these, the two young men and two young women, who had, each and all, their own lives to live, their own separate cares and joys. For even if blessed with the closest bonds of fraternity, every soul is more or less alone, or feels so, till the magic other soul appears, which, if fate allows, shall remove solitude forever. There may or may not be a truth in the doctrine of love at first sight, but it is, like the doctrine of instantaneous conversion, too rarely experienced to be much believed in. Ordinary men and women walk blindfold to the very verge of their fate, nor recognize it as fate till it is long past. Which fact ought to be, to both young folks and their guardians, at once a consolation and a warning.

Edna, when, immediately after the doctor's disappearance, the entrance of candles awakened Letty, told her sister frankly, and with considerable amusement, of the steadfast stare which for the moment had annoyed her.

"At least, I should have been annoyed had it been you, Letty. But with me of course it meant nothing; merely a little harmless curiosity. Certainly, as Mrs. Williams says, he has thorough 'doctor's eyes.' They seem able

to see every thing. As a doctor ought to see, you
know."

"And what color were they, and what sort of a face was
it altogether?"

"I really can not tell. A nice, kindly sort of face, and
that is all I know."

"But, Edna, if I am to marry him you ought to know.
So look hard next time, and tell me exactly what he is
like."

"Very well," said Edna, laughing; thankful for any
little joke that lightened the heavy depression which was
the hardest thing to contend with in Letty's present state.
And then she took to her work and forgot all about it.
Not until, after putting her sister to bed, she came down
again for one quiet hour, to do some needful sewing, and
institute a last and finally successful search among the odd
corners of her tired brain for the missing half-crown, did
Edna remember the doctor or his inquisitive stare.

"I wonder if he noticed what I was doing, and whether
he thought me silly, or was sorry for me. Perhaps he is
good at arithmetic. Well, if there could be any advantage in having a man belonging to one, it would be to
help in adding up one's weekly accounts. I shall advise
Letty to make that proviso in her marriage settlement."

While the sisters thus summarily dismissed the question
of their new neighbors, their neighbors scarcely thought
of them at all. Dr. Stedman sat by his brother's bedside,
trying by every means he could think of to make the weary
evening slip by, without forestalling the burden of the
still heavier night. He talked; he read a little out of an
old *Times*—first the solid leaders, and then a criticism on
the pictures forthcoming in the Royal Academy Exhibition, till, seeing the latter excited his patient too much, he
ingeniously shortened it, and went back to the heavy de-
bates and other masculine portions of the newspaper. But
in all he did, and earnestly as he tried to do it, there was
something a little clumsy, like a man—and one who is altogether a man—not accustomed to women's society and
influence. There was nothing rough or untender about

him; nay, there was exceeding gentleness in his eyes and voice; he tried to do his very best; but he did it with a certain awkwardness that no invalid could help feeling in some degree, especially such a nervous invalid as this.

The two brothers were very unlike—as unlike as the two sisters who sat below stairs. And yet there was a curious "family" expression; the kindred blood peeping out, pleadingly, amidst all dissimilarities of character and temperament. The younger was dark; the elder fair. The features were not unlike, but in one face delicate and regular; in the other, large and rugged. The younger had apparently lived altogether the student's life; while the elder had been knocked about the world, receiving many a hard hit, and learning, in self-preservation, to give a hard hit back again if necessary. Besides, an occasional contraction of the brow, and a slight projection of the under lip, showed that the doctor had what is called "a temper of his own;" while his brother's expression was altogether sweet, gentle, and sensitive to the last degree.

As he lay back on his pillow—for he had been put to bed immediately—you might have taken him for a boy of seventeen, until, looking closer into the thin face, you read there the deeper lines which rarely come under the quarter-century which marks the first epoch in a man's life. No; though boyish, he was not a boy; and though delicate-looking, not effeminate. His was the temperament which we so ardently admire in youth, so deeply pity in maturer years—the poetic temperament—half masculine, half feminine—capable of both a man's passion and a woman's suffering. Such men are, as circumstances make them, the angels, the demons, or the martyrs of this world.

He lay—restless, but trying hard to be patient—till the light failed and his brother ceased the reading, which was not specially interesting, being done in a slightly formal and monotonous voice, like that of a person unaccustomed to, and not particularly enjoying the occupation.

"That will do, Will. It's really very good of you to stay in-doors with me all this evening; but I don't like it.

I wish you would go out. Off with you to the beach. Is there a good beach here?"

"A very fine one. You shall see it by-and-by."

"Nay, my Bath chair could never get down these steep cliffs."

"Do you think I mean you to spend all your days in a Bath chair, Julius, lad?"

"Ah, Will, shall I ever do without it? Tell me, do you really, candidly, in your honest heart—you're almost too honest for a doctor, old boy—believe that I shall ever walk again?"

The doctor turned and gave him a pat on the shoulder —his young brother, five or six years younger than himself, which fact had made such a vital difference once, and the fatherly habits of it remained still. There was a curious twitching of his mouth, which, though large and firm, had much lurking softness of expression. He paused a minute before speaking, and then said, earnestly:

"Yes, I do, Julius. Not that I know it for certain; but I believe it. You may never be quite as strong as you have been; rheumatic fever always leaves behind great delicacy in many ways; but I have known cases worse than yours which ended in complete recovery."

"I wish mine may be, if only for your sake. What a trouble I must have been to you! to say nothing of expense. And you just starting for yourself too."

"Well, lad, it didn't matter—it was only for myself. If I'd had a wife, now, or half a dozen brats. But I had nobody—not a single 'responsibility'—except you."

"And what a heavy responsibility I have been! Ever since you were fifteen I must have given you trouble without end."

"Pleasure, too, and a deal of fun—the fun of laughing at you and your vagaries, though I couldn't laugh you out of them. Come, don't be taking a melancholy view of things. Let's be jolly."

But the mirth came ponderously out of the big fellow, whose natural expression was evidently grave—an enemy might have called it saturnine. And Dr. William Sted-

man looked like a man who was not likely to go through
the world without making some enemies, if only from the
very honesty which his brother spoke of, and a slight want
of pliability—not of sympathy, but of the power of showing it—which made him a strong contrast to his brother,
besides occasionally jarring with him, as brothers do jar
against brothers, sisters against sisters, friends against
friends—not meaning it, but inevitably doing it.

"I can't be jolly, Will," said Julius, turning away.
"You couldn't, if you had my pains. Ah me! they're beginning again—they always do at night. I think Dante
would have invented a new torment for his Inferno if he
had ever had rheumatic fever. How mad I was to sit that
week painting in the snow!"

"Let by-gones be by-gones, Julius. Never recall the
past except to mend the future. That's my maxim, and
I stick to it, though I am a stupid fellow — you're the
bright one of us two."

"And what good has my brightness done me? Here
I am, tied by the leg, my profession stopped—so far as it
ever was a profession, for you know nobody ever bought
my pictures. If it had not been for you, Will, what would
have become of me? And what will become of me now?
Well, I don't care."

"'Don't care' was hanged," said the elder brother, sen-
tentiously; "and you'll be hung, and well hung, I hope,.in
the Royal Academy next year."

The threadbare joke, so solemnly put forward and
laughed at with childish enjoyment, effected its purpose
in turning the morbid current of the sick man's thoughts.
His mercurial and easily-caught fancy, which even illness
could not destroy, took another direction, and he began
planning what he should do when he got well—the next
picture he should paint, and where he should paint it.
His hopes were much lower than his ambitions, for his
bias had been towards high art, only his finances made
it impossible to follow it. And, perhaps, his talent — it
scarcely reached genius — was more of the appreciative
than the creative kind. Yet he loved his art as well as he

loved any thing, and in talking about it he almost forgot his pains.

"If I could only get.well," he said, "or even a little better, I might find in this pretty country some nice usable bits, and make sketches for my next year's work. Perhaps I might do a sea-piece: some small thing, with figures in it—a fisherman or a child. One could study from the life here without ruination to one's pocket, as it used to be in London. And, by-the-bye, I saw to-day a splendid head, real Greek, nearly as fine as the Clytie."

"Where?"

"Here—at the parlor-window."

The elder brother smiled. "You are always discovering goddesses at parlor-windows, and finding them very common mortals after all."

"Oh, I have done with that nonsense," said Julius, with a vexed air; adding, rather sentimentally, "my day is over—I shall never fall in love again."

"Not till the next time. But this head? I conclude it was alive, and had a woman belonging to it?"

"Probably, though I only saw the head. Are there any lodgers here besides ourselves?"

"Two ladies—possibly young ladies; but I really did not think of asking. I never was a ladies' man, you know. Shall I make inquiries on your account, young Lothario?"

"Well, you might, for I should like a chance of seeing that head again. It would paint admirably. I only wish I had the luck of doing it—when I get well."

"When I get well"—the sad, pathetic sentence often uttered, often listened to, though both speaker and listener know by instinctive foreboding that the "when" means "never." Dr. Stedman might have shared this feeling in spite of his firm "I believe it" of ten minutes before, for in the twilight his grave face looked graver still. Nevertheless, he carefully maintained the cheerful, even jocular tone of his conversation with his brother.

"You might ask the favor of taking her likeness. I am sure the young lady could not refuse. No young ladies ever do. Female vanity and your own attractions seem to fill your port-folio wherever you go. But to-morrow I'll try to get a look myself at this new angel of yours."

"No, there is nothing angelic about her face; not much, even, that is spiritual. It is thorough mortal beauty; not unlike the Clytie, as I said. It would paint well—as an Ariadne or a Dido; only there is not enough depth of sadness in it."

"Perhaps she is not a sad-minded young woman."

"I really don't know, or care. What nonsense it is our talking about women! We can't afford to fall in love or marry—at least I can't."

"Nor I neither," said the doctor, gravely. "And I did not mean to talk any nonsense about these two young women—if young they are—for the landlady told me they had just come out of great trouble—being school-mistresses, with their school broken up, and one sister nearly dying through scarlet-fever."

"That isn't so bad as rheumatic fever. I remember rather enjoying it, because I was allowed to read novels all the time. Which sister had it? the Clytie one? That rare type of beauty runs in families. Perhaps the other has a good head too."

"I don't think she has."

"Why not?"

"Because I suspect I saw her just before I came up stairs to you—a little, pale, anxious-looking thing—not at all a beauty—sitting adding up her accounts. Very small accounts they were, seemingly; yet she seemed terribly troubled over them. She must be very poor or very stupid—women always are stupid over arithmetic. And yet she did not look quite a fool, either."

"How closely you must have watched her!"

"I am afraid I did, for at first I thought her only a little girl, she was so small; and I wondered what the creature could be so busy about. But I soon found she was a woman, and an anxious-faced little woman too. Most likely these two school-mistresses are as poor as we are; and, if so, I am sorry for them, being only women."

"Ah, yes," said Julius, absently; but he seemed to

weary of the conversation, and soon became absorbed in
his own suffering. Over him had evidently grown the involuntary selfishness of sickness, which Letty Kenderdine
had referred to; probably because she herself understood
it only too well. But her sufferings were nothing to those
of this poor young fellow, racked in every joint, and
with a physical organization the very worst to bear pain.
Nervous, sensitive, excitable; adding to present torment
by both the recollection of the past and the dread of the
future; exquisitely susceptible to both his own pains and
the grief and anxiety they caused to others, yet unable to
control himself so as in any way to lessen the burden of
them; terrified at imaginary sufferings, a little exaggerating the real ones—which were sharp enough—the invalid was a pitiable sight, and most difficult to deal with by
any nurse.

But the one he had was very patient—marvellously so
for a man. For hours, until long after midnight—for
Edna told her sister afterwards she had heard his step
overhead at about two in the morning—did the stout,
healthy brother, who evidently possessed in the strongest
degree the *mens sana in corpore sano*, devote himself to
the younger one, trying every possible means to alleviate
his sufferings; and when all failed, sitting down by his
bedside, almost like a woman and a mother, saying nothing, simply enduring; or, at most, holding the poor fellow's hand with a firm clasp, which, in its mingled strength
and tenderness, might have imparted courage to go through
any amount of physical pain—nay, have led even to the
entrance of that valley of the shadow of death which we
must all one day pass through, and alone.

Help, as far as mortal help could go, William Stedman
was the one to give; not in words, but in a certain atmosphere of quiet strength, or rather, in that highest expression of strength which we call fortitude. It seems easy to
bear with fortitude another person's sufferings; but that
is, to some natures, the very sharpest pang of all. And
with something of the same expression on his face as once
(Julius reminded him of the anecdote about one in the

morning), in their first school, he had gone up to the master and begged to be flogged instead of Julius—did William Stedman sit by his brother's bedside till the paroxysms of pain abated. It was not till nearly daylight that, the sufferer being at length quietly asleep, the doctor threw himself, dressed as he was, on the hearth-rug before the fire, and slept also—suddenly, soundly, and yet lightly; the sleep of a sailor or a mastiff dog.

Morning broke smilingly over the sea—an April morning, breezy and bright; and Edna, who had not slept well —not nearly so well as Letty—being disturbed first by the noises overhead, and then kept wakeful by her own anxious thoughts, which, compulsorily repressed in daytime, always took their revenge at night—Edna Kenderdine welcomed it gladly. Weary of sleeplessness, she rose early, and looking out of her window, she saw a man's figure pacing up and down the green cliff between her and the sea-line. Not a very stylish figure—still in the old coat and older wide-awake hat; but it was tall, broad, and manly. He walked, his hands folded somewhat ungracefully behind him, with a strong and resolute step, looking about him sometimes, but oftener with his head bent, thinking. Undoubtedly it was the doctor.

Edna watched him with some curiosity. He must have been up all night, she knew; and as she had herself lain awake, listening to the accidental footfall, the poking of the fire, and all those sick-room noises which in the dead silence sound so ominous and melancholy in a house, even to one who has no personal stake in the matter, she had felt much sympathy for him. She was reminded keenly of her own sad vigils over poor Letty, and wondered how a man contrived to get through the same sort of thing. To a woman and a sister nursing came natural; but with a man it must be quite different. She speculated vaguely upon what sort of men the brothers were, and whether they were as much attached to one another as she and Letty. And she watched with a vague, involuntary interest the big man who kept striding up and down, refreshing himself after his weary night-watch; and when at last

he came in and disappeared, probably to his solitary breakfast, she thought, in her practical, feminine soul, what a
dreary breakfast it must be; no one to make the tea, or
see that the eggs were boiled properly, or do any of those
tender duties which help to make the day begin cheerily,
and in which this little woman took an especial pleasure.

As she busied herself in doing them for Letty, who was
always the last down stairs, Edna could not forbear asking
Mrs. Williams how the sick lodger was this morning.

"Rather bad, miss. Better now; but was very bad all
night, his brother says; and he has just started off to
Ryde to get him some new physic."

"To Ryde—that is nine miles off!"

"Yes; but there was no help for it, he said. He inquired the short way across country, and meant to walk
it, and be back as soon as he could. I asked him about
dinner; but he left that all to me. Oh, miss, how helpless
these men-folk be! He only begged me to look after his
brother."

"Is the brother keeping his room?"

"No; he dressed him and carried him down stairs, just
like a baby, before he went out. Poor gentleman, it's a
heavy handful for him; and him with no wife or mother
or sister to help him; for I asked, and he said no, they had
none; no relations in the world but their two selves."

"No more have we; but then women are so much more
used to sickness than men are, and more helpful," said
Edna. Yet, as she recalled her own sense of helplessness
and entire desolation when she and Letty were landed in
this very room, wet and weary, one chill, rainy afternoon,
and the fire smoked, and Letty cried, and finally went into
hysterics, she felt a sensation of pity for her neighbors—
those "helpless men-folk," as Mrs. Williams called them,
who, under similar circumstances, were even worse off
than women.

"How is the poor fellow now?" she asked. "Have you
been in again to look at him? He should not be left long
alone."

"But, miss, where am I to get the time? And, besides,

he don't like it. Whenever I go in and ask if I can do any
thing for him, he just shakes his head and turns his face
back again into the pillow. And I don't think any thing
will do him much good; he isn't long for this world. I
wish I hadn't taken 'em; and if I can get 'em out at the
week's end—not meaning to inconvenience—and hoping
they will get as good lodgings elsewhere, which no doubt
they will—"

"You wouldn't do it, Mrs. Williams," said Edna, smiling, and turning upon her those good, sweet eyes, which,
Miss Kenderdine's pupils declared, "frightened" all the
naughtiness out of them.

The landlady smiled too. "Well, miss, maybe I
wouldn't; for I feels sorry for the poor gentleman; and
I once had a boy of my own that would have been about
as old as him. I'll do what I can, though he is grumpy
and won't speak; and that ain't pleasant, is it, miss?"

"No."

This little conversation, like all the small trivialities of
their life, Edna retailed for Letty's edification, and both
sisters talked the matter over threadbare, as people in sea-
side lodgings and out on a holiday have a trick of doing;
for holiday-making to busy people is sometimes very hard
work. They even, with a mixture of curiosity and real
compassion, left their parlor-door open, in order to listen
for and communicate to Mrs. Williams the slightest movement in the parlor opposite, where the sick man lay so
helpless, so forlorn, that the kindly hearts of those two
young women—certainly of one of them—forgot that he
was a man, and a young man, and wished they could do
him any good.

But, of course, under the circumstances, it would, as Letty declared, be the height of indecorum; they, unmarried
ladies and school-mistresses, with their credit and dignity
at stake, how could they take the slightest notice of a
young man, be he ever so ill?

"Yet I wish we could," said Edna. "It seems so heartless to a fellow-creature to let him lie there hour after
hour. If we might go in and speak to him, or send him

a book to read, I can't believe it could be so very improper."

And when they came back from their morning stroll she lingered compassionately in front of the closed window and drawn-down blind behind which the sick man lay, ignorant of, or indifferent to, all the glad sights and sounds abroad—the breezy sea, the pleasant country, rejoicing in this blessed spring morning.

"Do come in," sharply said Letty, who had in some things a keener sense of the outward proprieties than Edna. "Don't be nonsensical and sentimental. It would never do for us to encourage, even in the smallest degree, these two young men, who are certainly poor, and, for all we know, may be scarcely respectable. I won't allow it, sister."

And she passed hastily the opposite door, which Edna was shocked to see was not quite closed, and walked into their own, with Letty's own dignified step and air of queenly grace, which, wherever she went, slew men, young and old, in indiscriminate massacre.

She was certainly a rare woman, Letitia Kenderdine—one that, met anywhere or anyhow, would make one feel that there might have been some truth in the old stories about Helen of Troy, Cleopatra of Egypt, and such like—ancient queens of history and fable, who rode rampant over the necks of men, and whose deadly beauty proved a fire-brand wherever it was thrown.

"Yes," replied Edna, as she took off her sister's hat and shawl, and noticed what a delicate rose-color was growing on the sea-freshened cheek, and how the old brightness was returning to the lustrous eyes. "You are quite right, Letty, dear. It would never do for us to take any notice of our neighbors, unless, indeed, they were at the very last extremity, which is not likely to happen."

"Certainly not; and even if it did, I must say I think we ought not to trouble ourselves about them. We have quite enough cares of our own without taking upon ourselves the burden of other people's."

This was only too true. Edna was silenced.

CHAPTER III.

" L'HOMME propose, et Dieu dispose," is a saying so trite
as to be not worth saying at all were not its awful solemnity, in mercy as often as in retribution, forced upon
us by every day's history; more especially in those sort
of histories of which this is openly one — love - stories.
How many brimming cups slip from the lip, according to
the old proverb! how many more, which worldly or cruel
hands have tried to dash aside, are nevertheless taken and
guided by far diviner and safer hands, and made into a
draught of life all the sweeter for delay! And in lesser
instances than these, what a curious path Fate oftentimes
seems to make for mortal feet, leading them exactly whither they have resolved not to go, and shutting up against
them those ways which seemed so clear and plain!

For some days Fate appeared to be doing nothing as
regarded these four young persons but sitting invisibly
at their mutual threshold with her hands crossed, and
weaving no web whatever for their entanglement. They
went out and came in — but their going and coming
chanced to be at different hours; they never caught sight
of one another. Edna, moved by her kindly heart, every
morning made a few civil inquiries of Mrs. Williams after
the invalid; but Letty, seeing that no interesting episode
was likely to occur, ceased to care at all about the new-
comers. Indeed, as she was now rapidly getting well,
blooming into more than her ordinary beauty in the reju-
venescence that sometimes takes place after a severe illness, how could she be expected to trouble herself about a
sick young man in a Bath chair, and a stout brother who
was wholly absorbed in taking care of him? Except for
Edna, and her occasional inquiries and remarks concerning
them, Letty would almost have forgotten their existence.

But Fate had not forgotten. One morning the grim

unseen Woman in the door-way rose up and began her work.

The "last extremity" of which Edna had spoken suddenly occurred.

They had seen Dr. Stedman start off, stick in hand, for his evening walk across the cliffs—which was the only recreation he seemed to indulge in—he took it while his brother slept, Mrs. Williams said, between twilight and bedtime; otherwise he rarely left him for an hour. This night it was an unfortunate absence. He had scarcely been gone ten minutes when the landlady rushed into the Misses Kenderdine's parlor in a state of great alarm.

"Oh! Miss Edna, would you come? You're used to illness, and I don't know what's the matter. He's dead, or dying, or something, and his brother's away. Please come!—this minute—or it may be too late."

"Don't go!" cried Letty. "Mrs. Williams, it's impossible—impertinent of you to ask it. She can't go."

But Edna had already gone without a word.

She was not surprised at the landlady's fright. One of those affections of the heart which so often follow rheumatic fever had attacked the young man; very suddenly, as it seemed. He lay not on the sofa, but on the floor, as if he had slipped down there, all huddled up, with his hands clenched, and his face like a dead man's face. So like, that Letty, who, after a minute, had, in spite of her opposition, followed her sister, thought he really was dead; and, having a nervous horror of death, and sickness, and all kinds of physical unpleasantnesses, had shrunk back again into their own sitting-room, and shut the door.

Edna knelt down and lifted the passive head on to her lap. She forgot it was a young man's head; she scarcely even saw that it was beautiful—a poet's face, like that of Shelley or Keats. She only recognized that he was a sick human creature who lay there needing her utmost help; and, without a second thought, she gave it. She would have given it just the same to the ugliest, coarsest laborer who had been brought injured to her door, and have shrunk as little from dirt and wounds as she did now from the grace of the curly black hair and the gleam of the white throat, which she hastily laid bare to give him a chance of breath.

"No, he is not dead, Mrs. Williams. I can feel his heart beat. He has only fainted. Bring me some smelling-salts and a glass of water."

Her simple restoratives took effect — the patient soon opened his eyes.

"Go into our room; tell my sister to send me a glass of wine," whispered she; and the frightened woman at once obeyed.

But the glass was held to his lips in vain. "Don't trouble me," said the poor fellow, faintly, and half-unconscious still. "Don't, Will! I'm dying—I would rather die."

"You are not dying, and we can not allow it," said Edna from behind. "Drink this, and you will be better presently."

Instinctively he obeyed the cheerful, imperative voice, and then, coming more clearly to his senses, tried to discover whence it came, and who was holding him.

No vision of beauty; no princess succoring a wounded knight; or queen of fairies bending over King Arthur at the margin of the celebrated lake; nothing at all romantic, or calculated to fix a young man's imagination at once and forever. Only a little woman—a rather plain little woman too — who smiled down upon him. very kindly, but without the slightest confusion or hesitation; no more than if she had been his aunt or his grandmother. He did not even think her a young woman—not then—for his faculties were confused; the only fact he was sensible of was her womanliness and kindliness.

The conversation between them was also as commonplace as it could be.

"You are very good, madam; I am sorry to have troubled you — and all these women," looking round on Mrs. Williams and the servant with an ill-concealed expression of annoyance. "I am quite well now."

"You will be presently. But please don't talk. Drink

this, and then lie down again on your sofa till your brother comes back. Will he be long ?"

She had scarcely said it before the brother himself appeared. He stood a minute at the parlor-door. To say
he looked astonished at the scene before him is needless;
but his penetrating eye seemed to take it all in at a glance.

"Don't move, Julius. I understand. I wish I had not
gone out," said he; and kneeling beside him, felt his pulse
and heart.

"Never mind, Will; I am better now. Mrs. Williams
looked after me; and this lady, you see."

"Mrs. Williams fetched me, knowing I was accustomed
to illness," explained Edna, simply, as she resigned her post
to the doctor and rose to her feet. "I do not think it was
worse than a fainting-fit, and he is much better now."

"So I see. Thank you. We are both of us exceedingly indebted to you for your kindness," said Dr. Stedman,
rather formally, but in a manner which proved he was—as
Edna had said every doctor ought to be—really a gentleman. And then, taking advantage of his complete absorption in his brother's state to the exclusion of all standers-
by, she quietly slipped out of the room; thereby escaping
all further thanks, explanations, or civilities.

Letty, having recovered from her fright, and being re-
assured that there was not that dreadful thing "death in
the house," nor likely to be at present, became, as was natural, mightily interested in the episode which had taken
place in the opposite parlor.

"Quite a scene in a play. You must have felt like a
heroine of romance, Edna."

"Indeed I didn't; only rather awkward and uncomfortable — that is, if I felt any thing at all, which I am not
sure I did, at the time. He was a very sad sight, that
poor young fellow. Fainting in the reality is not half so
picturesque as they make it on the stage and in books.
Besides, I fear it is only an indication of worse things.
Heart-disease almost invariably follows rheumatic fever.
I know that."

"Of course. You know every thing," said Letty, with

the slight sharpness of tone which was occasionally heard
in her voice, and startled a stranger by the exceeding contrast it formed to her beautiful classical face. "But, for
all you say, it was a charming adventure. A sick young
man lying unconscious, with his head in your lap, and his
brother coming in and finding you in that romantic attitude."

"Nonsense!" cried Edna; a slight color, half shame-
faced, half-indignant, rising in her honest cheek.

"It isn't nonsense at all. It's very interesting. And
pray tell me every word they said to you. They ought
to have overwhelmed you with gratitude; and one or
both brothers — both would be better — ought to fall in
love with you on the spot. The result—rivalry, jealousy,
fury, and fratricide. Oh! what fun! To have two brothers in love with one lady at the same time! I wonder it
never happened to me; but perhaps it may some day."

"I earnestly hope not," said Edna.

But at the same time a horrible foreboding entered her
mind concerning these two brothers, who must inevitably
live under the same roof with Letty for some days, possibly weeks; who would have many opportunities of seeing
her—and nobody ever looked at the beautiful Letty who
did not look again immediately. For her charms were
not those recondite and variable ones of expression and
intellect; they were patent—on the surface—attractive at
once to the most refined and the coarsest masculine eyes.
Hitherto no young man had ever cast the merest glance
upon Letty Kenderdine without trying to pursue the acquaintance; and the anxious sister began to wish that her
own sympathies had not led her into that act of kindly
civility which might prove the "open, sesame" to a hundred civilities more, were the opposite lodgers so inclined.
Should it appear likely, she determined to make a dead
stand of opposition, and not allow the least loop-hole
through which they could push their way to any further
acquaintance.

This determination, however, she wisely kept to herself;
for in Letty's last little love-affair they two had held di-

vided opinions, and, with all her affection for her sister,
she had begun to find that sisters do not necessarily think
alike.   Their twelvemonths' living together, after an almost total separation since their school-days, had taught
Edna this fact—one of the sad facts which all human beings have to learn—that every one of us is, more or less,
intensely alone.   Before marriage—ay, and after any but
the very happiest marriage — absolutely and inevitably
alone.

"Don't speak so seriously," said Letty, laughing. "You
are not vexed with me?"

"Oh no!"

Where, indeed, was the use of being vexed with her?
or of arguing the point with her?   Edna knew that if she
were to talk to her sister till doomsday she could no more
make her understand her own feelings on this subject than
if she were preaching to a blind man on the subject of
colors.   To Letty love merely meant marriage, and marriage meant a nice house, a respectable, good sort of man
as master to it—probably, a carriage; and at any rate as
many handsome clothes as she could possibly desire.   She
did not overlook the pleasantness of the preliminary stage
of love-making, but then she had already gone through
that, in degree; in truth, her lovers had of late become to
her more of a worry than an amusement, and she was now
disposed to take a thoroughly sensible and practical view
of things.

Nevertheless, there was in her a lurking love of admiration *per se*, without ulterior possibilities, which had grown
by what it fed on—and there was no lack of provender in
Letty's case, for every man she met admired her.   Also,
she had in her a spice of feminine contradictoriness, which,
had she discovered any lack of admiration, would have
roused her to buckle all her beauty's armor on, and reme-
dy it, thus marring, by one fortuitous glance or smile, all
her sister's sage precautions.

Edna knew this; knew it by the way in which, while
protesting that she hoped no further acquaintance with
the two Stedmans would ensue through this very impru-

dent step on Edna's part, she talked all evening about them, and insisted on hearing every particular concerning them: what they did, said, and looked like ; what sort of a parlor they had, whether it was very untidy and bachelor-like.

" For, of course, neither of them is married, though the doctor is old enough to be; but doctors never can afford to settle early, especially in London. These people live in London, don't they ?"

" I really don't know. I have never inquired."

" Do inquire, then; for if Dr. Stedman should take it into his head to call—and it would be the least thing he could do, in acknowledgment of your kindness to his brother—"

" Oh, I hope not."

" So do I; for it might turn out exceedingly"—Letty cast a half-amused glance at herself in the mirror—" exceedingly awkward — for him, poor fellow ; of course, it couldn't affect me. Though big and rough—as he is, you say—he seems decidedly the most interesting of the two. And depend upon it, Edna, if we should happen to make acquaintance with these two brothers, he is the one that will fall in love with me."

" Why do you think so?" asked Edna, internally resolving that, if she could possibly prevent it, the poor honest-looking doctor should be saved from that dire calamity.

" Why? Because he's ugly, and I'm—well, I'm not exactly ugly, you know; and I always notice that plain people are certain to fall in love with me—probably just by the law of contrast. For the same reason you'll tell me, I suppose, that I ought to marry some very wise, grave fellow, possibly such an one as this doctor of yours, who would altogether look after me, take me in and do for me—admire me excessively, no doubt, but still save me all trouble of thinking and acting for myself. Heigh-ho! what a comfort that would be !"

" It really would !" said Edna, seriously, and then could not help smiling, for the hundredth time, at Letty's very

matter-of-fact style of discussing her loves and her lovers.
Her extreme candor was her redeeming point. She was
not a wise woman, but she was certainly not a hypocrite.
No need to fear that with Letty Kenderdine it would be
"all for love and the world well lost," or that if she married she would make otherwise than what even Belgravian
mothers would call "a very good marriage," and afterwards strictly do her duty to her husband and society, or
rather to society first, and then, so far as was practicable,
to her husband. And, Edna sometimes thought, judging
by the sort of lovers that came after Letty, with whose
characters and feelings she, Edna, was fully conversant—
for her sister had no reticence whatever concerning them
—men marry for no higher, perhaps even a lower, motive.
"I am rather glad," said she, suddenly, apropos of nothing, "certainly more glad than sorry, that I shall be an
old maid."

"Well, as I always said, you will be an extremely happy one," returned Letty; "and you ought to be thankful
to be saved from all the difficulties which fall to my lot.
There! don't you hear the opposite door opening? He is
stopping in the lobby—speaking to Mrs. Williams. Of
course, I knew what would come of all this. I was certain the young man would call."

But, in spite of Letty's tone of indignation, her countenance fell considerably when the doctor did not call, but
shut his sitting-room door again immediately, apparently
without taking the slightest interest in, or manifesting the
smallest desire to communicate with, his fair neighbor.
And another night fell, and another day rolled on, bright,
sunshiny, calm; it was most glorious weather; just the
"fullness of the spring," when

"A young man's fancy lightly turns to thoughts of love;"

and still Fate sat motionless at the threshold—nor ap-
proached a step nearer to make these young hearts beat or
tremble with premonitions of their destiny.

It was not until the last evening of the week, and three
days after Edna's act of unacknowledged, and, Letty de-

clared, quite unappreciated kindness, that the four inmates of Mrs. Williams's lodgings really met, face to face,
in a rencontre unplanned, unexpected, and impossible to
be avoided on either side. Yet it came about naturally
enough, and at the most likely place—the garden gate.

Just as the two sisters were setting out for the latest
of their three daily strolls, and the doctor was bringing
his brother home from his, the Bath chair stopped the
way. Letty, walking in advance, as she usually did, being
now as restless for going out as she had formerly been languid and lazy in stopping in, came suddenly in front of her
fellow-invalid.

She drew back—as has been said, Letty had an instinctive shrinking from any kind of suffering—and Julius, lifting up his heavy eyes, saw this tall, beautiful woman
standing with one hand on the wicket gate, and her hat in
the other, for she rather liked to go bareheaded in the sea-
breeze. Now it freshened her cheek and brightened her
eyes, until she seemed a vision of health as well as beauty
in the sight of the sick man, who was turning homeward
after a long afternoon's stroll, weary of himself, of life, of
every thing.

His artistic eye was caught at once; he recognized her
with a look of admiration that no woman could mistake;
though it puzzled Letty Kenderdine a little, being different from the bold, open stare she was so well used to. It
was a look, respectful and yet critical; as calmly observant as if she had been a statue or a picture, not a living
woman at all, and he bent upon investigating her good
and bad points, and appraising her value. Yet it was a
gaze of extreme delight, though delight of a purely artistic
kind—the pleasure of looking at a lovely thing; the recognition, open and free, of that good gift—beauty; when, or
how, or upon whomsoever bestowed. Therefore it was a
gaze that no gentleman need have blushed to give, nor
any lady to receive; even Edna, who, coming behind her
sister, met and noticed it fully, could not take offense at it.

And at sight of Edna the sickly face broke out into a
smile.

C

"It is you. I hoped I should see you again. I wanted
to thank you for your kindness to me the other day. I
told Will— Here, Will, I want you."

Dr. Stedman, who had been pushing the Bath chair
from behind, also stood gazing intently at the beautiful
vision, which, indeed, no man with eyes could possibly
turn away from.

"Will, do come and thank this lady—I forget her name;
indeed, I don't think I ever heard it."

This was a hint which Edna did not take; but, to her
surprise, it was unnecessary.

"Miss Kenderdine, I believe" (and he had got the name
quite pat and correct, which strangers seldom did), said
the doctor, taking off his hat, and showing short, crisp,
brown locks, curling tight round what would, ere many
years, be a bald crown. "My brother and I are glad to
have an opportunity of thanking you for your kindness
that day. It made a strong impression on him; he has
talked of you ever since."

"Yes, indeed; it was such a charitable thing for a
stranger to do to a poor sick fellow like me," added Julius,
looking up with a simplicity that had something almost
child-like in it. "Such a frank, generous, womanly thing!
I told Will he ought to go in and thank you for it, but he
wouldn't; he is such a shy fellow, this brother of mine."

"Julius, pray—we are detaining these ladies."

But Julius never took any hints, and often said and did
things which nobody else would ever think of; and yet,
coming from him, they were done in such a pleasant way
as never to vex any body.

"Nonsense! we are not stiff in our manners here: we
are at the sea-side; and then I am an invalid, and must be
humored, must I not, Miss Kenderdine? You don't mind
my detaining you here for two minutes, just to thank you?"

"No," said Edna, smiling. She wondered afterwards
that she had responded so frankly to the young man's
greeting, and allowed so unresistingly the introduction
which soon brought them all to speaking terms, and drew
Letty also into the quartette who, for the next five min-

utes or so, paused to talk over the garden gate. But, as she was forced to confess—when in their walk afterwards Letty reproved her, laying all the blame upon her, whatever happened—she could not help it. There was a charm about Julius Stedman which made every body do as he wished, and he evidently wished exceedingly to make acquaintance with these two young ladies. Not an unnatural wish in any man, especially in dull sea-side lodgings.

So he detained them as long as he civilly could, chatting freely to the one, and gazing silently at the other — the owner of that wonderful Clytie face. He put himself, with his unquestioned prerogative of illness, much more forward than his brother—though the doctor, too, talked a little, and looked also; if not with the open-eyed admiration of Julius, with a keen, sharp investigation, as if he were taking the measure, less artistically than morally, of this lovely woman.

Nevertheless—or, perhaps, consequently—the conversation that went on was trivial enough: about the sea, the fine coast, the lovely spring sunset, and the charming weather they had had these two days.

"Yes, I like it," said Julius, in reply to Edna's question. "It warms me through and through—this glorious sunshine! I am sure it would make me well if it lasted; but nothing ever does last in this world."

"You will speak more cheerfully by-and-by," said Edna. "I was pleased at this change of weather, because I knew it would do you and all sick people so much good."

"How kind of you to think of me at all!" returned Julius, gratefully. "I am sure you must be a very nice woman."

"Must I?" Edna laughed, and then blushed a little, to find herself speaking so familiarly not only with strangers, but with the very strangers whom she had determined to keep at arm's-length under all circumstances. But then the familiarity was only with her—Edna, to whom it signified little. Neither of the brothers had addressed Letty, nor offered her any attention beyond a respectful bow; and Letty had drawn herself up with considerable *hauteur*, adding to the natural majesty of her beauty a sort of "fall-in-love-if-you-dare" aspect, which, to some young men, might have been an additional attraction, but which did not seem to affect fatally either of these two.

They looked at her; with admiration certainly, as any young men might—nay, must have done—would have been fools and blind not to have done; but that was all. At first sight neither seemed disposed to throw himself prone under the wheels of Letty's Juggernaut chariot; which fact relieved Edna's mind exceedingly.

So, after some few minutes of a conversation equally unembarrassed and uninteresting, the young people parted where they stood, all four shaking hands over the gate, Julius grasping Edna's with a grateful pressure that would decidedly have startled her, had she not recognized by instinct the impulsive temperament of the young man. Besides, she was utterly devoid of self-conscious vanity, and accustomed to think of her own relation to the opposite sex as one that precluded any special attentions. Her personal experience of men had been solely in the character of confidante to Letty's lovers. She used to say, laughing, "She was born to be every body's sister, or every body's maiden aunt."

And so the ice was broken between these four young people, so strangely thrown together in this solitary place, and under circumstances when the world and its restrictions—whether needed or needless—were, for the time being, more or less set aside. They met, simply as four human beings, through blind chance, as it seemed, and wholly ignorant that the innocent wicket gate, held open so gracefully by Letty's hand for the Bath chair to pass through, was to them an opening into that enchanted garden which is entered but once. Which most of us—nay, confess it! all of us—dream about continually before entering; and passing out of—even for happier Edens—seldom leave without a sigh of regret. For it is the one rift of heaven which makes all heaven appear possible; the ecstasy of hope and faith, out of which grows the Love which is our strongest mortal instinct and intimation of immortality.

CHAPTER IV.

It is an undoubted fact, that when that event happens, the most vital in human life—the first meeting of two persons who are to influence one another's character and destinies in the closest manner, for good or ill, happiness or misery, nay, even for virtue or crime—the sky does not fall, no ominous signs appear in the outside world; nay, the parties concerned, poor puppets as they are, or seem to be, are usually quite unconscious of what has befallen them, and eat, drink, and sleep just as composedly as ever.

Thus the two Misses Kenderdine, after shaking hands with the two Stedmans over the gate, went calmly on their usual stroll along the cliffs, discussing in feminine fashion their new acquaintances, and speculating about them with an indifference that was perfectly sincere; for though these school-mistresses were young enough to have the natural lot and future of womanhood running a good deal in their heads, especially at holiday time, when they had no more serious business in hand, and Letty's continual "difficulties" always kept the subject alive, still they were neither of them silly school-girls, in love with every man they met, or fancying every man in love with them. Letty, perhaps, had a slight tendency in the latter direction, which her experience rather justified than not; but Edna was free from all such folly, or only regarded the question of love and matrimony in its relation to her sister.

So they discussed freely and openly the two young men.

Edna had been most interested in the invalid, as was natural; her heart warmed towards every kind of suffering; while her sister had chiefly noticed the big healthy-looking brother, who was evidently "a man with no nonsense about him," by which Letty meant no sentiment; for she, who had been haunted by sentimental swains, poets addressing verses to her, and artists imploring to sketch her portrait, disliked sentiment above all things.

"Besides, this doctor does really seem a gentleman, in spite of his shabby coat. He might be spruced up into a very good-looking fellow if he had somebody to see after him. You are quite sure he is not married, Edna? And where did you say he lived? I wonder if it is in a respectable street, and what sort of a practice he has got."

"Letty," cried Edna, turning sharply round, half amused, half angry, "you are not surely going to—".

"No, you foolish child; not being quite a simpleton. I am not surely going to—to marry him—your friend with the shabby coat. Nor even to let him fall in love with me, if I can help it. But if he does, you can't blame me. It's all my unfortunate appearance."

Edna attempted no reply—where was the use of it? Indeed she shrank back into total silence, as was her habit when the sense of painful incongruity between herself and her sister, their thoughts, motives, and actions, rose up more strongly than usual. She wished there was no such thing as falling in love—as Letty put it—or that Letty would fall in love honestly and sincerely, once for all, with some good man—she began not to care much who it was, if he were only good—marry him and have done with it. These perpetual "little affairs" of her sister's could not go on forever. Edna was rather weary of them; and wished, more earnestly than she liked to express, that she could see Letty "settled"—fairly sheltered under the wing of a worthy husband who would at once rule her and love her—pet her and take care of her; for indeed she needed taking care of more than most women of six-and-twenty. Perhaps Dr. Stedman might be the very sort of man to do this. He looked like it. There was a steadfast honesty of purpose in his eyes, and a firmness about his mouth, which seemed to imply sterling worth. But, though a good man, his expression was not exactly that of an amiable man; and Letty was a person likely to try a husband's temper considerably at times. Besides, what if he were poor? Indeed the fact seemed self-evident. A poor man—as she said herself, and Edna confessed the truth of this—would never do for Letty Kenderdine.

Edna's thoughts had galloped on thus far in a perfect steeple-chase of fancy, when she suddenly pulled up, reflecting how exceedingly ridiculous it was. She almost despised herself for speculating thus on so slender a foundation, or no foundation at all, and bent her whole attention to the outer world.

Every thing was so beautiful in the still evening—the sea as calm as the sky, and the cliff-swallows skimming airily between both. Even Letty, whose thoughts there is no need to follow, for she never thought much or long about any thing, noticed them, and called them "pretty little things;" while Edna, who had a great love for birds, watched them with a curious tenderness — the creatures that came so far from over the waters—guided unerringly, —to make their nests here; as (Edna still firmly believed in her deepest heart, though her twelvemonths' life with Letty had somewhat shaken the out-works of that girlish faith) Heaven guides all true lovers that are to be husband and wife—leads them from farthest corners of the world, through storm and trial, danger and death, to their own appointed home in one another's arms.

So she left her sister's lot—her own she never thought of—in wiser hands than hers; trusting that He who mated the swallows and brought them hither from across the seas, and made them so content and happy, hovering about in the spring twilight, would in time bring Letty a good husband, and relieve her sisterly heart from the only real care it had—the unknown future of this beautiful, half-foolish, half-worldly-wise woman, who, though her very flesh and blood, was so unlike herself that it puzzled Edna daily more and more both to understand her and to guide her.

The two sisters went back to their dull lodgings, which, in common with all lodgings, looked especially dull and unhome-like at this hour. They sat down to their innocent milk supper, and the one glass of wine which Letty still indulged in, as a last relic of invalidism, though saying each day she would give it up. And then they settled themselves to sewing, at least Edna did, Letty declaring she

never could sew with the poor light of two mould candles.
She amused herself with lying on the sofa and talking, or
chatting, the sort of desultory chat which people who live
together naturally fall into—it is only strangers who maintain " conversation." Besides, Letty's talk was never conversation; it rarely rose beyond ordinary facts or person-
alities; generally of a trivial kind. Clytie-like though her
lips were, they did not drop pearls and diamonds; but then
they never dropped toads and adders. She was exceedingly good-natured, and never said sharp or unkind things
of any body; in this having the advantage of Edna, who
sometimes felt sorely tempted to be severe and satirical,
then blamed herself, and took refuge in mild generalities,
. as now.

The two brothers would have been more amused than
flattered had they known that on this momentous evening
of their first rencontre with the two young ladies, which
meeting had conveyed to both an impression of undefined
pleasantness, as the society of all good women ought to
give to every good man, their fair neighbors' conversation
was, from the time of re-entering the house, strictly on the
subject of clothes.

"Alas!" Letty broke out, almost as soon as supper was
over, declaring the matter had been on her mind all day—
the spring weather was coming on fast, and they had only
their winter garments with them, and no possibility of
getting more.

"For we can't buy every thing new, and our last summer's things are locked up at home; and besides, I almost
forget what we have."

"Nothing very much, I fear."

"We never have," said Letty, in a melancholy voice.
"When I was in situations I was obliged to dress well;
but now? Just think, Edna, to-morrow is Sunday, and we
have only our brown bonnets and our winter cloaks; and
it will likely be as hot as to-day, and the sunshine will
show all their shabbiness. It is very provoking; nay, it
it is exceedingly hard."

"It is hard, especially for you, Letty."

And Edna glanced at her beautiful sister, upon whom any thing looked well; yet whose beauty would have borne the most magnificent setting off that wealth could furnish. How splendid she would have looked in silks, laces, and jewels—the prizes that in all ages there have been found women ready to sell their souls for! Was Letty one of these? Edna could not believe it. Yet she knew well that dress, and the lack of it, was a much severer trial to her sister than to herself—that Letty actually suffered, mentally and morally, from a worn-out shawl or an old-fashioned bonnet; while as to herself, so long as she was neat and clean, and had colors matching—no blues and greens, pinks and scarlets, which poverty compelled to be worn together—it did not materially affect her happiness, whether she had on a silk dress or a cotton one.

This catastrophe of the winter bonnets was annoying; but it was a small annoyance—not worth fretting about, when they had so many more important cares, and many a blessing likewise. Her mind, which had been wandering alternately back to the house and the school to which in a short time they must return, and dwelling on a few pleasant fancies left by the evening walk, felt suddenly dragged down into the narrow ways of ordinary life—made narrower than they need to be by this hopeless way of looking at them. She did not like it; for, monotonous and commonplace as her life had been—ever since she was twelve years old—first school life, then governess life in a dull country city family, there was in this young school-mistress's soul a something which always felt like a little bird that would stretch its wings, feeling sure there must be a wide empyrean waiting for it somewhere. In her long pauses over her needle-work this little bird usually sat pluming its feathers and singing to itself, till some chance word of Letty's silenced it—as was wisest and best. For Letty would not have understood the little bird at all.

Edna fastened its cage-door, and determined to make the best of things.

C 2

"Yes, as you say, it is hard; but be patient this one Sunday, and before the next I will see what can be done. Suppose I take the coach to Ryde, and choose two plain straw bonnets and trim them myself—with green, perhaps. You always look so well in .green. Then we should be quite respectable while here, and they would last us as second-best all summer."

Letty brightened up amazingly. "That is a capital thought, Edna. You are the very cleverest girl! I always said, and I will say it, a great deal cleverer than I am, if the men could only find it out."

"They never will, and I don't want them," said Edna, laughing. "And now let us come to bed, for it is quite time."

As the sisters passed up stairs, both cast a glance on the shut parlor-door opposite, behind which was complete silence, as usual of evenings. The brothers did not seem to have such long tongues as the sisters.

"I wonder how they contrive to amuse themselves, these two young fellows," said Letty, yawning. "I hope they are not as dull as we are sometimes."

"Men never are dull, I suppose," replied Edna, in her glorious maiden ignorance. "They have always something to do, and that alone makes people cheerful. Besides, they don't dwell on trivial things, as we do; their minds are larger and clearer—at least, the best of them must be so," she corrected herself, reflecting that she was speaking more out of her ideal than her actual experience of the race. And with a feeling of weariness at the smallness into which her daily gossip with Letty sometimes degenerated, Edna thought she would really like, just for a change, to have a good, sensible talk with a man. She wondered what those two men down stairs talked about when they were alone, and whether their chief conversation, corresponding with that in the next parlor, was on the subject of clothes. And the idea of Dr. Stedman discussing the shape of his new hat, or Mr. Stedman becoming confidential with his brother on the question of coats and trowsers, proved so irresistibly ludicrous that Edna burst into one of her hearty fits of laughter—her first since Letty was ill—which did her so much good that she was sound asleep in five minutes.

And what of the two men fated to influence, and be influenced by, these two young women, in the way that human lives do act and react upon one another, in a manner so mysterious that all precautions often seem idle—all plans vain—all determinations null and void—and yet we still go on working, planning, and resolving—deliberately laying out the pattern of our own and others' future, of which we can neither forecast, nor control, nor, alas! recall, one single day.

They did not talk over their neighbors; it is not man's way, or not the way of such men as, with all their faults, these two Stedmans were—honest young fellows, from whom neither sin nor folly had rubbed off the bloom of their youth, or led them to think and talk of women as, God forgive them! men sometimes do—men, who were born of women, who were hung as innocent babies at some woman's breast.

They came in-doors, Julius with evident reluctance.

"Why didn't you give me another turn on the cliff, Will? I wanted two or three more minutes to study that head."

"Miss Kenderdine's?"

"Isn't it grand, now? Bring me my sketch-book, and I'll have a try at the profile. Finest profile I ever saw. It might be useful some day, when I get well."

"You'll be well sooner than you think, old boy."

And that was literally all which passed concerning the two sisters.

The brothers spent their usual silent evening, Julius drawing, and William immersed in a heap of medical literature which lay on a table in the corner, into which he plunged at every possible opportunity. For he knew that time was money to him, in these early days when he had more leisure than fees; and besides, he had a genuine love of acquiring knowledge, all the stronger, perhaps, that he was of too cautious, modest, and self-distrustful a tempera-

ment to strike out brilliant ideas of his own. But he had
the faculty, perhaps safer for ultimate success, of acquiring and assimilating the ideas of other men. And consequently he had a keen delight in what is called "hard
reading."

His head, as he bent it over the chaotic mass of books,
had a finer expression than its ordinary one, which was a
little heavy, and sometimes a little cross. But both these
expressions originated in a sort of undeveloped look he
had, as if in him the perceptive and the practical had been
well cultivated, while the fancy lay dormant. A strong
contrast to that sweet, sensitive, poetic head of his brother's, where the balance lay in precisely the opposite direction. Any superficial observer would have wondered how
they got on together at all, except for the patent fact that
people sometimes fit into one another precisely because
they differ, when the difference is only difference and not
contrariety.

"There! I think I've got it at last!"

"Got what?" said the doctor, rousing himself and rub-
bing his fingers through his short curly locks till they
stood out all round his head like a *chevaux de frise.*

"That profile, of course. Come over and tell me if you
think it like. Pretty well, I think, for a study done from
memory. I must get her to sit to me. Will, couldn't
you manage it somehow? Couldn't you cultivate their
acquaintance?"

"I? Nonsense! I never knew what to say to women."

"Then how, in the name of fortune, do you mean to
make yourself into a London physician? If a doctor can't
be sweet to women he never earns even salt to his por-
ridge."

"As probably I never may. And then I'll keep on being a poor hospital doctor, or doing a large practice gratis,
as I do now."

"More's the pity."

"Not at all. It is practice. And it saves one from
rusting to death, or eating one's heart out in disappointment before the good time comes, as I suppose it will

come some time. And now give me your sketch to look at."

He examined it minutely, deliberately rather than enthusiastically, taking exception to certain points of feature both in it and the original, but, on the whole, very laudatory of both.

Still, Julius put up the port-folio half dissatisfied.

"You are so confoundedly cool about things. Why, Will, it's the finest subject I ever had. A perfectly correct face. Not a feature out of its place, and the coloring glorious. What a blessing to have such a model always at hand! I could understand Raffaelle's carrying off the Fornarina, and Andrea del Sarto marrying his beautiful Lucrezia, if only for convenience."

"You scape-grace!" cried the elder brother, laughing. "If I thought you were going to make a fool of yourself—"

"No, no; my fool-days are done. I'm nothing but an artist now. Don't make a mock of me, Will!—a poor, helpless fellow that can't even walk across a room."

"Yes, you could if you tried. I told you so yesterday. Will you try?"

Julius shook his head. "That was always your motto —'Try!' You should paint it on your carriage when you hunt up the Heralds' College to get arms for your two-horse brougham, in which you come to visit me in a two-pair back in Clipstone Street, or Kensal Green Cemetery. I don't know which, and don't much care."

The elder brother turned away. He was used to these sort of speeches—hardened to them, indeed; yet they could not fail slightly to affect him still, with the sort of feeling—half pity, half something less tender than pity—. with which we are prone to regard weaknesses that we ourselves can only by an effort comprehend.

"Well! in the mean time, as to your walking. I have often told you, Julius, some of your ailments are purely nervous. I mean, not exactly imaginary," seeing that Julius winced, "but in the nerves. And the nerves are queer things, my boy: very much guided by the will, which is a queerer thing yet."

"What do you mean? That I could walk if I tried?"

"Not precisely. But that if you were forced to walk
—if some strong impulse came—say a fire in the house,
and you were compelled to escape for your life—you would
find you could do it. At least that is my opinion."

"Opinions are free, of course. I wish for your sake I
could gratify you, William. I would not then be detaining you here from your practice, your profession, and all
the enjoyments of your life, in waiting upon a miserable
fellow who had much better be in his grave."

The quick, irritable pride—the readiness to take offense
—William Stedman was familiar with these vagaries too.
But the next minute they were gone, as they always were.
In the sweet nature no bitterness ever lingered long. Ju-
lius held out his hand to his brother with a child-like ex-
pression of penitence.

"I beg your pardon, Will. You're the best old fellow
alive. Give me your hand, and I'll try to walk, or at least
to stand."

"That's right."

"Will it—will it be very painful?"

The doctor hesitated; and as he looked at his brother
there came into his face that deep tenderness—wholly a
man's tenderness—which none but strong men ever feel,
and rarely feel except to women.

"Painful, lad? Yes, it may be painful. I am afraid it
will be, at first. I wish I could bear it for you. Which
is a silly speech, because I can't. Still, won't you try?"

"I will—with somebody to help me."

Ay, that was the key to his whole nature—that sensitive, loving, delicate nature. He could do almost any
thing with somebody to help him; without that, nothing.

The brother held out a steady hand; and then slowly,
shrinkingly, trembling all over with nervous apprehension,
Julius tried to raise himself in his chair and stand upon
his stiff limbs. So far he succeeded; but when he attempted to move them, the pain, or the dread of pain, was
too much for him. He fell back white and exhausted.

"It won't do, Will; it won't do."

"Not this time. Wait a few minutes, and then—"

"Must I try again? Oh, couldn't you be kind to me, and let me rest?" said the poor fellow, piteously.

"If I did, it would not be real kindness. Let me talk to you a little common·sense—you're not an invalid now, nor a baby either. Will you listen to me?"

Julius opened his eyes from the sofa where his brother had tenderly laid him down, and saw Will sitting on the table opposite, playing with a paper-cutter, but keenly observant all the while.

"Yes, I'll listen. But it will be useless; you can't give me my legs again. Oh, Will, it's easy for you to speak—such a big, strong, healthy fellow as you are! And I was the same once, or nearly so, till I threw my health away. It's too late now."

"Too late, at twenty-five? Bosh! Look here, lad. As I told you before, a doctor has a pretty severe handful with fellows like you. He has to fight against two things —the reality and the imagination. You are ill enough, I know—at least, you were when you were down with that rheumatic fever."

"By George, I was ill! Never suffered such a horrible pain in all my life. Don't tell me that was fancy."

"No; but the pain has left you now. Your last bad attack was the night you came here. I do not believe you will have any more. Your feet don't swell now; your joints are supple; in fact, your legs are as sound as my own. Yet there you sit, and let them stiffen day by day; or rather, I'm such a fool as to let you, because I happen to be brother as well as doctor. Once for all, Julius, do you wish to be a cripple for life?"

"No. Oh, my God, no!" replied Julius, with a shudder.

"Then try once more, before it is too late, and you really do lose the use of your limbs. Walk, if only three steps, to prove to yourself that walking is possible."

Julius shook his head mournfully.

"It is possible," cried Will, almost angry with earnestness. "On my honor as a doctor, there is no physical reason why you should not walk. I am sure of it."

"Of course it is only my 'fancy,' which you are always throwing in my teeth. I suppose I could jump up this minute and run a hurdle-race across the cliff for your amusement. I only wish I could, that's all! If you are right—and of course you always are right—what an awful humbug I must be!"

"I never said that—I never thought it," replied the elder brother, very patiently—far more patiently than his looks would have given reason to expect. "You are no humbug: no more than was a certain patient of mine, who fancied he could not use his right arm; went about with it in a sling; won unlimited sympathy; learned to write with his left hand; for he was an author, poor fellow!"

"Ah! according to you, half the 'poor fellows' in the world are either authors or artists."

"He would come to me," William went on, "with the saddest complaints and the most hopeless forebodings about his arm. Yet if I got him into an argument, and made him forget it, he would slip it out of the sling, and clench and flourish it in his own excitable manner; nay, I have seen him hammer it on the table as orators do. And when I smiled he would suddenly recollect himself, pull a pitiful face, and slip it back into its sling as helpless as ever."

"The hypocrite!"

"Not a bit—no more a hypocrite than you or I. He was an exceedingly honest, good fellow, but he was afflicted with nerves. He had not the sense to fight against them manfully at first, till afterwards they mastered him. He had a great dread of pain: his imagination was so vivid, and he yielded to it so entirely, that at last he could not distinguish between what he felt and what he feared, until his fancies became only too sad realities."

"How did he end?" said Julius, roused out of the contemplation of himself and his own sufferings.

"I can not tell, for I lost sight of him."

"But how do you think he would end?"

William was startled by the excessive earnestness of

the question. "I could not say—indeed, I should hardly like to speculate. In such cases, these delusions are only the beginning of the end."

"Isn't it a strange thing," said Julius, after a long pause, "that we none of us know, have not the dimmest idea how we may end? Here you and I sit, two brothers, brought up together, or nearly so; living together, with one and the same interest, and—well, old fellow! with a decent amount of what folk call brotherly love—yet how shall we both end?"

He put his thin hand on William's arm and looked at him, or rather looked beyond him into vacant space, with that expression of sad foreboding constantly seen in faces like his, which is at once cause and effect, prevision and fulfillment.

But it fell harmlessly on the unsuperstitious doctor.

"How shall we end? I trust, lad, as we began — together. And that is as much as either of us knows, or ought to know. I don't like to look far ahead myself; it does no good, and is often very silly. Come, we both have preached quite enough, let us practise a little. Will you walk back to your arm-chair?"

"You are the most obstinate, determined fellow. I do think, if I were lying dead, you would coolly walk in with your galvanic battery to galvanize me to life again."

"Perhaps I should, because I should never believe you dead. Fellows of your temperament take a vast deal of killing. Besides, I don't want you to be killed. There's a deal before you yet. Will Stedman can never set the Thames on fire, but perhaps Julius Stedman may."

Julius again shook his head, but smiled, and made an effort to rise.

"Give me your hand, Will. It's just like learning to walk again, as if I were a baby. And you did teach me to walk then, you know. You'll have to do it again now."

"Very well. Here is a finger; now toddle away, and don't be frightened, you old baby."

Julius tried, walked two or three steps with difficulty, and many an expression of suffering, then he succumbed.

"I can't, Will, I can't do it; or, at least, it isn't worth
the pain—'*Le jeu ne vaut pas la chandelle*,' as I used to say
so often. It wasn't true then; it is now. Never mind
me: let me be a cripple for life, or let me die."

"Neither the one thing nor the other. It isn't likely,
and I'll not allow it. Cheer up, my boy! You've made
a beginning, and that was all I wanted. You have had
plenty of exercise for to-night, and now for a sound sleep
till morning."

So saying he took his brother up in his arms, lifting the
thin, slight figure as easily as if it had been a woman or a
child, and carried him off to bed.

CHAPTER V.

A BRIGHT, cheery, sunshiny Sunday morning, such a Sunday as makes every honest heart glad, down to the young
'prentice-boy who sings, in that pleasant old English song—

> "Of all the days throughout the week
> I dearly love but one day,
> And that's the day that comes between
> The Saturday and Monday:
> For then I'm dress'd in all my best
> To walk abroad with Sally."

And though not dressed in all her best, and having no one
(save Edna) to walk abroad with, even Letty Kenderdine
enjoyed this Sunday; ay, though she had to attire herself
for church in the obnoxious brown bonnet and well-worn
cloak—the cloak of two winters. But under it her tall
figure, now lithe and upright with renewed health, looked
so exceedingly graceful, and above the brown bonnet-
strings, carefully tied, bloomed such apple-blossom cheeks,
that when she saw herself in the glass even Letty was contented. Perhaps all the more so because her beauty had
not been quite unbeheld.

Passing through the hall, Dr. Stedman, who chanced to
open his door at the same moment, had bowed to her with
a courteous "good-morning," not pausing to say more;

though she declared to Edna he looked as if he should
have liked it, and she was certain he blushed. However,
he had given the mere salutation and walked rapidly on
ahead, till the sisters lost sight of him.

"Very good manners. He evidently does not wish to
intrude," observed Letty.

"No gentleman would," said Edna, "unless quite sure
that we desired his company."

"I wonder where he is going? Probably to church—
so you see he must be quite respectable."

A little lurking devil in Edna's spirit inclined her to begin and argue that question, and prove how many bad
people went to church, and how many good people conscientiously staid away; but she restrained it, and soon
forgot the evil spirit in the delicious calm of their walk,
through lanes green with budding hedge-leaves and sweet
with the scent of primroses, to the tiny old village church.
Such a contrast it was to their London church—so different was this day to their terrible London Sundays, with
the incessant stream of feet pattering along the dusty,
glaring pavement, church-goers and holiday-makers all
hurrying on to their worship, their amusement, or their
vice, with much the same countenance, and perhaps with
not such a vital difference in their hearts! Edna often
used to think so, and then rebuked herself for her uncharitableness.

But, in truth, she hated London—she hated, above all
things, London Sundays. Her Sundays here, in the gray
little church, with a green vision of the outside world
showing through its unpainted windows and open door,
recalled to her the sweet peaceful Sabbaths of her childhood, when she was a little country girl in Hampshire, and
was taken across fields and woods to just such a village
church as this. As she sat there, in the free seats (which
Letty did not like at all), there came back into her head a
poem which, in her dreary school-days at St. John's Wood,
she had learned, and the school-mistress had reproved her
because there was "love" in it. But Edna had fancied
it because there was in it a feeling like those country Sun-

days; and oh! how unlike the Sunday at St. John's Wood!
It was something about—

> "There the green lane descends,
> Through which I walked to church with thee,
> O gentlest of my friends!

> "The shadow of the linden-trees
> Lay moving on the grass,
> Between them and the moving boughs,
> A shadow, thou didst pass.

> "Thy dress was like the lilies,
> And thy heart was pure as they:
> One of God's holy messengers
> Did walk with me that day."

And so on, and so on—sweet stray verses, which all the
service long "beat time to nothing" in Edna's brain. A
strangely simple, yet acute and tenacious brain—a strangely young heart, that in the midst of all its cares could go
back upon lots of silly childish poetry. Yet she did so,
and recalled the exact state of mind she was in when she
learned it—poor little sixteen-year-old girl, brimming over
with romantic dreams, none of which had ever come true.
No, not one; nor did she expect it now; yet they were to
this day vivid as ever. And as, with a half-comical appli-
cation to the present, her fancy went over the lines—

> "Long was the good man's sermon,
> But it seemed not so to me;
> For he spake of Ruth the beautiful,
> And still I thought of thee.

> "Long was the prayer he uttered,
> Yet it seemed not so to me;
> For in my heart I prayed with him,
> And still I thought of thee."

—she still felt, as she remembered to have done then, that
it would be the summit of earthly happiness to go peacefully to church—just such a village church as this, and on
just such a summer Sunday morning—and sit there, with
the beloved of one's heart, worshipping and loving, with

the prayer that has its root in love, and the love that is worth nothing unless it is a perpetual prayer.

"What a dear little church this is!" she whispered to her sister as they went out.

"Very; but a rather common congregation. I saw scarcely any one above the class of farmers, except in the rectory pew. And did you notice a bonnet there—straw, with a green trimming and a wreath of pink daisies all round the face? That is how I should like my bonnet, Edna. Please, remember."

"Very well."

"Dr. Stedman did go to church. He sat just behind us. Didn't you see him?"

"No. In truth, I had forgotten all about him."

"Hush! there he is."

He might have overheard the remark, for he passed close by the sisters, passed again with only a bow—not manifesting the slightest intention of stopping and speaking, like the rest of the congregation, who lingered in friendly groups all the way between the church-porch and the lichgate. Presently his long strides took him far away down the road.

"What very odd manners!" remarked Letty, a little annoyed.

"I think they are the manners of a gentleman who has the sense not to intrude upon two ladies who have neither father nor brother to make his acquaintance desirable—or even possible," said Edna, determined to hold to her resolution, and allow no loop-hole of civility through which the enemy might assault their little encampment, and bring about that passage of arms for which Letty was evidently accoutring herself—making ready for a tournament which, in Edna's mind, was either foolish child's play, or a battle royal for life and death.

Not that any idea of so serious a crisis struck her on that bright Sunday morning. She simply thought that her sister wanted a bit of flirtation, and was resolute she should not have it. At which Letty sulked a little all the afternoon, and spent a long, leisurely, lazy Sunday, with-

out referring again to either Doctor Stedman or his
brother.

After tea she insisted she was strong enough to go to
church a second time, but recalled her wish when she
looked out on the sweet Sabbath evening. "We'll take a
walk instead, if you are not too good, Edna."

Edna was not in the least too good. She longed to be
out in the green lanes, enjoying the birds' Sunday hymns,
and the incense of the Sunday flowers, and the uplifting
of the elm-trees' tall arms, in a dumb thanksgiving for
being again clothed with leaves: all creatures, great and
small, seeming to feel themselves happier and merrier on
a Sunday than on any common day. So she brought
down Letty's hat—deposing the obnoxious brown bonnet
—wrapped her up well in a warm shawl, and went out
with her, having first cast a glance to see if the opposite
door were shut. It was, and the blinds were down. The
brothers seemed seldom or never to go out of evenings.

The sisters crossed the threshold with light steps and
lighter hearts. But as they did so the grim invisible
Woman, sitting there, laughed at them, knowing she had
her will—not they.

And what of the two divided from them by just a wall
on this momentous, monotonous Sunday—the two young
men, about whom, whether they thought or not, they said
nothing?

Julius Stedman had been terribly depressed all day.
There came upon him one of those moody fits to which,
even in health, he had been subject, and which now were
so severe as to try to the utmost both body and mind; and
the cloud did not lift off for hours. Except during church-
time, his brother never left him, but hovered about him
with a tenderness, less brotherly than sisterly, alternately
reasoning and jesting, reproving and persuading, but all in
vain. He lay silent, shutting out daylight and cheerfulness, refusing to do any thing, or to suffer any thing to be
done for him. At last, *apropos* of nothing that William
could discover, unless it was the ringing of the bells and
the closing of the hall-door, indicating the departure of

somebody to evening church, Julius said, "I should like to go out."

The doctor remonstrated. It was late—the dew would soon be falling.

"What do I care? What need I care? It will do me no harm. Or if it did, what matter? You can't cure me, Will, with your cleverness. You had better kill me off quick."

"How? Mention the easiest way."

"Oh, any thing. I hate this shilly-shally work — one day better, the next day worse. Your prognostications were all wrong. This place does not cure me, and never will."

"Shall we go back to London?"

"Horrible! No. Besides, didn't you tell me you wanted a fortnight's quiet reading before your hospital lectures began?"

"I'll manage about that, if you would like to go home. In fact, though it isn't much of a home we have, I think we should be better off there than here."

Then, with the contrariness of sickness, Julius veered round, and argued energetically, almost irritably, on the other side.

Dr. Stedman could not repress his annoyance. He was a man who always knew his own mind, and his brother's indecision tried him severely.

"Have it which way you like," he said, sharply. "You are as bad to deal with as any woman. Stay or go—which you choose; only let me know, that I may take my measures accordingly."

"As bad as a woman," repeated Julius, mournfully. "Yes, I suppose I am. Not half a man, and never shall be. Ah! I wish I had some woman about me; she would pity me; she would understand me. Nay, Will, don't look savage. I didn't mean to vex you."

"Nor did you vex me; so don't be fancying that among other nonsense," returned Will, with some impatience. "Just let us try to have an ounce of common sense between us. The larger matters we can settle to-morrow.

At present the question is, Will you or will you not go out
this evening? Say yes, and I'll go and fetch the chair."

"Thank you. But it's late, and it's Sunday evening."

"Pshaw!" The doctor rose, searched for his hat, and
was off in a minute.

In ten minutes more the brothers were out on the cliffs,
in their accustomed mode of progression, along the familiar way. Doubtless, a weary life for them both; an unnatural life for two young men, in the very flower of their
age, and both in the most critical time of their career; a
time when to most men every week, every day is of moment as regards their future. Yet here they were, passing
it in compulsory idleness. No wonder both were silent,
and that the lovely evening did not steal into their hearts
as it did into those of the two young women. Nay, their
forced companionship seemed to throw the brothers wider
apart than it had done the sisters. True, Will and Julius
never quarrelled, as Letty and Edna sometimes did—burst-
ing into a thunder-storm of words, ending in tears and kiss-
es of reconciliation—womanish but safe. On the contrary, each fortified himself behind his masculine armor of
steely reticence, smooth and cold, feeling all the while that
within it he was a dull fellow—a solitary fellow—even
with his own brother beside him. Such lonely moments
come to all people—before marriage (Heaven help them
if they come after marriage!)—and it would be well if
brothers and sisters, fathers and mothers, recognized this
fact—as a law of God and necessity—that all the love of
duty never makes up for the love of choice.

What poor Julius was thinking of as he sat, helplessly
propelled along, and looked listlessly on the sweet landscape that he had neither strength nor heart to paint—
what William felt as he expended in pushing the Bath-
chair the manly strength that would have enjoyed a good
twenty-mile walk across the island, geologizing, botaniz-
ing, and what not—must remain alike unknown. Certainly, neither brother communicated his feelings to the other.
They were uncommonly dull company this evening, and
that was the truth of it.

The cliffs were deserted—all the good people at church. Only, just as they were returning home, Julius pointed out two figures standing on the cliff-top, sharp against the sky.

"Two ladies, I think they are—a very tall one and a very short one."

"It is probably the Misses Kenderdine. They were out, for I saw their door open as we passed."

"Hurry back then, Will. Don't let us meet them. They will only look at me with their confounded pity. I hate being pitied. Make haste!"

The doctor did his best, but there were some steep little ascents and descents which required all his skill and strength. In one of these his pilotage failed. In turning past a large stone the wheel came off, and the chair toppled over, landing its occupant ignominiously on the grass.

A slight, almost ridiculous accident, if it had not happened to an invalid, and to such a nervous invalid as Julius Stedman. As it was, his brother was seriously alarmed. But Julius, whose state could never be counted on with certainty for five minutes at a time, seemed to·take his disaster easily enough. Nay, the little excitement roused his mobile temperament into healthy vitality. He sat on the grass, perfectly unhurt, and laughing heartily.

"I never knew such a 'spill.' Done as cleverly as if you had done it on purpose—perhaps to attract the attention of those ladies. They evidently think we have had a frightful accident. See how they are running to the rescue—that is, the little one; the other is too majestic to run. She stalks down, Juno-like, to offer her benign aid to me, miserable mortal! And, by Juno, what a gait she has! Never did I see such a handsome creature! No, I thank you, Miss Kenderdine," added he, when, a second time led away by her impulse of kindness, Edna came hastily down to the scene of disaster. "No, I'm not killed —not this time. But I seem always destined to fall into sudden misfortune and have you appearing to me as my guardian angel."

Edna did not laugh, for she caught sight of Dr. Stedman's anxious face, and guessed at once that the position

of affairs was rather serious—the chair useless, no carriage
attainable, the dews beginning to fall heavily, and they on
the cliff-top, at least a quarter of a mile from home, with
an invalid who could not walk a step, and was too heavy
to be carried.

"What is to be done?" said she, in a low tone, to the
elder brother, while the younger, oblivious of his disaster,
became absorbed in conversation with Letty, who, arriving
stately and slowly, had just begun to hope, with condescending interest, that he had not hurt himself. "I see
how things are. What must we do?" repeated Edna, in unconscious fraternity. "Shall I run and fetch assistance?"

"No; it would only annoy him. Besides, there is no
need. We must get him to walk home. I know he could
walk if he tried."

Edna looked amazed—a little indignant.

"You think me cruel, I know; but we doctors are
obliged to be so to some sort of patients. And it is the
real truth. He is quite capable of walking a short distance, and I shall be rather thankful for any thing that
forces him to acknowledge it. Am I very hard-hearted,
Miss Kenderdine?"

"I can not say. I suppose you know best."

This little conversation was carried on in confidence
over the broken wheel, but there was no time for discussion. Every minute the air grew more chill and the grass
more dewy; the tide was rising, and the wind that came
in with it began to blow freshly from over the sea. To
healthy people it was delicious—intoxicating in its pure
saltness; but to the invalid, though apparently he did not
notice it, being engaged talking to Letty, who was sym-
pathizing with him in the most charming manner—to a
person in Julius Stedman's condition, Edna felt that it
might be most dangerous.

"We must get him home somehow at once, and I see
but one way," said the doctor, with a professional air, decisive and dictatorial, which at any other time would have
amused Edna. "Will you help me, Miss Kenderdine? If
I support him on one side, will you let him lean on you at

the other? I am sorry to trouble you—very sorry; but it is a case of emergency. And if, as you said, you are accustomed to sick-nursing—"

"Yes; and I think I can do this. I have almost carried Letty many a time. Though I am small, I am very strong."

"I can see that."

"But how will you persuade him to walk?"

"Will you suggest it? It might come better, coming from a stranger. Try, please; for we have not a minute to lose."

Nobody knew exactly how it was done—probably by the invalid's being taken by surprise, and left no chance of refusing; but it was done. Between his two supporters Julius was marched remorselessly on, half in jest, half in earnest, across the smooth down. And then, no doubt, it was rather pleasant to be assisted in his steps by one charming girl, and have his progress watched and encouraged by another. Be that as it may, Julius did walk, with the assistance of his brother and Miss Kenderdine, the whole quarter of a mile; and when he reached the garden gate, so far from being exhausted, as they had expected, he turned, with his countenance all beaming—

"How cleverly I have done it! I do think I shall get back the use of my limbs. Will said so—but I never believed him. I say, old fellow, don't be too conceited—but you were right, after all."

The doctor smiled. Edna saw something in his face that touched her even more than the delighted excitement in that of the invalid.

"Oh, if you knew what it feels like!" said Julius to Edna. "To have been tied and bound for weeks to that chair—to feel as if one should never walk any more; and now, I do believe, if you would let me, I could walk quite alone."

"Try," said the doctor, composedly.

"Oh, do try!" cried Edna, eagerly.

The young man did try, and succeeded. Very tottering steps they were, and not many of them, for his brother would not allow it; but he did really walk—alone and unassisted. And only those who know what it is to be de-

prived for a season of the power of locomotion, or of any
power which we use so commonly and thanklessly that we
need to lose it before we fully recognize its blessing, can
understand the ecstasy which lit up every feature of the
poor fellow's face, and was reflected in the faces round
about him.

"I declare I am just like a baby—a baby first learning
to walk," said Julius, viewing first one leg and then the
other—patting them and looking down upon them as if
they were quite new acquaintances or lately-recovered
friends. "Don't laugh at me, please, you two young ladies. Will, there, won't; he knows I always was a simpleton. And then I have been so ill, and the future has
looked so terrible. Don't laugh at me."

"We are not laughing," said Letty, whose good-nature
had really been roused—so much so as to forget herself,
her "unfortunate appearance," and the sense of dignified
propriety due to both, in the warm human interest of the
moment. "Indeed, we are exceedingly glad to see you
better—are we not, sister?"

But Edna was so moved that she was actually crying.

"How good you are!" said Julius, taking her hand and
pressing it warmly. While the whole four stood silent,
something—they knew not what—seemed to come creeping round them like an atmosphere of peace, and kindliness, and mutual sympathy—compelling them into friendliness, whether they willed it or not. And as they stood
at the front door, the soft, gray, misty twilight was drawing a veil over the sea, and the robin-redbreast, from his
nest at the cliff's edge, gave one or two good-night war-
bles over his mate and his little ones, and the first star
came out, large and bright, in the zenith. This sunshiny
Sunday was making a good end.

"Come in, now," said the doctor, for nobody seemed disposed to stir. "At least, we must. Julius, say good-night,
with many thanks, to these two ladies. Are you quite
warm, lad? I wish I had ordered a fire."

"Ours is lit," said Edna; and, with a glance at her sister,
she did on the impulse of the moment what seemed a sim-

ple thing enough, yet was the very last thing which, an
hour ago, she would have thought of doing—the thing of
all others she had determined not to do—she invited the
brothers into their parlor.

"It will prevent all danger of a chill," said the little
woman, turning to Dr. Stedman with quite a grandmotherly air. "Your room will be warm in half an hour; and
meantime he can lie down. We have a capital sofa; indeed, Mrs. Williams told us it was better than yours, and
we offered to exchange."

"Do not think of such a thing," said Julius. "I shall
soon be well; indeed, I feel myself well now. It is astonishing what good this evening has done me; or rather, not
astonishing—a little society cheers one up so much. Well,
I may go in and sit by that nice blazing fire?"

"By all means, since these ladies are so kind."

The doctor helped his brother in, made him comfortable
on the sofa ("and how cleverly he did it too—wouldn't he
be uncommonly good to his wife, that great big fellow!"
remarked Letty afterwards), and then was about depart-
ing, as if he hesitated to consider any one but Julius included in the invitation.

Letty said, in her most stately but most fascinating manner, "she hoped Dr. Stedman would remain." So he remained.

It was the first evening they ever spent together—these
four; indeed, it could scarcely be called an evening, for Dr.
Stedman carried his brother away remorselessly at the half-
hour's end. Its incidents were unimportant, and its conversation trivial, as is usually the case with first acquaintance. Only in books, seldom or never in real life, do
youths and maidens dash into the Romeo-and-Juliet passion of the instant. Nowadays people—even young people—rarely fall in love; they walk into it deliberately and
open-eyed, or slip into it gradually unawares. It is all one.

> "Come he slow, or come he fast,
> It is but Love that comes at last."

The only notable fact in the evening's entertainment

was that, ere he sat down, Dr. Stedman pointedly took out
his card and laid it before the sisters.

"I think, Julius, before we intrude upon these ladies'
hospitality, we ought to tell them who and what we are.
Miss Kenderdine, my brother is an artist, and I am a doctor. There are only we two; our parents are long dead,
and we never had a sister. We live at Kensington, where
I have taken the practice of the late Dr. Young."

"We knew Dr. Young," replied Edna, with very considerable relief; "and we heard he had a high opinion of
the gentleman who afterwards succeeded him. That must
have been yourself?"

Dr. Stedman bowed. "Then," he added, smiling, and in
his smile the not quite good-tempered look before spoken
of certainly disappeared—"then I may be considered to
have given in our certificates of character?"

"Not mine," observed Julius from the sofa. "I may be
a most awful scape-grace for all these ladies know; a ne'er-
do-weel, hanging round the neck of my respectable brother
like a millstone on an old man of the sea; a poor artist—
disreputable, as most poor artists are. Nobody can expect
the luxury of a character unless he is rich; and I am as
poor as a church mouse, I assure you, Miss Kenderdine.
All our money came to Will there; his grandfather's pet
he was, and he left him his heir, but he halves it all with
me, and—"

"Julius, what nonsense you are talking!"

"I always do talk nonsense when I'm happy; and I am
so happy to-night I can't think what has come over me.
So now you know all about us, Miss Kenderdine; and you
may either make friends of us or not, as you choose."

"Say, rather, acquaintance; friendship does not come
all in a minute," said the doctor, regarding his brother,
who sat looking so handsome and bright, pleasant and
lovable, with something of the expression, deprecating yet
proud, with which a parent regards a spoiled child, for
whom he feels bound to apologize, but can not quite see
the necessity, and thinks every body must secretly be in
as admiring an attitude as he himself. In fact, the big

brother's evident admiration of the sickly one struck the sisters as something quite funny—if it were not so touching and so unusual in its way.

"Well, then—we being two lonely brothers, and they two sisters, thrown together in this not too lively abode—will they kindly permit our acquaintance, after the pattern of Queen Elizabeth's celebrated letter—'Yours as you demean yourselves, Edna Kenderdine and—I have not heard your sister's Christian name."

"Letty—Letitia," said the owner of it, looking downward.

This was the only information vouchsafed to the two guests by their hostesses. As Letty said, after they were gone, the two brothers, who were evidently gentlemen, must have seen at a glance that she and her sister were gentlewomen; and any further facts were quite unnecessary.

Edna thought so too; still, with her exceeding candor, and perhaps a lurking pride, she would have liked them—the doctor especially—to know that Letty and herself were only school-mistresses.

CHAPTER VI.

WHY do people take to loving one another—or liking, the customary and safe preliminary to loving? And how does the love first come? Through what mysterious process do young folks pass, by steps rapid or slow, according to circumstances and their own idiosyncrasy, out of the common world—the quiet, colorless, everyday world—into that strange new paradise from which there is no returning? No, none! We may be driven out of it by an angel with a flaming sword—out into the wilderness, which we have to till and keep, changing its thorns and thistles into a respectable ordinary garden—we may pass out of it, calmly and happily, into a new earth—safe and sweet, and homelike; but this particular paradise is never found again—never re-entered more.

Why should it be? All life is a mere progression—a
pressing on and on; and death itself—we Christians believe—but a higher development into more perfect life.
Yet as nothing good is ever lost, or wholly forgotten, one
can imagine even a disembodied spirit sitting glorious before the great white throne, recalling with a tender sweetness the old earthly heaven which was first created by that
strange state of mind—that intoxicating idealization of
all things within as without, as if every thing were beheld
with new eyes—the eyes of a creature new-bound; the
condition which silly folk call being "in love."

It has its sillinesses—no one will deny; its weaknesses
and madnesses; but it has its divine side too, chiefly because then, and not till then, comes the complete absorption
of self into some other being dearer and better, higher and
nobler than one's self, or imagined so; which is the foundation of every thing divine in human nature. If men or
women are ever good at all—ever heroic, unselfish, self-
denying—they will be so when they first fall in love; and
if the love be worthy, that goodness will take root and
grow. As a tree is known by its fruits, so a noble love,
be it happy or unhappy, ennobles a whole life. And I
think no friends—no parents especially—if they are real
friends, real parents, true as tender, generous as wise, can
see two young people standing at the enchanted gate
without a prayerful thankfulness—ay, thankfulness. For
it is the gate of life to them, whatever be the end.

Neither friends nor kindred stood by these four to watch
or warn them, to help or to hinder their footsteps, in entering this unknown paradise; they walked into it deliberately, day by day and hour by hour, from that first Sunday night when Julius Stedman lay on the Misses Kenderdine's sofa, talking to one and gazing at the other,
with all his heart both in his lips and eyes.

He was the grand foundation of the acquaintance, the
corner-stone which seemed to make it all safe and right
and natural. The sacredness of sickness was upon him
and around him; for after the exertion of that night he
fell back considerably, and for some days made his brother

and his friends—in the anxiety they grew into friends—very miserable about him. The Misses Kenderdine were by no means strong-minded women, to fly in the face of the world, and make acquaintance with, or suffer themselves to be made acquaintances by, any stray young man they happened to meet. They had a keen sense of decorum; but then it was the decorum of true womanliness, the pure simplicity of soul which sees no harm in things not really harmful; the sweet dignity of maidenhood, which, feeling that, known or unknown, met or unmet, there can be to any woman but one man alive who is a possible husband, regards the rest of the sex with a gentle kindness—a placid indifference—nothing more.

At least such was Edna's condition, and by the strong influence of her character she turned Letty into the same, or an imitation of the same, for the time being. After a long consultation between themselves, the sisters agreed that it would be ridiculous in them to stand aloof from the poor sick fellow in the next room, and his grave, anxious brother, who seemed wholly absorbed in nursing him, because these happened to be young men, and they themselves young women; and no regular introduction in society had taken place between them.

"But we know all about them, nevertheless," argued Edna. "I quite well remember that when I was urged to send for Dr. Young to you, and found he had died suddenly, his successor was very highly recommended. It must have been the same Dr. Stedman. Had I sent, and had he attended you in the fever, how very funny it would have been!"

"Yes, indeed. Suppose we tell him what a near escape he had of either killing or curing me!"

"I think not, dear. As you say, there is no necessity for them to know any thing about us. I do not mean even to tell them that we live at Kensington; but it is a satisfaction to know something about Dr. Stedman, and it warrants us in being kind and civil a little to that poor sick lad—he looks no more than a lad. And how very ill he seemed this morning!"

D 2

So Edna reasoned with herself, most simply and sincerely; as she drifted—they all drifted—into that frank association, which, the first barrier being broken, was sure to come to people living in the same house, having nothing in the wide world to do but to go out and come in, and watch each other's goings out and comings in, innocently enough; but yet with a certain interest that appeared to waken up into new life the whole party, especially the invalids.

For Letty was a little of an invalid again. She took a slight chill; and Dr. Stedman prescribed for her in a very reticent, formal, but still pleasant and friendly way, which further helped on the intimacy between them. And as for Edna, her chief friend, as she openly declared, was Julius. He took to her suddenly and completely, with a kind of child-like dependence, so affectionately persistent that there was no withstanding it. Soon it became quite natural for him to send for her in to sit with him when his brother went out, to beg her to accompany them and "see that nothing happened to them" in the daily walk that Will shortly began to insist upon, first round the garden, and gradually lengthening, to the total abolition of the Bath-chair. He talked and jested with her alternately, for she was a merry as well as earnest little woman; he tyrannized over her, making her see to his little comforts, which she did in quite a motherly, or, rather, as he declared, a "grandmotherly" way; sometimes he even presumed to tease her, but all in such frank, boyish, and yet perfectly gentlemanly fashion, that the result was inevitable—Edna grew exceedingly fond of him.

"Fond of" is the word—that gentle tenderness which almost invariably, though not always, precludes the possibility of any thing more.

This firm alliance, open and free, between Julius and Edna, made things progress amazingly, and threw the two others together more than Letty's sister would, a week ago, have dared to risk. But then Dr. Stedman, the more she knew of him, seemed the more unlikely to fall into the ranks of Letty's victims, being exceedingly sedate and

middle-aged for his years, and apparently not at all disposed to make the best of his opportunities. He would
walk by Letty's side for hours without detaching her
from the others, or talking to her very much himself;
he seemed to like looking at her as any man might, and
that was all. Obviously he was incapable of flirtation,
did not seem to understand what it meant, carried on all
conversations with the sisters in the most open, grave, and
courteous earnest; as Letty declared, it would have been
quite impossible for her to set up a flirtation with him,
even had she tried.

. To do her justice, she did not try. She too was subdued by the shadow of heavy sickness, which she had so
lately escaped, and which still hung over the two brothers.
Her sympathy was aroused; she thought less of herself
and her charms, and was consequently more charming than
she had ever been in her life.

Did the young men see and feel it? This extraordinary
fascination, half of soul, half of sense, which breathes in
the very atmosphere of a beautiful woman, if she has any
thing womanly in her at all. And Letty had a good deal.
There was in her not a particle of ill-nature, that "envy,
malice, and all uncharitableness," which women have sometimes sore need to pray against. She was always gentle
and lady-like, and extremely sweet-tempered. If, taken
altogether, her character was chiefly made up of negatives,
her beauty was a thing so positive that it supplied all deficiencies, at least for a long time. In the eyes of men,
probably for always.

Julius had his wish, and made sketches innumerable,
sometimes open, sometimes surreptitious, of her flexible
figure and lovely face. Of evenings he used to repeat
them from memory, and make compositions out of them.
Dr. Stedman was called out of his medical researches for
endless criticism upon Miss Kenderdine — they always
called her Miss Kenderdine, and her sister Miss Edna,
though why, nobody knew—as the gardener's daughter,

> "Gowned in pure white that fitted to the shape,
> Holding a branch to fix it back,"

Miss Kenderdine in mediæval costume, as Kreimhild in the
Niebelungenlied, and Miss Kenderdine with her hat off,
and sea-weeds in her hair, standing with the tide rolling
in upon her feet, musing pensively with head bent forward
—a veritable Ariadne of Naxos.

"That's the best, I think," said Will, whose comments
were always sharp, short, and decisive.

"I think so too," replied the other, lingering over his
work with an artist's delight. "There is a wonderful deal
of the Ariadne in her face naturally."

"Yes. The features are of the true Greek type—sensu-
ous without being sensual, pleasure-loving, but not coarse.
She ought to marry a rich man, and then she would do
uncommonly well."

"Probably; so would most women," said Julius, with
some sharpness.

Will did not notice that, but still gazed in keen criticism on the sketch.

"Ay, it's like her; a true Ariadne face—that, Theseus
lost, would take up very comfortably with Bacchus."

"Horrible!" cried the artist. "I never knew such a
matter-of-fact, abominably blunt fellow as you. You
might as well say that if Miss Kenderdine were disappointed in love she would take to drinking."

"She might. I have seen some terrible cases of female
Bacchants under similar circumstances. But I beg your
pardon. You need not tell her I said so. Besides, she is
never likely to be disappointed in love," added the doctor,
as he put down the sketch-book, and ceased the conversation.

It was the only conversation that during the first fortnight the brothers held concerning their new acquaintances. Indeed, there was not time, for, excepting the late
working hours — after nine or ten o'clock — scarcely an
hour passed when the occupants of the two parlors did
not meet, or sit waiting, expectant of the chance of meeting. Not that any walks or talks were purposely or sys-
tematically planned — still they always seemed to come
about, and at length both sides seemed to make reasons
or excuses for them.

"We are just a lot of children out on a holiday," said Julius one day, when they were all sitting eating their combined lunch on a primrose bank, with larks singing madly overhead, the salt wind freshening all their faces, and far away the outline of white cliffs and blue sea stretching into infinite brightness—infinite peace. "Just mere children, Miss Edna, and oh, do let us enjoy ourselves as such. We shall have hard enough work when we get home."

"That is true," said Edna, with a half sigh; and she too gave herself up to the enjoyment of the moment.

None the less enjoyable that it was, strangely enough, the first time in their lives that these two young women had had any frank association with men—good, pleasant, clever men. To Letty the opposite sex had always come in the form of lovers—not always satisfactory, especially in the amazing plurality with which they had blessed Letitia Kenderdine; while Edna knew nothing about men at all. That cheerful, frank intercourse—social, moral, and intellectual—which, within limits, does both sexes a world of good, was to her not only a novelty, but an exceeding pleasure. She was not a stupid woman—indeed it sometimes dawned upon her that she might have a few brains of her own, since she could so readily enter into the talk of these two men, who both, in their way, were undoubtedly clever men—thoughtful, original, and with no folly or coarseness about them, such as would at once have repelled these maidenly gentlewomen. Neither of the brothers attempted in the slightest degree to make love to Letty, and both treated Edna with a grateful politeness, a true heart courtesy, that did her own heart good. For, she argued to herself, it was not like the civilities shown to Letty; it must be sincere, since it was shown to a poor, plain little school-mistress. She had taken care to let their new friends know they were only school-mistresses, teaching tradesmen's daughters in a London suburb—so much, no more; and she had noticed with approbation that neither brother had made the slightest further inquiry; nor had their respective positions in life, or pecuniary affairs, or family connections, been again referred to.

Thus they spent day after day, these four young people, in as complete an Arcadia as if there were no such a place as the common, working-day world, no sound of which ever reached them. This little Isle of Wight, which was not then what it is now, but far simpler, far lonelier, far lovelier—though it is lovely yet—might have been an enchanted island of the sea—an Atlantis, such as weary mariners sailed after in vain—where no one toiled and no one suffered; no one hated, or quarrelled, or betrayed; but all within was as sweet and peaceful as without, and where these young people seemed to live a life as innocent as the birds, and as peaceful as the primroses.

Letty even forgot her new bonnet, Edna never took that expedition to Ryde; it seemed a pity to waste a day thereon; and for two Sundays more the sisters went contentedly to church in their winter's clothes. But it was spring in both their hearts all the while.

This was, they agreed, the most wonderful spring they had ever seen. The primroses were so large; the hyacinths so innumerable and intensely blue, and the trees came into leaf with such especial luxuriance—all in a minute, as it seemed; some days you could almost see them growing. The twenty-ninth of May the oaks were full enough to shelter a moderate-sized King Charles; and on a certain country walk Edna discussed eagerly with Julius that celebrated historical fact, which he had tried to illustrate by a large cartoon in the previous year's exhibition at Westminster Hall.

"Did you compete for the prizes?" she asked, walking along by his side, while the others went on ahead, this being their usual way, because Letty disliked being hindered with Julius's still feeble steps.

"I tried, but I failed. I always do fail, somehow."

"That is hard. I wonder why it should be so, when you are so very clever," said Edna, innocently.

"Perhaps other people—Will especially—think me cleverer than I am. I don't know how it is," added he, mournfully, "but I always seem to miss the exact point of success. I get near it, but I never touch it. I am afraid my life has been—always will be—a failure."

"Many lives are, that do not show it outside," replied Edna, more sadly than her wont. For she too, on that sunshiny day, with all things luring her to enjoyment, had become slightly conscious of something lacking. Did the others feel it, she wondered? Was Letty, there, as happy as she looked, when stopping with Dr. Stedman on the summit of the steep cliff, up which she herself had managed to climb with Julius, indulging him with the fancy that he was helping her, while, in reality, she supported him—a common fiction.

"My brother and your sister have got on ahead of us," said Julius, pausing, breathless. "They seem capital friends. He admires her extremely, as, indeed, every body must do. She is the most beautiful person we ever saw."

"Yes; all people say that. I am quite used to hearing it now."

"Of course you are, which must be my apology for making the remark. The fact is so patent that it ceases to be either a compliment or an impertinence."

"It would never be an impertinence, said as you say it," replied Edna, gently, for she saw that the young man was a little annoyed in some way. "Yet, I will confess, you are the first person whom I ever heard call my sister handsome without its making me angry."

"What an odd observation to make! How it might be misinterpreted!"

"How? That it meant I was jealous of her? Oh, how very funny! What an altogether ridiculous idea! Me jealous of my sister because she is so beautiful, while I myself am—well—"

"Never mind what you are," interrupted Julius, blushing, for he felt he was treading on the very bounds of incivility.

"Oh, but I do mind a little. I confess I should like to have been handsome, too. But as it can't be, it can't be; and I have now grown quite used to being plain." ·

Julius was fairly puzzled. It had been his trial, and a not inconsiderable one, in his acquaintance, or friendship, or whatever it was, with this sweet little woman, that she was so plain. To his keen artist eye her want of complexion, of feature, and general brilliancy of effect, was sometimes really annoying. She would have been so attractive, so original, so altogether charming—if only she had been a very little prettier.

Of course he would not betray this, and yet he did not like to tell an untruth, or to pay a silly compliment, which the candid Edna could at once have discovered and scorned. A bright thought struck him, and he compromised with it.

"Plain, are you? Every body doesn't think so; Will doesn't. The very first night he saw you, when you sat adding up your accounts, he told me what a nice face you had."

"Did he? I am sure I am very much obliged to him."

"And your sister?" continued Julius, still watching the other two with an intentness that might have seemed peculiar had not Edna now become accustomed to his artist way of staring—"quite in the way of business," as he took care to explain. "What does your sister think of Will?"

"I really can not tell," replied Edna, smiling. "In truth I have not the slightest idea."

She might have added—once she thought she would, and then despised herself for such an unsisterly betrayal —that Letty's thoughts did not much matter, as she was not in the habit of thinking long or seriously about any thing. So she held her tongue, and the brotherly earnestness of her companion's next speech shamed her still more.

"I hope she likes him; she ought—you both ought, for I am sure he likes you, which is a great deal to say for Will, as he does not usually get on with young ladies. Yet he is a wonderfully good fellow, Miss Edna; a fine fellow in every way, as you would say if you knew him."

"I have no doubt of it."

"Brothers don't often pull together as well as we do, yet we are very unlike, and I have tried him not a little. When I get strong—if I ever do get strong—"

"You certainly will. Dr. Stedman said so to me only yesterday."

"What was he saying about me? You see, Will and I don't talk much either of or to one another, and I should like to know what he could find to say."

Edna hesitated a moment whether or not to repeat this, the only bit of confidence that had ever passed between herself and the doctor, and which had at once amazed and puzzled her for the time: it seemed so very uncalled for. Then she thought she would tell it, for it could do no possible harm out of its anxious brotherly affectionateness. And it might even do good, by rousing Julius out of that languid indifference to the future, that loose grasp of life, with its duties and pleasures alike, which was such a sad, nay, a fatal thing to see in a young man of his age.

"It was very little your brother said; only he told me his firm conviction that you had no real disease or feebleness of constitution. You would be all right if you could once be roused out of your melancholy and moody fits by any strong feeling of any kind: made to take care of your health, work hard, though not too hard, and finally marry and settle."

"Did he say that? Did he want me to marry?"

"Very much indeed," replied Edna, laughing. "No match-making mother was ever more earnest on the subject. He said that a good wife would be the best blessing that could happen to you, and the sooner it happened the better."

"Were those his words? Exceedingly obliged to him!"

From the tone Edna could hardly tell whether the young man was pleased or vexed, but he blushed extremely: so much so that she began to blush too, and to question within herself whether she had not gone a little too far, and in her sublime grandmotherly indifference had overstepped the boundary of maidenly propriety. But at this instant the other two returned, and the conversation became general.

Edna was glad Dr. Stedman had called hers "a nice face." It showed that he liked her, and she had rather

thought the contrary. Scarcely from any expression or
non-expression of the fact, but because he did not seem a
person who would easily like any body: but once liking,
his fidelity would be sure for life. Or so at least fancied
Edna in her simple speculations upon character, in which
she was fond of indulging—as most people are who do not
take very much trouble in thinking about themselves.
She must think about something, and not being given to
lofty musings or abstract cogitations, she thought about
her neighbors; and, for the remainder of that walk, about
that special neighbor who had been her first acquaintance
of the two; since Dr. Stedman had more than once declared, when they were jesting on the subject, that his acquaintance with the sisters dated from the moment when
he had been moved to such deep sympathy by Miss Edna's
arithmetical woes.

She was glad he liked her, for she liked him; his keen
intelligence, less brilliant than Julius's, but solid, thorough, and clear; his honesty of speech and simple unpre-
tending goodness—especially his unvarying goodness to
his brother, over whom his anxiety and his patience
seemed endless; and Edna could understand it all.. In
the few private talks she and Dr. Stedman had together,
their conversation seemed naturally to turn upon the nearest subject to both their hearts—their respective sister
and brother.

Was he falling in love with Letty, or fearing Julius
would do so? Either chance was possible, and yet improbable; nay, in the frank pleasure of their intercourse,
Edna had almost ceased to dread either catastrophe. Now,
as they turned homeward along the cliff, she noticed that
Dr. Stedman looked exceedingly thoughtful—almost sad
—that he either walked beside Letty, or, when she was
walking with his brother, he followed her continually with
his eyes.

No wonder. Edna thought she had never seen her sister so irresistibly attractive. If half the men in the world
were on their knees at Letty's feet, it would have scarcely
been unnatural. And yet—and yet—

Edna did not like to own it to herself—it seemed so unkind, unsisterly; still, if, as a perfectly unprejudiced person, she had been asked, was Letty the sort of girl likely to carry away captive Dr. Stedman, she should have said no. She should have thought a man with his deep nature would have looked deeper, expected more. With all her love for Letty, Letty would have been the last person in the world whom, had she been a man, she, Edna, would have fallen in love with; if Dr. Stedman had done so, she was a little surprised and—it must be confessed—just a trifle disappointed.

Chiefly so, she argued internally, because she felt certain that Letty would never look at him, and then it might turn out such an unlucky business altogether—the worst yet; for the doctor was not a person to take things easily, or to be played fast and loose with, as was unfortunately rather Letty's way. Edna felt by instinct that he would never be made a slave of—much more likely a tyrant. And if he should be very miserable—break his heart perhaps—that is, supposing men ever do break their hearts for love—Edna would have been so very sorry for him.

She watched him closely all the road home. She did not even ask him to come in to tea, as both brothers seemed half to expect, and as had been done more than once before the quartette started together for their evening ramble. Nevertheless, one was arranged—to look at a wreck which had been washed ashore the previous winter, and which Julius wished to make into a sketch for a possible picture. And though there was some slight opposition from Edna, who thought the walk would be too long for Letty, and from Dr. Stedman, for the same reason as regarded his brother, Julius was obstinate, and carried his point.

So they parted; for the brief parting of an hour or two, which scarcely seemed such at all.

Letty threw off her hat and lay down, with both her arms over her head, in an attitude exquisitely lovely.

"I am quite tired, Edna; that doctor of yours does take such gigantic strides, and he talks on such solid subjects, it quite makes one's head ache to follow him. I wonder why he chose me to walk with, and not you; but these wise men like silly women. I told him so. At least I owned I was silly; but of course he didn't believe it."

"Of course not. But what was he talking about?"

"Oh, nothing particular," said Letty, with a slightly conscious air. "Men all talk alike to me, I fancy."

Edna asked no more questions.

DOCTOR STEDMAN.

CHAPTER VII.

"Will, do you mean to sit over your books all evening? Because if you do I'll not wait for you any longer, but take myself off at once."

"Where? Why, were you waiting?"

"Don't pretend that you have forgotten." Julius spoke with some of his old irritability. "We were to walk as far as the wreck; and unless we start in good time the tide will have risen, and we shall not be able to pass the point; which would be uncomfortable for ladies."

"Did the ladies decide to go? I thought Miss Edna rather objected."

"Miss Edna's objections were overruled. I arranged the matter."

Will smiled.

"Yes—I did. I'll not have her and you always getting your own way. I must have mine sometimes. I'm not your patient now, Will, and I have just as much right to enjoy myself as you have."

"Did any body say you hadn't, my boy? Who hinders you? Carry out any plans you fancy, provided they do you no harm."

The doctor rose, put a mark in his book, and prepared to clear his " rubbish " away.

"So, Will, you are going. I thought you would go, though you made believe to be so indifferent about it."

The elder brother flushed up, for there was an undertone of rudeness in the younger's speech not exactly pleasant. But Will was too well accustomed to the painful irritability of illness to take much heed of it. He only said:

"For many reasons, I don't consider the expedition very wise; but if these young ladies are determined to go, they will be all the better for having a man to take care of them."

"They will have one in any case. I am going. No need for you to trouble yourself concerning them."

The sharpness of this speech made Dr. Stedman turn round. He was not a man of many words, nor yet a very sensitive man — that is, he felt deep things deeply and strongly, but the small annoyances of life passed harmlessly over him. He had always had something else to think about than himself, and the way people treated him. For this reason he often did not even see when Julius was annoyed; but he did now, and turned upon the brother a full, frank, good-natured smile.

"What are you vexed about, lad? Do you want to have your friends all to yourself? If so, I'll stay at home and read. I dare say Miss Edna—"

"Stop there. Yes, Will, I am vexed with you, and I have good reason to be."

"Out with it, then."

"What business had you to go talking to Miss Edna about me? Why open up to her my weaknesses and follies, which nobody knows but you, and you only too much? Why should these two girls—for whom, mind you, I care not a straw, except that they are pleasant companions—be taught to criticise me and pity me?"

"Pity you?"

"Of course they do—a poor fellow with not a half-penny of money, and no health to earn it—wholly dependent upon you."

"That is not quite true."

"Yes, it is; and they must despise me—any girls would. There are times when I despise myself."

This outburst was so sudden, vehement, and inconsequent, as it seemed, that Will Stedman, though tolerably used to the like, scarcely knew what to answer. When he did, he spoke gently, as to a passionate child who was talking at random.

"Indeed, Julius, I had no thought of annoying you in what I said, which was, in truth, very little; and I felt I was saying it to a friend of yours, who was quite welcome to repeat it to you if she chose."

"But why talk to her at all about me? What are my concerns to her? If a friend, she isn't an old friend. Three weeks ago we had neither of us set eyes on either of these women. I wish we never had. I wish to Heaven we never had!"

Will replied a little seriously:

"I can not exactly see the reason of that. They are both pleasant enough, and, so far as we can judge, very excellent women."

"I hate your excellent women!"

"You don't hate these, though, I am sure of that, lad," said the doctor, smiling. "Be content; I have done you no harm. I said not a word against you to Miss Edna— quite the contrary."

"But, I repeat, why speak of me at all?"

"Perhaps I had my own reasons."

"What are they? I insist upon knowing!" and Julius rose and walked up to his brother with a dramatic air.

Will was comparing his watch with the clock on the mantel-piece. He paused to wind up and set both before he replied:

"Since you compel me to speak—and perhaps after all it's best—it has struck me more than once, Julius, that you would very well like—and, moreover, it would not be a bad thing for you—to spend your life, as you have pretty well spent the last fortnight, with such a sweet, good, sensible little woman as Edna Kenderdine."

Julius threw himself back into his chair, and burst into shouts of laughter.

"Was that it? And so you were saying a good word for me to her! What a splendid idea! You are the queerest old fellow that ever was."

"But, Julius—"

"Don't interrupt. Do let me have my laugh out. It's the best joke I've ever heard. You dear old boy! What on earth have I ever done or said to make you take such a ridiculous notion into your head?"

The doctor looked a little bewildered.

"It did not seem to me so ridiculous; and, at any rate, it is hardly civil to the lady to suppose so. She is about your own age—perhaps a year older; but that would not signify much. She is healthy, bright, active, clever—"

"But oh, so plain! Now, Will, in the name of common sense, do you think I ever could fall in love with a plain woman?"

The child-like directness and solemnity of the appeal broke down Will's gravity; he, too, laughed heartily.

"Never mind. I've made a mistake, that's all. I don't know whether I'm glad or sorry. But still, it is a mistake; and I beg your pardon—Miss Edna's too—for mixing her name in such talk. I am certain no idea of the kind has ever entered her head."

"I trust not—nay, I am sure not," replied Julius, warmly. "She's not an atom of a flirt—quite different from any girl I ever knew—the best, kindliest, sweetest little soul.

But I would as soon think of marrying her—or, indeed, of marrying any body—"

"Wait till your time comes. Meanwhile, shake hands, and forget all this nonsense. Only, if ever you do fall seriously in love, come and tell it to your brother. He'll help you."

"Will he?" said Julius, eagerly.

But at that moment, sweeping past the window, plainly visible beneath the half-drawn Venetian blind, came the violet folds of Letty Kenderdine's well-known gown— the much-abused winter gown which had in its old age ·been complimented, and sketched, and painted, as making the loveliest bit of color, and the most charming drapery imaginable. ·

"There they are: we must not keep them waiting," said Dr. Stedman, as he took his hat and went out at once to the sisters.

The three sat talking very merrily on the bench at the cliff edge for several minutes, till finding Julius did not appear, his brother went in to look for him. He had started off alone, leaving word that they were not to wait —he might possibly join them on their return.

"Perhaps he wants to make a sketch or two alone," said the doctor, apologetically. "We will go without him."

"Certainly," said Letty, who was a little tenacious of the disrespect of delay. "Dr. Stedman, your brother is a most peculiar person ; and I can never understand peculiar people."

"He is peculiar in the sense of being much better than other people," replied the doctor, who—whatever he might say to Julius—never allowed a word to be said against him, which idiosyncrasy at once amused and touched Edna. With the new idea she had taken concerning him, she resolved to watch William Stedman rather closely, and when, before they had gone half a mile, Julius turned up, and attached himself very determinedly, not to her side, but her sister's, she fell into the arrangement with satisfaction. It would give her opportunities of observing more narrowly this big, quiet, grave man, who was not nearly so easy to read as his volatile, impulsive, but clever, affectionate brother.

So they descended the steep cliffs, and walked along underneath, just below high-water mark, where the wet sand was solid to their feet: a little party of two and two, close enough to make neither seem like a *tête-à-tête*, and yet sufficiently far apart to give to each a sense of voluntary companionship. But the conversation of neither seemed very serious; for Letty's gay laugh was continually heard, and Edna made, ever and anon, sundry darts from her companion's side to certain fascinating islands, formed by deeper channels intersecting the damp sand, and which had to be crossed through pools of shallow sea-water, crisped by the wind into wavelets pretty as a baby's curls. Edna could not resist them; but whenever Dr. Stedman fell into silence—which he did pretty often—she quitted him, and ran with the pleasure of a child to stand on one or other of these sand islands, and watch the long white rollers creeping in, each after each, as the tide kept steadily advancing upon the solitary shore.

Very solitary it was, with the boundless sea before, and the perpendicular wall of cliff behind, and not an object to break the loneliness of the scene, except that loneliest thing of all—the stranded ship. She lay there, fixed on the rock where she had struck, with the waves gradually reaching her and breaking over her, as they had done night and day, at every tide, for six months.

Julius regarded her with his melancholy poet's eyes.

"How sad she looks—that ship! Like a lost life."

"And what a fine ship she must have been! How very stupid of the sailors to go so near the rocks!"

"How very stupid of any body to do any thing which is not the best and wisest thing to do! Yet we all do it sometimes, Miss Kenderdine."

"Eh, Mr. Stedman? Just say that again, for I did not quite understand. You do say such clever things, you know."

E

"That was not clever, so I need not say it again. Indeed I'd better hold my tongue," replied Julius, looking full at Letty Kenderdine, with the sudden thirst of a man who is looking for perfection, has been looking for it all his days, and can not find it. And Letty, with those blue eyes of hers—the sort of azure blue, large and limpid, which look so like heaven, except for a certain want of depth in them, discoverable not suddenly, but gradually —Letty

"Gave a side glance and looked down,"

in her long-accustomed way, thinking of nothing in particular, unless it was that the evening was coming on, misty and gray, and the sands were wet, and she had only her thin boots on.

She meant no harm, poor girl! She was so accustomed to be admired, to have every body looking at her as Julius Stedman looked now, that it neither touched nor startled her, nor affected her in any way—especially as the look was only momentary; and the young man returned immediately to his ordinary lively talk—the chatter of society—in which he was much more *au fait* than his brother, and which Letty could respond to much more easily. Indeed she had felt the change of companionship to-night rather an advantage, and had exerted herself to be agreeable accordingly. Though no one could say she smiled on one brother more sweetly than on the other; for it was not her habit either to feel or to show preference. She just went smiling on, like the full round moon, on all the world alike, as she had nothing to do but to smile. Did any hapless wight fall, moon-struck—who was to blame? Surely not Letitia Kenderdine.

And, meanwhile, Edna too had been enjoying herself very much, in a most harmless way, clambering over little rocks, and trampling on sea-weed—the bladders of which "go pop," as the children say, when you set your feet upon them — a proceeding which, I grieve to say, had amused this young school-mistress as much as if she had been one of her own pupils. Finally, by Dr. Stedman's assistance—for the rocks were slippery, and she was often

glad of a helping hand—she gained the farthermost and
most attractive sand island, and stood there, with her hat
off, letting the wind blow in her face, for the sake of
health and freshness; she was not solicitous about bloom
or complexion.

Yet Edna was not uncomely. There was a fairy grace
about her tiny figure, and an unaffected enjoyment in her
whole mien, which made her interesting even beside her
beautiful sister. While she was looking at the sea, Dr.
Stedman stood and looked at her, with a keen observation
—inquisitive, and yet approving—approving rather than
admiring; not at all the look he gave to Letty. And yet,
perhaps, any woman, who was a real woman, would rather
have had it of the two.

"You seem to enjoy yourself very much, Miss Edna.
It does one good to see any person past childhood who
has the faculty of being so thoroughly happy."

"Did I look happy? Yes, I think I am: all the more
so because my happiness, my sea-side pleasure, I mean,
will not last long. I want to get the utmost out of it I
can, for we go home in three days."

"So soon? When did you settle that?"

"At tea-time to-day. We must go, for we have spent
all our money, and worn out all our clothes. Besides, it
is time we were at home."

"Have you taken all precautions about fumigating,
whitewashing, etc., that I suggested?" (For she had told
him about the fever, and asked his advice, professionally.)

"Yes; our house is quite safe now, and ready for us.
And most of our pupils have promised to come back. We
shall be in harness again directly after the holidays. Ah!"
she sighed, hardly knowing why, except that she could
not help it, "I have need to be happy while I can. We
have a rather hard life at home."

"Is it so?" Then, after a pause, "Forgive me for asking, but have you no father living, no brothers? Are
there only you two?"

"Only us two."

"It is a hard life, then. I have seen enough of the world

to feel keenly for helpless women left to earn their livelihood.   If I had had a sister I would have been so good to
her."

"I am sure you would," said Edna, involuntarily.   And
then she drew back uneasily.   Was it possible that he
could be thinking of her in that light—as a sister by marriage, who might one day take the place of a sister by
blood?   Was that the reason he was so specially kind to
her?

She could not have told why—but she did not quite like
the idea, and her next speech was a little sharp, even
though sincere.

"Yet, on the other hand, however kind a brother may
be, it is great weakness and selfishness in a sister to hang
helplessly upon him—draining his income, preventing him
from marrying, and so on.   If I had ten brothers, I think
I would rather work till I dropped than I would be dependent on any one of them."

"Would you?   But would that be quite right?"

"Yes, I think it would be right—for me, at least.   I
don't judge others.   Let all decide for themselves their
own affairs, but, as for me, if I felt I was a burden upon
any mortal man—father, brother, or—well, perhaps husbands are different, I have never thought much about that
—I believe it would drive me frantic."

"You independent little lady!" said Dr. Stedman, laughing outright.   "And yet I beg your pardon," he added,
seriously.   "I quite agree with you.   I don't see why a
woman should be helpless and idle any more than a man.
And a woman who, if she has to earn her daily bread, sets
bravely to work and does it, without shrinking, without
complaining, has my most entire respect and esteem."

"Thank you," said Edna, and her heart warmed, and
the fierceness that was rising there sank down again.   She
felt that she had found a friend, or the possibility of one,
did circumstances ever occur to bring them any nearer
than now.   Which, however, was not probable, since, as
to these Stedmans, she had determined that when they
parted—they parted; that this brief intimacy, which had

been so pleasant while it lasted, should become on both sides as completely ended as a dream. Indeed, it would be nothing else. The sort of association which seemed so friendly and natural here, would, in their Kensington life, be utterly impossible.

"Things are hard enough even for us men," said Dr. Stedman, taking up the thread of conversation where Edna had dropped it. "Work of any sort is so difficult to obtain. There is my brother, now. He drifted into the career of an artist almost by necessity, because to get any employment such as he desired and was fitted for was nearly impossible. Even I, who, unlike him, have had the advantage of being regularly educated for a profession—would you believe it?—I have been in practice three years and have hardly made a hundred pounds. If I had not had a private income—small enough, but just sufficient to keep Julius and me in bread and cheese—I think we must have starved."

"So he has told me. He says he owes you every thing—more than he can ever repay."

"He talks great nonsense. Poor fellow! if he has been unsuccessful it has neither been through idleness nor extravagance. But he has probably told you all about himself. And you, I find, have told him what I yesterday said to you concerning him."

"Was I wrong?"

"Oh no. If it had been a secret I should have said so, and you would have kept it. You look like a woman who could keep a secret. If I ever have one I will trust you."

What did he mean? Further hints on the matter of sisterhood? Edna earnestly hoped not. Perhaps the fatal time had passed over, since the people who fell in love with Letty usually proposed to her suddenly—in two or three days. Now Dr. Stedman had been with her a whole fortnight—every day and all day long—and, so far as Edna knew, nothing had happened. If the sisters went away on Thursday nothing might happen at all.

She dismissed her fears and went on with her talk, in which the two others soon joined—the pleasant, desultory

talk, half earnest, half badinage, of four young people al-
lied by no special tie of kindred or friendship, bound only
by circumstance and mutual attraction—that easy liking
which had not as yet passed into the individual appropria-
tion which, with the keen delights of love, creates also its
bitter jealousies. In short, they stood, all of them, on the
narrow boundary-line of those two conditions of being
which make hapless mortals—especially men—either the
best or the worst company in the world.

They strolled along the shore, sometimes two and two,
sometime falling into a long line of four, conversing rather
than looking around them—for there was nothing attractive in the evening. A dull, gray sky, and a smooth, leaden-
colored sea, had succeeded those wonderful effects of evening light which they had night after night admired so
much; yet still they went on walking and talking, enjoying each other's company, and not noticing much beyond,
until Dr. Stedman suddenly stopped.

"Julius, look there; the tide is nearly round the point.
We must turn back at once."

Letty gave a little scream. "Oh, what will happen!
Why did we go on so far? Edna, how could you—"

"It was not your sister's fault," said Dr. Stedman, catching the little scream and coming anxiously over to Letty's
side. "I was to blame; I ought to have noticed how far
on the tide was."

"But oh, what will happen? Edna, Edna!" cried Letty,
wringing her hands.

"Nothing will happen, I trust, beyond our getting our
feet wet. Perhaps not that, if we walk on fast. Will
you take my arm?"

"No, mine," said Julius, eagerly, and his brother drew
back.

"Do not be alarmed, Miss Edna; but indeed I see you
are not," said the doctor, striding on, while she kept pace
with him as well as she could with her little, short steps.
"We two will just walk on as fast as we can. There is
no real danger. At worst we shall only get a good wet-
ting; but that would be very bad for our invalids."

"Very bad. Letty—Mr. Stedman—please come on as fast as you can."

"Will!" shouted out Julius, "is it spring or neap tide?"

"I do not know; only get on. Don't lag behind."

"Get on yourself, and leave us alone."

"That isn't your habit, I'm sure, Miss Edna," said Will Stedman.

"What isn't my habit?"

"To get on by yourself and leave others to get on alone, as my brother has just advised my doing."

"Oh, he did not know what he was saying."

This was all that passed between them, as walking as rapidly as they could, though often turning uneasily back to watch the other two, the elder brother and sister reached the point where a "race," that is, a line of rocks reaching right up to the cliff, made the sea more turbulent, and where the cliff itself, jutting out a considerable way, caused the distance between it and high-water mark to be scarcely more than a foot—in spring-tides nothing at all. It was not exactly a dangerous place—not in calm weather like this. At most, a wade up to the knees would have carried a wayfarer safely beyond the point; but still it was an uncomfortable place to pass, and when Dr. Stedman and Edna reached it, they found the worst had come to the worst—there was no passage remaining, or merely a foot or two left bare, temporarily, at each ebb of the wave.

There were no breakers, certainly; nothing more threatening than the long slow curves of tide that came creaming in, each with a white fringe of foam, over the smooth sand; but whenever they met not sand but rocks, they became fiercer, and dashed themselves about in a way that looked any thing but agreeable, and rendered footing among the sea-weed and sharp stones extremely difficult.

Edna and Dr. Stedman exchanged looks—uneasy enough.

"You see?"

"Yes, I see. It is very unfortunate."

"Will she be frightened, think you? Your sister, I mean. She seems a timid person."

"Rather, and she dislikes getting wet. How fast the

tide comes in! Is there no chance of climbing a little
way up the cliff?"

"No, the cliffs are perpendicular. Look for yourself."

But the doctor looked uneasily back, his mind full of the
other two.

"How slow they are! If they had only been here now
we might cross at once, and escape with merely wet feet.
There would be just time. Julius!" he shouted, impatient-
ly—"Julius, do come on!"

"He can not," Edna said, gently. "Remember, he can
not walk like you."

"Thank you; you are always thoughtful. No; I suppose there is no help for it. We may as well sit down
and wait." He sat down, but started up again immediately. "I beg your pardon, Miss Edna, but would you
like to go on? I can easily take you past the point, and
return again for them. Will you come?"

"No, oh no." And she, too, sat down on the nearest
stone; for she was very tired.

It was full five minutes before Julius and Letty reached
the point, and by that time the sea was tumbling noisily
against the very foot of the cliff. Julius at once saw the
position of things and turned anxiously to his brother.

"Will, this is dreadful! Not for us, but for these ladies.
What shall we do?"

Letty caught at once the infection of fear.

"What is so dreadful? Oh, I see. Those waves, those
waves! they have overtaken us. I shall be drowned!
Oh, Dr. Stedman, tell me—am I going to be drowned?"

And she left Julius's arm and clutched the doctor's, her
beautiful features pallid and distorted with fear. Also
with something else besides fear, which shows plainly
enough in most faces at a critical moment like this, when
there awakes either the instinct of self-preservation, said
to be nature's first law, or a far diviner instinct, which is
not always—yet, thank God! it is often—also human
nature.

Dr. Stedman was an acute man. No true doctor can
well be otherwise. He said little, but he observed much.

Now, as he looked fixedly down upon the lovely face a curious change came over his own. More than once, without replying, he heard the piteous cry—sharp even to querulousness—"Shall I be drowned?" and then gently released himself from Letty's hold.

"My dear Miss Kenderdine, if any were drowned, there would be four. But I assure you nothing so tragical is likely to happen. Look at the line of sea-weed all along the shore; that is high-water mark; farther the tide will not advance."

"But the point—the point."

"Even at the point the water is not more than six inches deep. It could not drown you."

"But it will spoil my boots, my dress—every thing. Oh, Edna, how could you be so foolish as to let us come?"

Edna, indeed, did feel and look very conscience-smitten, till Dr. Stedman said, rather abruptly,

"There is no use regretting it, or scolding one another; we were all equally to blame. Don't let us waste time now in chattering about it."

"No, indeed. Let us get home as quickly as we can. Letty, take hold of me, and try to wade through."

But Letty, tall as she was, shrank in childish terror from the troubled waters, and several more precious minutes were wasted in conquering her fears, and finding the easiest passage for her across the sands. Meantime the line of sea-weed began to be touched—nay, drifted ominously higher and higher by each advancing wave, until Dr. Stedman noticed it.

"Look!" he said in an under-tone to Edna; "last tide may have been neap, but this is evidently a spring-tide. It makes a great difference. We must go on without losing more time. How shall we divide?"

"I'll help Letty."

"No, that is scarcely safe—two women together. Shall I take your sister, and you my brother? You can assist him best! Poor fellow! this is more dangerous for him than for any of us. Julius!" he called out, "don't waste more time; take Miss Edna and start."

E 2

Julius turned sharply upon his brother:

"Excuse me, but we have already made our plans. Come, Miss Kenderdine."

Will Stedman once more drew back, and would not interfere, but he looked seriously uneasy.

"What must be done?" he said again to Edna. "I wanted you to walk with Julius. She can not take care of him—she is too timid. She will only hang helplessly upon him, and drag him back when he ought to get on as fast as possible."

"Is there danger—real danger?"

"Not of drowning, as your sister thinks"—with a slight curl of the not too amiable mouth—"but of my brother's getting so wet and exhausted that his illness may return. Look! he is staggering now, the tide runs so strong. What can I do?"

"Go and help them. Get them safe home first."

"But you?"

"I can not cross by myself. I see that," said Edna, looking with a natural shiver of dread at the now fast-rising waves. "But I can stay here. I should not be afraid, even if I had to wait till the tide turns."

"That will be midnight. No, about eleven, I think."

"Even so, no harm will come to me; I can walk up and down this beach, or else I could clamber to that ledge on the cliff where the cliff-swallows are building. The highest tide could not reach me there. I'll try it. Good-bye."

She spoke cheerfully, reaching out her hand. Dr. Stedman grasped it warmly.

"You are the bravest and most unselfish little woman I ever knew."

"Then you can not have known many," said she, laughing; for, somehow, her courage rose. "Now, without another word, go."

He went, but returned again in a minute to find poor Edna clambering painfully to her ledge in the rock. He helped her up as well as he could, then she again urged him to leave her.

"I can not. It seems so wrong—quite cruel."

"It is not cruel—it is only right. You and I are far the strongest. We must take care of those two."

"I have taken care of him all my life, poor fellow!"

"That I can well believe. Hark! is Letty screaming? Oh, Dr. Stedman, never mind me. For pity's sake go and help them safe home."

"I will," said he, "and then I'll come back for you in a boat, if possible, only let me see you safe. One step more. Put your hand on my shoulder. You're all right now?"

"Quite right, and really very comfortable, considering."

"This will make you more so, and I don't need it."

He took off his coat and threw it up to her, striding off before she had time to refuse.

"Miss Edna!" and to her great uneasiness she saw him looking back once more. "You'll not be frightened?"

"Not a bit. Oh, please go!"

"Very well, I am really going now. But I'll never forget this day."

Edna thought the same.

CHAPTER VIII.

EDNA sat on her ledge of rock, to the great discomfiture of the cliff-swallows, for a length of time that appeared to her indefinite. She had no means of measuring it, for the very simple reason that the sisters had only one reliable watch between them, and, when it gave her no trouble, Letty usually wore it. Now, in her long, weary vigil, Edna's mind kept turning regretfully and with a childish pertinacity to this watch, and wishing she had had the courage—she did think of so doing once, and hesitated— to borrow Dr. Stedman's. It would have been some consolation, and a sort of companion to her, during the hour or two she should still have to wait before the tide went down. That was, supposing Dr. Stedman found it impossible to get the boat; which, when the evening began to close in, and still there was no sign of him, she thought must have been the case.

EDNA WAITING.

She was not exactly alarmed: she knew that the highest spring-tide could never reach the ledge where she sat
—where the birds' marvellous instinct had placed their
nests. Her position was safe enough, but it was terribly
lonely; and when night came rapidly on, and she ceased
to distinguish any thing except the momentary flashes of
foam over the sea—for the wind had risen, and the white
horses had begun to appear—she felt sadly forlorn—nay,
forsaken. The swallows ceased their fluttering and chattering, and becoming accustomed to her motionless presence, settled down to roost; soon the only sound she heard
was the waves breaking against the cliff beneath her feet.
She seemed to hear them quite close below her: so the
spring-tide must have been a high one; and she felt thankful for this little nook of safety—damp and comfortless as

it was: growing more so, since, with the darkness, a slight
rain began to fall.

Edna drew Dr. Stedman's coat over her shoulders, as
some slight protection to her poor little shivering, solitary
self: thinking gratefully how good it was of him to leave
it, and hoping earnestly he had got home safely, even
though in ignominious and discreditable shirt-sleeves.
And, amidst all her dreariness, she laughed aloud to think
how funny he would look, and how scandalized Letty
would be, to see him in such an ungentlemanly plight,
and especially to walk with him through the village.
But while she laughed the moral courage of the thing
touched her. It was not every gentleman who would
thus have made himself appear ridiculous in a lady's eyes
for the 'sake of pure kindness.

And then, in the weary want of something to occupy
her mind and to pass the time away, she fell into vague
speculations as to how all this was to end: whether Dr.
Stedman really wished to marry Letty; whether Letty
would have him if he asked her. One week would show;
since, after Thursday, circumstances would be so completely changed with them all that their acquaintanceship must,
if mere acquaintance, die a natural death. No "gentlemen visitors" could be allowed by the two young school-
mistresses; so that even though the Stedmans lived within a mile of them—which fact Edna knew, though they
were not aware she knew it—still they were not very likely to meet. People in and near London often pass years
without meeting, even though living in the next street.
And if so—if this association, just as it was growing quite
pleasant, were thus abruptly to end—would she be glad
or sorry?

Edna asked herself the question more than once. She
could not answer it, even to her own truthful heart. She
really did not know.

But she soon ceased to trouble herself about that or
any thing; for there came upon her a feeling of intense
cold, also—let it not disgrace her in poetical eyes, this
healthy-framed and healthy-minded little woman!—of

equally intense hunger: during which she had a vision of
the bread-and-cheese and beer lying on the parlor-table,
so vivid and tantalizing that she could have cried. She
began to agree with Dr. Stedman that it was rather cruel
to have left her here—at least for so long—so much longer than she had anticipated.

Surely they had all got home safe by this time. Nothing had happened—nothing was likely to happen; for she
had seen them with her own eyes cross safely the perilous
point and enter upon the stretch of level sand. With a
slightly sad feeling she had watched the three black figures moving on—two together and one a little apart—
till they vanished behind a turn in the cliff. Beyond that
nothing could be safer, though it was a good long walk.

"And that young man is weak still," thought Edna,
compassionately. "Of course he could not walk quickly;
and Letty never can. Besides, when she learned I was
left behind she might have been unwilling to go home
without me."

But while making this excuse to herself Edna's candid
mind rejected it as a fiction. She knew well that, with
all her good-nature, Letty was not given to self-denial:
being one of those theoretically-virtuous people who are
content to leave their heroisms to be acted out by some
one else. But the doctor: he was a man—a courageous
and kindly man, too. He surely would never leave a
poor, weak woman to spend the night upon this dreary
ledge of rock.

"He said he would bring a boat; but he may not be
able to get one, or to pilot it in this darkness and among
all these rocks. It would not be safe." And this thought
conquered all her personal uneasiness. "Oh, I hope he will
not try it. Suppose he did, and something were to happen to him! I wish I had told him I would wait till the
tide went down. Rather than any risk to him I would
have sat here till daylight."

And with a kind of vague terror of "something happening"—such terror as she had never felt concerning any
one except Letty—nay, with her very slightly, for in their

dull, peaceful lives had occurred none of those sudden
tragedies which startle life out of its even course, and
take away forever the sense of security against fate—
Edna sat and listened for the sound of oars, of voices—of
any thing; straining her ears in the intense stillness until
the sensation became actual pain.

But she heard nothing except the lap-lap of the tide going down—either it was going down, for it sounded faint-
er every minute, or else she herself was sinking into a
state of sleepy exhaustion, more dangerous than any danger yet. For if she fainted or dropped asleep she might
fall from her narrow seat and be seriously hurt. She
thought, should he come and find her there, lying just at
his feet, with a limb broken, or otherwise injured, how
very sorry Dr. Stedman would be!

All these fancies came and went, in every form of ex-
aggeration, till poor Edna began to fancy her wits were
leaving her. She drew herself as far back against the
rock as possible, crouching down like a child, leaned her
head back, and quietly cried. Then excessive drowsiness
came over her: she must, for some minutes at least, have
actually fallen asleep.

She was roused by hearing herself called: in her confused state she could not think where or by whom; and
her tongue was paralyzed and her limbs frozen just as if
she had the nightmare.

"Miss Edna—Miss Edna!" the shouting went on, till
the cliffs echoed with it. "Where are you? Do answer
—only one word!"

Then the voice ceased, and a light like a glow-worm began to wander up and down the rocks below. Edna tried
to call, but could not make herself heard. The whole
thing seemed a kind of fever-dream.

At length, sitting where she was, she felt a warm hand
touch her. She uttered a little cry.

"You are alive," some one said. "Thank God!"

Though she knew it was Dr. Stedman, and tried her utmost to appear the brave little woman he had called her,
Edna's strength failed. She could not answer a word, but

fell into a violent fit of sobbing, in the which the doctor soothed her as if she had been a child.

"There now. Never mind crying—it will be a relief. You are quite safe now; I have come to fetch you home. Oh, if I could but have got back here a little sooner!"

And then Edna was sufficiently her natural self to ask eagerly if no harm had befallen Letty or his brother—if they were both safe at home?

"Yes, quite safe. But it was a long business. Twice I thought Julius would have broken down entirely."

"And my sister?"

"Your sister is perfectly well, only a good deal frightened."

"Was she very uneasy about me?"

"Not overwhelmingly so," said Will Stedman, with that slight hardness, approaching even to sarcasm, which came occasionally into his voice as well as his manner, giving the impression that if very good he was not always very amiable. "But come! we are losing time; and I have to get you safe home now. I have no boat. I was delayed; they were so long in reaching home that when I went after a boat the water was too shallow to make it available—the men refused it."

"How did you come, then?"

"I waded. But the tide is down now. We may easily walk—that is, if you can walk. Try."

Edna stretched her poor cramped limbs, and attempted to descend. But she grew dizzy; her footing altogether failed her.

"I can't stand," she said, helplessly. "You will have to leave me here till morning."

"Impossible."

"Oh no! Indeed, I don't much mind."

For in her state of utter exhaustion any thing—even to lie down there and die—seemed easier than to be forced to make a single effort more.

"Miss Edna," said the doctor, with all the doctor in his tone—calm, firm, authoritative—"you can not stay here.

You must be got home somehow. If you can not walk, I must carry you."

Then Edna made a violent effort, and succeeded in crawling, with both hands and feet, down the cliff-side to the level sands. But as soon as she stood upright and attempted to walk, her head swam round and consciousness quite left her. She remembered nothing more till she found herself lying on the sofa in their own parlor, opposite a blazing fire, with Letty—only Letty—sitting beside her.

"Mrs. Williams! oh, Mrs. Williams! come here! She's quite herself now. My sister—my dear little twin-sister! Oh, Edna, I thought you were dead. I have been near breaking my heart about you."

And Letty hugged and kissed her, and hung over her, and gave her all manner of things to eat, to drink, and to smell at—with an affection the genuineness of which was beyond all doubt. For Letty was no sham; she had a real heart, so far as it went, and that was why Edna loved her. All the better that it was a keen-eyed love, which never looked for what it could not find, and had the sense not to exact from the large, splendid, open-bosomed *Gloire de Dijon*, the rich depths of perfume that lie hidden in the red moss-rose.

"Yes, Letty dear, I must have frightened you very much," said she, clinging to her sister, and trying to recall, bit by bit, what had happened. "It must have been a terrible suspense for you. But indeed I could not help it. It was impossible for me to get home. How did I ever get home at all?"

"I don't know, except that Dr. Stedman brought you. You were quite insensible when he carried you in, and he had a deal of trouble to bring you to. Oh, it was such a comfort to have a doctor in the house! and he was so kind!"

"Where is he now?" And as Edna tried to raise her head a faint color came into her white face.

"He has just gone away. He said it was much better that, when you came to yourself, you should find nobody

beside you but me—that he had to sit up reading till
about three in the morning; and if you were worse I was
to send for him—not otherwise. He told me not to fright-
en myself or you. He was not uneasy about you at all;
you would soon recover, you were such an exceedingly
healthy person. Indeed, Edna, he must be a very clever
doctor: he seemed to understand you as if he had known
you all your life."

Edna smiled, but she felt too weak to talk. "And you
—how did you get home?"

"Oh, it was terrible business. I was so frightened.
And that young Julius Stedman—he was no help at all.
He is but a poor stick of a fellow for all practical purposes, and gets cross at the least thing. Still, when we
reached home, and his brother started off again to fetch
you, he was very kind also."

"I am sure he would be."

"He sat with me all the time we were waiting for you;
I sent for Mrs. Williams, so it was quite proper—but, in-
deed, I was too miserable to think much about propriety.
I only thought, What if you were drowned, and I were to
lose my dear little sister—my best friend in all this world?
Oh, Edna, Edna!"

And once again Letty kissed and embraced her, shed-
ding oceans of tears—honest tears.

Mrs. Williams, too, put her apron to her eyes. She had
grown "mighty fond" (she declared afterwards) of these
two young ladies. She was certain they were real ladies,
though they had only one bottle of wine in the cupboard,
and their living was as plain as plain could be. So she,
too, worthy woman! shed a few glad tears over Miss
Edna's recovery, until Edna declared it was enough to
make a person quite conceited to be thought so much of.
And then, being still in a weak and confused state, she
suffered herself to be carried off to bed by Mrs. Williams
and Letty.

It was a novelty for Edna to be taken care of. Either
she was very healthy—though so fragile-looking—or she
did not think much about her own health, which is often

the best method of securing it; but for years such a thing
had not happened to her as to lie in bed till noon, and
have Letty waiting upon her. It was rather pleasant
than otherwise for an hour or two, until Letty began to
weary a little of her unwonted duties, and Edna of the
dignity of invalidism. So she rose, and, though still feeling dizzy and strange, crept down stairs and settled herself in her usual place, with her work-basket beside her.

There Dr. Stedman found her, when, having sent a preliminary message through Mrs. Williams, he came, in the
course of the afternoon, to visit his patient.

His patient he seemed determined to consider her. He
entered the room with a due air of mental gravity—nay,
a little more formal than his customary manner—touched
her pulse, and asked a few unimportant questions, after
a fashion which quite removed the slight awkwardness
which Edna felt, and was painfully conscious she showed,
towards him.

"Yes, she will soon be quite well," said he, turning to
Letty. "Your sister is thin and delicate-looking, Miss
Kenderdine, but she will take a great deal of killing, she
has such a thoroughly pure constitution. You need not
be in the least alarmed about her. Still, I will just look
after her for a day or two, professionally—I mean in an
amateur professional way—if she will allow me."

Letty was overflowing with thanks. Edna remained
silent. She disliked being Dr. Stedman's, or indeed any
doctor's patient; but her position would have been still
more difficult had he appeared to-day in the character of
her brave preserver, who had waded through the stormy
billows like a Norse hero, and carried her back in his
arms—as she now was sure he had carried her, for he
could have got her home in no other way. But he had
said nothing about this, and, apparently, nobody had asked him. Nor did he refer to it now, for which reserve
Edna was very grateful. She would not have known
what to say, nor how to thank him, but his delicate silence
on the matter made all things easy.

Likewise Letty, who was not given to penetrate too

deeply below the surface of things, seemed blessed with a
most fortunate lack of inquisitiveness. She made no reference to last night, but sat talking sweetly to the doctor
in the character of affectionate nurse and sister, looking
the while so exquisitely lovely that Julius, who, on his
brother's suggestion, had been invited in to see Edna, was
driven to beg permission to make a sketch of her on the
spot, in the character of a guardian angel.

Nobody objected—for the young artist was treated like
a spoiled child by them all. And, as it was a wet day—
so wet that nobody could think of going out, and every
body would be dull enough in-doors—they agreed to share
their dullness and spend the afternoon together; for, as
some one suggested, their time was drawing short now.

So Julius brought in his sketch-book and fell to work.
After a long discussion as to what sort of an angel Miss
Kenderdine was to be made into, it was finally decided
that she would do exactly as one of the Scandinavian Val-
kyriæ, who wait in the halls of Odin to receive the souls
of the departed slain.

"Is that the business of guardian angels?" asked Will
Stedman. "I should have thought they would have done
better in taking care of the living than making a fuss over
the dead."

Julius looked annoyed. "Pray excuse Will, Miss Kenderdine. He is not at all poetical; he always takes a matter-of-fact view of things. Now, just the head bent, with
a pitying sort of expression, if you can manage it. Thank
you—that will do exactly."

And Julius, with that keen, eager, thirsty look, which
for the last few days had begun to dawn in his face, gazed
at Letty Kenderdine, who smiled as usual, calm and moon-
like. Even as Andrea del Sarto's Lucrezia might have
smiled on him, and as dozens more as lovely women to
the end of time will continue to smile, maddeningly, upon
the two types of men with whom such charms are all-pow-
erful—the sensualist, who cares for mere beauty, and it
alone; the poet, who out of his own nature idealizes physical perfectness into the perfection of the soul.

But there is a third type which unites both these.
Was it to this that William Stedman belonged?—that is,
in his real heart, though his eyes might have been temporarily no wiser than his neighbors'.

He seemed a little changed in his manner since yesterday—graver, and yet franker and freer. He made no attempt to interfere with his brother's complete engross-
ment of Letty, though he watched the two very closely at
intervals. This Edna saw, and drew her own conclusions
therefrom; but they were erroneous conclusions. Nevertheless, they made her resolve more strongly than ever
that with next Thursday this intimacy should entirely
cease. That one or both of these brothers should fall in
love with Letty was a catastrophe to be avoided, if possible. They were two good men, she was sure of that, and
they should neither of them suffer if she could help it.
No: just two days more, and the acquaintance with the
Stedmans should come to a natural and fitting close.

This being decided, Edna threw herself unresistingly into
the pleasures of it while it lasted. For it was a pleasure
—she had ceased to doubt that. No good, simple-hearted,
sensible woman could help enjoying the society of two
such men, each so different, and yet each acting as a set-
off to the other. Julius, when he flung himself into conversation, was not only clever but brilliant; William said
little, but whatever he did say, he said it to the point.
True, as his brother had accused him, he did now and then
take a matter-of-fact view of things; but his matter-of-
factness was neither stupid nor commonplace. He might
be slow, or obstinate, or hard to please, but he was not a
fool—not a bit of it; in spite of his grave and solid temperament, most people would have considered him an exceedingly clever man, in his own undemonstrative way.

So Edna thought. And since he chose to talk to her,
she talked to him back again, and enjoyed the exercise.
For there could hardly have been a greater contrast than
these two. Edna Kenderdine, though so quiet, was not a
passive, scarcely even a calm woman. Whatever she felt,
she felt acutely. Life and energy, feeling and passion,

quivered through every movement of her small frame,
every feature of her plain but sensitive and spiritual face
—more so to-day than usual, through the excitement left
behind by her last night's peril. Also by another sort of
excitement, for which she could not at all account, but
which seemed to make her whole being thrill like a harp
newly tuned, which the lightest touch causes to tremble
into music.

She could not think how it was: she ought to have been
miserable, leaving that pleasant place to go back to London, and work, and endless anxieties. Yet she was not
miserable; nay, she felt strangely happy during the whole
of this day, wet as it was, and through great part of the
next day — except the hour or two that she occupied in
packing.

There, in the solitude of her own room — for Letty,
whose back was quite too long for packing, was sitting on
the bench outside, between the two Stedmans—poor Edna
felt just a little sad and dull. They had had such a happy time, and it was now over, or nearly over: ay, forever!
—such times do not return. People say they will, and
plan renewed meetings of the same sort; but these seldom
come about, or if they do, things are different. Edna, in
her level existence, had not known enough either of happiness or misery to feel keenly the irrecoverableness of the
past; still she had sense enough to acknowledge that a
time such as she and Letty had had for the last fortnight,
so exceptional in its circumstances and its utter unworld-
liness of contentment, was never likely to occur twice in
their lives.

First, because two hard-working, solitary women were
never likely again to be thrown into such close yet perfectly
harmless and blameless relations with two such young men
as the Stedmans—thorough gentlemen, refined in act and
word, never by the slightest shadow of a shade crossing
the boundary of those polite and chivalric attentions which
every man may honorably pay to every woman; men, too,
whom they could so heartily respect, who apparently led a
life as pure and simple as their own. At this time it was

with the young men, as with the young women, such an innocently idle life. When they met again, if they ever did meet, they would all be in the whirl of London, absorbed in work—the restless, jarring, selfish work of the world—in which they might both seem and be quite different sort of people, both in themselves and to one another.

So thought Edna, as she hastened her packing in order to go down to the others—who did not seem to want her much, she fancied. Still, she wanted them: there were several things she would like still to talk about to Dr. Stedman, and why should she not talk to him as long as she could?

As she closed her trunk the heavy fall of the lid felt like closing a bright chapter in her existence. She had an instinct that such seasons do not come often, and that when they do they are brief as bright. She did not weep—this cheerful-hearted Edna, who had, and was always likely to have, enough to do and to think of to keep her from unnecessary grieving. She locked her box, having placed inside it the little mementos they were carrying home—a pebble which Letty had picked up on the beach, supposed to contain the possibility of a valuable brooch, if they could afford to have it cut and set; a piece of some queer sort of sea-weed which Dr. Stedman had given her, telling her that, if hung up in a dry place, it would prove a faithful barometer for months and years; also, pressed between her blotting-book's leaves, the very biggest of primroses, a full inch in diameter, which she had gathered in a competition with Julius Stedman. All these trifles, and a few more, which were nobody's business but her own, she locked up fast: but as she did so Edna sighed.

CHAPTER IX.

In this love-tale I find I am telling the story of the women more than of the men—which is not unnatural.

But, in truth, of the men there is as yet little to be told. Their passion had not arrived at the demonstrative stage.

Every thing they did was done quite as usual. No doubt they seized every opportunity of joining their fair neighbors—watched them out and in; met them constantly on the cliff and down the shore; contrived in short, by some means or other, to spend with them nearly the whole of the last three days; but beyond this they did not go. And even this was done by tacit understanding, without prior arrangements. Men are much more delicately reticent in love-affairs than women. Many women, even good women, will chatter mercilessly about things which a man would scorn to reveal, and think himself a brute to pry into.

On the Wednesday night the brothers had sat till ten o'clock in the Misses Kenderdine's parlor—the visits were always there. On no account would the sisters have penetrated into that bachelor sanctum, of which, in its chaos of bachelor untidiness, they had sometimes caught a glimpse through the open door—to Edna's pity and Letty's disdain. The young men themselves felt the contrast between their masculine chamber of horrors and the feminine sitting-room opposite, which, humble and bare as it was, looked always cheerful, neat, and nice.

"What a muddle we do live in, to be sure!" said Will, when they returned this last evening to their own parlor. But he sat down to his books, and Julius to his drawing, and there they both worked away till nearly midnight, without exchanging ten words.

At length Will rose and suggested his brother's going to bed.

"We have to be up early to-morrow, you know."

"Have we?"

Will smiled. "Didn't I hear you settling with the Misses Kenderdine to see them off by the coach? It starts at seven A.M."

"I said I would go; but that does not imply your going."

"Oh, I should like to go and see the last of them," said Will.

"It may not be the last. There is no necessity it should be. They live in London, and so do we."

"Do you know their address?" Will asked, abruptly.

"No. Do you?"

"Certainly not. They did not tell me, and I should have thought it a great piece of impertinence to inquire."

"Should you? Perhaps you are right. I assure you I have never asked them—though I intended to ask to-morrow. But one wouldn't do the ungentlemanly thing on any account. So I suppose, if they give us no special invitation to call on them, they will drift away like all the pleasant things in this world, and we shall never see them more."

Julius spoke sentimentally—nay, dolefully; but with a complete resignation of himself to fate, as was his character. He never struggled much against any thing.

Will moved restlessly among his books—piling and repiling them in a vain effort at order. At last he let them be, and lifting up his head, looked his brother steadily in the face.

"Yes, I suppose at seven to-morrow morning we shall see the last of them. And I think it ought to be so."

"Why?" said Julius, sharply, taking at once the opposition side, as was also his character.

Dr. Stedman paused a minute before speaking, and the blood rose in his rugged brown face as he spoke.

"Because, Julius, in plain English, two young men can not go on in this sort of free-and-easy way with two young women—at least, not in any place but here, and not here for very long—without getting talked about, which would be very unpleasant. For the men it doesn't matter, of course, which makes it all the more incumbent on us to be careful over the women."

"Careful! What nonsense!"

"No, it isn't nonsense, though perhaps my speaking about it may be. But I've had it on my mind to speak, and it's better out than in."

"Very well, then. Preach away."

And Julius stretched himself along the sofa, his arms over his head, listening with a half-vexed, half-contemptuous air.

F

"Well, lad," said Will, stoutly, "I think that for a man, because he likes a girl's society, to daunder after her and hang on to her apron-strings till he gets her and himself talked about, is a piece of most arrant folly—not to say knavery; for he gets all the fun and she all the harm. It's selfishness—cowardly selfishness—and I won't do it! You may, if you choose; but I won't do it!"

"Do what?" said Julius, with an irritable and most irritating laugh. "What's the use of blazing up and striking your hand on the table as if you were striking me—which, perhaps, is what you're after? Come on, then!"

"Do you suppose I'm an idiot?"

"Or I either? What harm have I done? Was I going to offer myself on the spot to either of your fair friends? A pretty offer it would be! A fellow who has not a half-penny to bless himself with. Why, she'd kick me out of doors, and serve me right, too. No—no!" and Julius laughed again very bitterly: "I know women better than that. Pray compose yourself, Will. I'm not going to be a downright fool."

"You quite mistake me," said Will, gravely. "Any man has a right to ask the love of any woman—even if he hasn't a half-penny. But he has no right to pay her tender attentions, and set people gossiping about her, and perhaps make her fancy he likes her, when he either does not like her, or doesn't see his way clear to marry her. It's not to be done, lad—not to be done."

"And have I any intention of doing it? You foolish old fellow—what crotchets you take up! Why—hang it —if I had never flirted more than I have here—"

"I hate flirting," broke in Will, tearing a sheet of foolscap violently in two. "Women may like it; but men ought to have more sense. What's the use of philandering and fooling when you mean nothing, and it all ends in sheer waste of time? If ever I marry, I vow I'll go up to the woman and say, 'Mary' or 'Molly.'—"

"Her name is Molly, then? That's information."

"I mean, I'd ask her point-blank to marry me. If she said 'Yes,' well and good."

"And if 'No?'" said Julius, with a keen look.

"I'd walk off, and never trouble her more. If a girl doesn't know her own mind, she isn't worth asking—certainly not asking twice. She never would be asked twice by me."

"Wait till your time comes—as you once said to your obedient, humble servant. Go on, Will. I'm waiting for another sermon, please. Plenty more where that last came from, I know."

Julius seemed determined to turn the whole into a laughing matter; and at last his brother was fain to laugh too.

"One might as well preach to a post—it always was so, and always will be! Come, I've said my say, and it's done. Let us dismiss the subject."

"Not a bit of it," replied Julius, who, with his other womanish peculiarities, had a most provoking habit of liking to have the last word; "only just tell a fellow what you are driving at. What do you want us to do about these girls? Shut ourselves up in our rooms, and stare at them from behind the key-hole without ever daring to bid them good-bye?"

"Rubbish! We'll just meet them, as you said, at the coach, wish them a pleasant journey, and there it ends."

"Does it?" said Julius, half to himself; while his soft, sad look wandered into vacancy, and he leaned his arm behind his head, in his favorite listless attitude, in which there was something affected and something real; his small, slight figure, dark, meagre face, and brilliant eyes, making equally natural to him both languor and energy. A true Southern temperament—made up of contrarieties, if not contradictions, and never to be reckoned on long together in any way.

But he ceased to argue, either in jest or earnest; and soon the two brothers parted for the night; quite amicably—as, after all their little warfares, they were in the habit of doing; for neither of them were of the sullen sort; and, besides, Will had a doctrine—learned at the big public school where he had been educated, fighting

his way of necessity from bottom to top—that sometimes
after a good honest battle, in which either speaks his
mind, men, as well as boys, are all the better friends.

Julius went to bed. But far into the small hours Will's
candle burned in the parlor below, as was his habit whenever he had spent a specially idle day.

Edna, too, sat up late, for to her always fell the domestic cares of packing, arranging, and settling every thing.
Not that Letty did not try to help her; but she helped
her so badly that it was double trouble—every thing had
to be done over again. Letty's unconscious, good-humor-
ed incapacity was one of the things which tried her sister
most, and caused her to hope that whenever the of-course-
certain husband did appear, he might be a man sensible
and practical, and sufficiently rich to make his wife independent of those petty worries which a cleverer and
braver woman would breast and swim through, and perhaps even gain strength and energy from the struggle.

As it was, whenever they had any thing to do or to suffer, Edna's first thought was, how to get Letty out of the
way. She had sent her to bed early, and, creeping in tired
beside her, was only too thankful to find her sound asleep.
And Letty slept still when in the gray dawn of the morning Edna woke, with the consciousness that something had
to be done, or something was going to happen, which came
with a sharp shock upon her the minute she opened her eyes.

She took her watch to the window to see the time cor-
rectly, and stood gazing out upon the sea, which lay so
lonely and quiet—dim and gray—just brightened in the
eastward by those few faint streaks in the sky which
showed where the sun would rise ere long.

A strange unquietness came into Edna's spirit—hitherto as placid as that sea before the sun rose—a sense of
trouble, of regret, for which she could not account. For
though she was of course sorry to leave this place, still
she might come back again some day. And now she was
going home with Letty quite strong again, and herself
also ready to begin their work anew. Why should she
grieve? She ought to be very glad and thankful.

Perhaps she was only tired with the excitement of last night—when the two Stedmans had staid later and talked more than usual; pleasant, refreshing talk, such as clever, good men can make with good, and not stupid women; talk difficult to be detailed afterwards, if indeed any conversation written down does not seem as tame and lifeless as yesterday's gathered roses. But it had left a sweet aroma behind it, and while it lasted it had made Edna feel happy, like a creature long pent up in horrible cities, who is set free upon its native mountain, and led cheerily up the bright hill-side, at every step breathing a fresher and purer air; at every glance seeing around prospects wider and fairer; the sort of companionship, in short, which makes one think the better of one's self because one can appreciate it and enjoy it. How keenly she had enjoyed it Edna knew.

And now, with a slight spasm or constriction of the heart, she recognized that it was all over, that this morning was the very last day. She should probably never meet the Stedmans more.

She was not "in love." She did not for a moment fancy herself in love with either of them, being no longer of that unripe age when girls think it fine to be in love with somebody; but she was conscious that all was not right with her; that the past had been a delicious time, and that she began to look forward to her school-life, and her home-life, alone with Letty, with a sense of vacancy and dreariness almost amounting to dread. Be sorry for her, you who can understand this state of mind! And ye who can not—why, she had need to be sorry for you!

She stood looking at the sombre sea—at the smiling, hopeful dawn, then went back to her bed, and, hiding her face in the pillow, wept a few tears. But there was no time for crying or for sleeping; she had still a great deal to do, and they must leave soon after six; so, early as it was, she rose.

Her neighbors were early stirring too, though it was, after all, Will who accomplished this, rousing his brother into sufficient energy to be in time. The impulse of over-night had faded out, and Julius now seemed very indifferent whether or not he wished the sisters good-bye.

"If we are never to see them again, what does it matter to see them now?" said he, carelessly. "Or, indeed, what does it matter in any case? Women only care for fellows with lots of money."

"In one sense, perhaps—the matrimonial; but I thought we had decided that this was not the sense in which your civilities were to be construed."

"Our civilities, Will. You have been quite as sweet upon them as I have."

"Then there is no reason why our civilities should not be continued to the end. Get your hat, man, and let us start to the coach-office."

"Now?"

"Yes, now. We are better out of the way here. We'll not bother them with any last words."

And the doctor, who looked a little jaded, as if he had sat up most of the night—which indeed he had—contrived to stay out, and keep his brother out, on the breezy cliffs during the half hour that there was any chance of staircase meetings, or interference, for good or ill, with the proceedings of the Misses Kenderdine. But all this half hour the young men never once referred to their friends—or regretted their departure. They lounged about, read the newspaper, and talked politics a little, until, suddenly taking out his watch, Will said:

"Now, if we mean to be in time, we had better be off at once."

They walked up to the coach-office. In those days, and at that early season of the year, there was only a diurnal coach which passed through the village, taking up any chance passenger by the way. It was just the usual old-fashioned stage, with outside and inside places, and was rarely full; still, to-day, as it came lumbering up the hilly street, it looked to be so.

"Suppose they can't get seats," suggested Julius.

"Not impossible. I wish I had suggested their booking places over-night."

Small, trivial sentences about such a trivial thing!—save that all the manifold machinery of life hangs pivoted upon trifles.

The brothers found the two sisters standing waiting amidst a conglomeration of boxes, at which Julius shrugged his shoulders and winked aside at Will in thankful bachelorhood. But the four met and shook hands as usual, just as if they were starting for their conjoint walk this merry, sunshiny, breezy morning.

"What a fine day! I am glad you have good weather for your journey. We thought we might be allowed to come and see you off. Can we be of any use, Miss Kenderdine?"

Dr. Stedman addressed himself to Letty, who looked nervous and fidgety.

"Thank you, thank you. It is so troublesome, travelling; especially without a gentleman to take care of us. Edna, are you sure the boxes are all right? Did you count them? Two trunks, one bonnet-box, one—"

"Yes, all are right. Don't vex yourself, dear," said Edna, in her soft *sotto voce*, and then she was aware that Dr. Stedman turned to look at her earnestly, more earnestly than usual.

"Let me help you! you are carrying such a heap of cloaks and things, and you look so tired. Are you able for the journey to-day?"

"Oh yes, quite able. Besides, we must go."

Will made no reply, but he took her burdens from her, arranged her packages, and stood silently beside her till the coach came up.

Julius too, his languor and indifference dispersed as if by magic, placed himself close to the blooming Letty, paying her his final politenesses with remarkable *empressement*.

"Yes, I am sorry to leave this place," she said, in answer to his question. "We have had a pleasant time; and we are going back to horrid school-work. I hate it."

"No wonder. Still, your pupils are somewhat to be envied."

"Eh?" said Letty, not detecting the compliment, her

miud being divided between Julius, the boxes, and the
approaching coach. "Look, Edna, it is quite full. We
shall have to go inside—nay, the inside is full too. What
must we do? Oh, Edna, what must we do?"

"It was my fault," said Will Stedman. "I ought to
have told you it was better to secure places. Coachman,
is there no chance whatever for these ladies?"

Coachman shook his head, remorseless as Fate; and
Fate, laughing from under the coach-wheels, and making
mouths at them from the dickey, set at naught all the excellent schemes of these four young people.

The two sisters regarded each other in mute consterna-
tion.

"How very, very foolish I was!" said Edna, in extreme
vexation. "Can nothing be done? Dr. Stedman, will
you think for us? We *must* go home to-day."

"Po'-chay, ma'am — po'-chay to Ryde," suggested the
landlord.

"How much would that cost?"

A serious sum was named. Edna looked at and counted
her money. No, it was not to be done. She saw Dr. Stedman watching her, and blushed crimson.

He came near her, and said, almost in a whisper, "Excuse me, but at a journey's end one sometimes runs short.
If—"

Edna shook her head, and set her little mouth together,
firm as Fate—whom she fancied she was thus resisting: at
which Dr. Stedman blushed as deeply as herself, and retired.

There was no help for it. Several boats crossed daily
from Ryde; but to get to Ryde from this out-of-the-way
place was the difficulty.

"No, Letty," said Edna, "not being able to travel about
in post-chaises, we must e'en put up with our misfortune.
We can go by the coach to-morrow morning. I dare say
Mrs. Williams will take us in for one night more. Things
might be worse, you see."

But as she watched the coach roll away, Edna, though
she spoke cheerfully, looked a great deal more annoyed
and troubled than her sister did; and Dr. Stedman saw it.

"You have a tell-tale face," said he. "This has vexed you very much, I perceive."

"Of course it has. Many reasons made it important for us to go home."

"Your sister takes it easy enough, apparently."

"She always—" and Edna stopped herself. Why should she be discussing Letty with a stranger—with any body?

"I beg pardon," said Dr. Stedman, abruptly, and disappeared.

But when they had all escaped out of the condolences of the little crowd round the inn-door, and were ignominiously retracing their steps to Mrs. Williams's lodgings, he overtook them, breathless.

"Stop, Miss Edna. I have found a way out of your difficulties. There will be a post-chaise here at noon, bringing a wedding-couple from Ryde. It will take you the return-journey for merely coach-fare. If you cross at once you will be able to start from Portsmouth to London to-night. Will that do?"

"Admirable," said Edna, turning back. "Let me go and settle it at once."

"It is settled—I took the liberty of settling it with the landlord, whom I know. Always provided you were satisfied. Are you?"

"Quite."

"Thank you. And now you have only to repay me the coach-fare—inside places for two," said the doctor, holding out his hand with a smile.

Edna laughingly and, as it occurred to her long after, most unsuspiciously, gave him the money; and he walked on beside her, receiving silently her expressions of gratitude. She did indeed feel grateful. It was so new to her to have the burdens of daily life thus taken off her, and in such a considerate way, simply a man doing a man's part of kindness to a woman—nothing more. It made her remember his words: "If I had had a sister I would have been so good to her." Though while Edna recalled them, there was a strange sting in the remembrance.

At the familiar door they all stopped, rather awkward-

ly, till Dr. Stedman said, with something beyond his usual
formality:

"I wonder, Julius, if these ladies would consider it presumption in us to offer them our bachelor hospitality for
the next few hours? It might be more convenient, and
they would at least get a dinner."

"Oh, they must—they must," cried Julius. "Say you
will, Miss Edna," and he caught hold of her hand in his
boyish, affectionate way. "Come and dine with us; it
will be such fun. And we will go a long walk before
then. Oh, I am so much obliged to Fate and that grim
coachman! We'll have such a jolly day!"

He was evidently in a state of considerable excitement,
which relieved itself in almost puerile pranks, and incessant flow of talk, and a pettish assertion of his own will,
which was, as Edna declared, "exactly like a baby." Nevertheless, she and the others only laughed, and gave way
to him.

Evidently the catastrophe about the coach had produced in none of the little party any permanent depression; and it was with almost exuberant spirits that they
prepared to make the very most of this sweet, stolen day
—all the sweeter, Julius insisted, because it was stolen—a
clear robbery out of the treasure-house of Destiny, who
had not many such.

"At least not for us," added he, with the dash of melancholy which ran through his merriest moods. "So I'll
take the residuum* of my pleasures as I used to take the
spoonful of sugar at the bottom of an emptied coffee-cup,
which I was always told it was such ill-manners to touch,
though it was the best bit of the draught. And yet we
have had a good draught of happiness this fortnight—
have we not, Miss Edna? Our coffee of life was thoroughly well-made—strong and clear, with plenty of milk
in it."

"The milk of human kindness?"

"Yes; and some water too. We had only too much
water on Monday night. But I beg your pardon." For
Edna still turned pale, and then red, whenever there was

the slightest allusion to her painful adventure; so that now all reference to it had tacitly ceased.

"I think," said Dr. Stedman, "since our friends have gained an extra day of sea-air they had better make use of it. So come away all of you down to the shore."

There they wandered for hours, as merry as children, tossing the shingle at one another, or entombing themselves in it as they sat; writing names and sentences with umbrella-sticks on the sand, or building out of it castles and moats for the incoming tide first to fill and then to wash away. Some mixture of seriousness there was; for sea-side folly has always a touch of solemnity in it; and there is but a step between the babyish pranks on the sand and the awfulness of the silent ocean beyond. But still, whatever they did, or whatever they talked about, these four were very happy. It was a day—one of those single, separate days which stamp themselves upon the memory for years, both from their heavenly beauty, externally, and their moral atmosphere of pleasantness and peace. A day never to be forgotten in its innocent Arcadian enjoyment, to which all things seemed natural; and they themselves felt not like modern work-a-day men and women, but creatures of some perfectly ideal world—shepherds and shepherdesses of some long-past golden age.

They dined, nevertheless—upon cold mutton and suet dumplings, which was the best Mrs. Williams could provide; and they dined heartily and merrily. It might have been a little "incorrect," this bachelor entertainment to two young maiden ladies. In the midst of the meal a grave doubt of this struck Edna; but it was a merry meal, for all that, with not one bit of sentiment about it, or regret that it was the first and last. For still, with all their mutual friendliness, the sisters withheld their address, and the brothers were too courteous to ask for it.

Suddenly, in midst of the gayety, Dr. Stedman said, "It is nearly three. Your carriage will be at the door in five minutes." And for that five minutes every body was rather silent.

Edna sat at the window, taking a farewell look at the

beautiful sea; and Dr. Stedman came and looked at it
with her.

" You are better now than in the morning, I hope ?"

" Yes, the salt air always does me good."

" It will be very late before you reach home to-night.
Are you afraid ?"

" Oh no."

" You seem afraid of nothing."

" Not of many things—outside things. Why should I
be ? And it would do no good. I am not like a careful-
ly-guarded young lady; I am a poor school-mistress, who,
whether she likes it or not, must face the world."

" Do you find that very hard ?"

" Sometimes — only sometimes; for I am young and
strong, and not given to despondency. It may be otherwise when I get older."

And a vague cloud came over Edna as she spoke; a fear
that it not only might but would be thus; that the days
would come when her strength would fail, and her courage
sink, beaten down; when she would be dull, weary, lonely,
and old.

" Are you afraid of growing old ?" said Dr. Stedman
again. " I am—a little."

" Why should you be ?" said Edna, forgetting the question in the confession, and turning to look inquiringly at
him. " Old age can have no terrors for you. A man is
so different from a woman."

" He is — horribly different — in some things. Miss
Edna—I would give the whole world if I were more like
you."

These words, spoken in a tone that seemed at once ap-
pealing, apologizing—nay, almost caressing, so low and
soft was it, quivered through Edna from head to foot.
But before she had time to answer or think of answering,
the post-chaise was at the door—a goodly equipage—all
in its bridal splendor—white favors and all.

Letty jumped up in delight. " Oh, how nice ! We shall
get to Ryde so comfortably. And think of our starting
from the very door. So kind of you to order it, Dr. Sted-

man. It is almost as good as if we had our own carriage. Ah, Edna! shall we ever have our own carriage?"

"Possibly—I should say not improbably," said Dr. Stedman, dryly, as he handed the beautiful woman, with careful courtesy, to the chaise, which she seemed to step into as if she were born to a carriage.

Julius hung back, and made his adieux with a cynical air.

"Mrs. Williams thinks the white favors a lucky omen, Miss Kenderdine. She hopes to see one or both of you two young ladies back again ere long—in a similar equipage. I trust the owner may be a duke at least."

"Eh?" said Letty, not comprehending, but smiling still.

"Mrs. Williams says, next time you come here, she hopes it will be in your own carriage, and married to some rich gentleman—possibly a duke."

Letty bridled. "Oh, Mr. Stedman, you are so funny! Good-bye!"

So they parted—all four with the smile on their lips, shaking hands cordially, and keeping up their jests even to the last moment; expressing all manner of mutual good wishes, but not a hint or hope of future meetings. They parted—as completely as two ships that had crossed one another's track in the mid-ocean—paused alongside for a short space of kindly greeting—then divided, steadily and finally, to sail on round the world their several and opposite ways.

Edna knew it must be thus—that it was best it should be. Some instinct, forestalling experience, warned her of the fact—proved fatally by how many wrecked lives!— that men ought to be nothing to women, and women nothing to men, except in the merest ordinary friendship—unless they are either akin by blood, or deliberately choose one another in love and marriage: that all so-called "Platonic attachments," sentimental compromises which try to steer clear of both, and institute pseudo-relations which nature never meant, almost always end in misery—blameless, but still heart-deep, life-long misery. Edna wished to avoid every thing of the kind—both for herself and her sister. Nothing had happened; nobody had proposed to Letty, and she was thankful thus peacefully, friendly, and kindly to close all associations with the Stedmans.

Yes, they had parted just as (she said this to herself again and again during the long drive)—just as she most desired them all to part—like ships on the ocean, never to sail in company again. Still, she felt that for some days to come her own little vessel would sail rather drearily, and flap its canvas idly in the breeze, scarcely noticing whether or not there was sunshine on the sea, which looked so limitless, and yet which she must cross—and cross alone.

"I wonder," she thought to herself, "which of us will grow old the fastest or live the longest—Dr. Stedman or I?"

CHAPTER X.

KENSINGTON twenty years ago was not like the Kensington of to-day. It seemed much quieter and farther from London. No great Exhibitions had beaten down the smooth grass of Hyde Park and stamped out the green lanes of Brompton, which then formed a barrier between "the old court suburb," as Leigh Hunt tenderly calls it, and the metropolitan vortex. Down the long, dusty miles of the Knightsbridge road crawled a few uncomfortable omnibuses—forming the chief communication with London—except for those fortunate people who had carriages of their own. Consequently, to middle-class respectability, Kensington was a rather retired place. Townified, certainly, but then its queer winding streets, its old-established shops and old-fashioned houses, above all, its palace and ancient church, gave it a dignified quaintness which half atoned for the want of the country. And but a little way beyond it were many ruralities: lanes and gardens, haunted by larks in the day-time and nightingales at eve; here and there a real field—not yet become a brick-field; and several "lovers' walks," where, between the tall hedge

of May or wild roses, young people thus circumstanced
might exchange a kiss safely and unobserved.

About half a mile from where the Misses Kenderdine
lived was a canal, along the banks of which ran a slip of
waste ground, where bloomed as if by stealth many a real
country flower : bind-weed—the little pink creeping sort
and the large white one, that in late summer mounts the
hedges and stars them with its dazzling, short-lived bells;
abundance of those flowers which grow on commons and
waste ground—bright yellow hawk-weed, and the delicate
primrose-tinted kind; with various tiny plants, pleasant
enough to observant eyes, and of which there used to be
plenty in these regions, till London, gradually growing,
has forced them to give place to coarser weeds.

To this place Edna often came, between or after school-
hours, to fancy herself in the country and get a breath of
air, for the sisters' house was somewhat small and close.
Not that it was an ugly house; creepers, jasmine, and
grape-vine half covered it, and it was open, front and back,
to a view of market-gardens. Nobody can find it now—
it has been completely swept from the face of the earth;
pulled down and built upon, with all its surroundings.
Year by year genteel terraces and squares are growing
where the cabbages—acres of them—once grew. So if I
say, with the lingering tenderness that its inhabitants also
learned to speak of it, that it was not an ugly house,
there is no one who can contradict me.

It boasted three stories, of two rooms each, the most important of which were the sitting-room, the drawing-room
above, made into a school-room, and a large (or they called
it large) bedroom overhead, where the two sisters slept.
Thus, at a glance, may be seen their small establishment,
of which the only other inmates besides themselves were
one servant and a cat. A very microscopic, maidenly establishment, simple even to poverty, and yet it had its
happiness—to Edna at least—for it was their own. Every
atom of furniture had been bought with their own money
—bought and paid for—which is more than can be said of
many magnificent mansions. Every corner, from attic to

basement, was theirs to do with as they liked. And to
these governesses, who had lived for years in other people's houses, any nook they could call their own and do
what they chose in, possessed a certain charm, of which
the novelty was not even yet exhausted. In this nest of
theirs, narrow as it was, the two sisters had not been unhappy—Edna especially had been the merriest little bird
—till now.

It chanced that after the pleasant spring came a very
hot summer; weeks of settled drought. By August the
leaves were almost burnt off the trees, and the dusty, languid air that seemed to creep, or rather to stagnate, over
the lanes and market-gardens, and the line of road between Kensington town and Holland House, was almost
stifling, even at twilight, when Edna insisted on their going out, just for health's sake.

"Oh, Edna," Letty would say, drearily, as she crawled
along the heated pavement and looked up at the handsome houses, nearly all with closed windows—"every
body is gone out of town. Why can't we go too? It's
very hard for us to be teaching school here when all the
world is away at the sea-side. I wish we were there also.
Don't you?"

"No," replied Edna. "One holiday is enough for one
year. No."

But she knew she was telling a falsehood; that in her
heart of hearts she had a frantic longing for the sight of
the sea, for the sound and smell of briny waters, lapping
on shingle and sand, for even a handful of sea-weeds, damp,
salt, and living—not like that poor dead mummy of a sea-
weed that still hung up in a corner of the room, though
Letty had begged her more than once to take it down, it
looked so "nasty," for its meteorological powers had sig-
nally failed. Yet still she let it hang there—a thing that
had missed its destiny, and was of no mortal use to any
body—except as a memento of a very pleasant time.

That pleasant time had passed out of all memories.
Even Letty scarcely mentioned it now—three months
was far too long for Letty to remember any thing or any

body. At first she had found home extremely dull, had
talked incessantly of the Isle of Wight and of the two
Stedmans, wondering whether they had come home—if
when they did come they would make any effort to renew
the acquaintance.

"It would be possible, nay, easy, to find out our address, for our boxes were marked 'Kensington,' and there
is the post-office to inquire at. If I were they I would
hunt us out, and call. In which case, Edna, you know,
we must be polite to them. They might mean nothing."

"Probably not. What would you wish them to
mean?"

"How sharp you are with me! Of course, if Dr. Stedman did call upon us two single ladies, he could have but
one intention in doing so. Not that he ever gave me any
reason to suppose any thing," added Letty, looking down
with her half smile, that implied an expectation of being contradicted in her assertion. But no contradiction
came.

"Of course, a man so poorly circumstanced couldn't be
expected to come forward at once; but then you see—"

Edna would see nothing. Every time the conversation
took this turn she resolutely avoided it: to speak her
mind, or to open her heart to this her only sister, became
every day more impossible. Not that there was less affection between them, but there was a clearer perception
and a sadder acceptance of the great difference in thought
and feeling, which sometimes happens—that alienation of
nature which no nearness of blood can atone for, or prevent, or cure.

Sometimes, when in the long bright June evenings Letty persisted in walking out regularly—not down the actual street where Dr. Stedman lived (Edna knew it well,
and kept half a mile from it always), but up and down
the long green alleys of Kensington Gardens, looking
round at every corner, and fancying every tall figure—or
two figures, a taller and a shorter—must surely be the
two Stedmans—the patient elder sister would grow excessively irritable, and then Letty, who was invariably

good-tempered, would wonder at her, and fear she was
not well, and pet her and caress her in a fashion harder to
bear than the interminable talkativeness.

But when week after week crept by, and the Stedmans
gave no sign, Letty's interest in her lost admirer or ad-
mirers died out. Besides, school-time began, and the
small worries of the present completely extinguished the
past. Then, when her sister seemed quite to have forgotten them, poor Edna's memory of those happy sea-side
days woke up with a vividness quite horrible in its pain,
and in its sharp consciousness of what that pain was, whence
it arose, and to what it tended.

I will tell no untruth about my poor Edna, nor make
any pretenses concerning her, which she herself would
have been the first to scorn. I believe that no woman,
gifted with common sense and common feeling, ever "falls
in love," as the phrase is, without knowing it: at least
not when the love comes suddenly, and for one who heretofore has been a stranger, so that no gradual previous relations of intimacy have disguised the true state of things
for a while, as sometimes occurs. She may refuse to acknowledge the fact, even to herself; but she knows it—
knows it at the very core of her heart—in all its sweetness, and in all its bitterness too.

Long before those three months had gone by, Edna
Kenderdine, who had met so few men, and had never taken
the smallest interest in any man, began to find out that
she was never likely again to meet such an one as Dr. William Stedman—never likely, in all her future life, to have
such a happy fortnight as that she spent in the Isle of
Wight, when her anxiety for her sister was over, and she
and Letty were roaming about the sweet country and
pleasant sea-shore, and meeting the two Stedmans every
day and all day long.

Only a fortnight—fourteen days—a short time on which
to build—or to wreck—a life's happiness; yet many have
done it before now, and will do it again. Fate sometimes
compresses into a few days the events and experience of
years. People love in divers ways, and marry under in-

finitely varied circumstances, concerning which no person
can judge, or has a right to judge, any other; yet there is
but one true love—leading to the one perfect marriage, or
else leading through dark and thorny yet sacred ways to
that perpetual virginity of heart and life which is only
second to marriage in its holiness and happiness.

This love had come to Edna, and she knew it.

She did not fall into romantic ecstasies of joy or grief
over it, though let not even these be condemned; they are
natural in the time of passionate youth—the Juliet-time.
But Edna was a woman—not a girl, though her heart was
as fresh as if she were sixteen. She said nothing—she
betrayed nothing; externally she was the school-mistress
only; but within she was conscious of the great change
which only comes once in a lifetime, and after which no
woman is ever quite the same again.

Of her lover—or her love, a tenderer and nobler name—
she did not sit and think all day long—her days were too
busy for that; but she thought of him in every idle or solitary minute, and often when neither idle nor alone; till
day by day she learned to mingle him in all her doings
and all her dreams. Him—the one "him" in the world
to her now, whom by a magic sympathy she seemed already to understand, faults and all, better than any other
human being she had ever met.

For she did not think Dr. Stedman faultless; she had
seen in him a good many things she would have liked different, and had to apologize for—shortcomings of temper,
roughness, and hardness, which seemed the result of circumstances. Still he was himself drawn to her, or rather
she to him, by a strange attraction, and, as a whole, very
near her ideal of what a man should be.

But it is idle reasoning about such things, and soon
Edna ceased to reason, and was content only to feel. All
the stronger because in her intense humility it never occurred to her that the feeling could be reciprocated. She
accepted with a strong, silent courage the lot which had
befallen her—a great misfortune, some would say. But
she did not call it so, though she recognized to the full its

sadness, hopelessness, and — no, she was not so cowardly as to add, its humiliation.

She had done nothing wrong in loving, even though she loved a man who had never asked her to marry him, who had apparently no intention of asking her, whom, in all human probability, she would never meet again. Well, let it be so; she had met, for once in her life, the man who she felt could have satisfied her whole heart, reason, conscience—whom, had he asked her, she would have married, and whom otherwise she would remember tenderly to the day of her death. This is, next to a thoroughly happy marriage, the best lot which can befall any woman.

I linger over Edna Kenderdine because I like to linger over her, just here: the picture of a woman who is brave enough to love, unloved, the best and highest; embodied to her, as it was to her mother Eve, in a man. For Milton's celebrated line,

"He for God only, she for God in him,"

is so far true that no woman can love either lover or husband perfectly, unless—in a sense—she sees God in him, and sees in him, beyond herself, the desire for God only. And if so, her love is neither an unhappy nor an unfortunate love, however it may end.

One fact proved incidentally how utterly removed from the selfishness of all personal feeling was this ideal admiration, this self-existent, up-looking, and outloving love which had taken such sudden and strong hold of Edna's heart, and after lurking there awhile, sprung up, forced into being not by the sunshine of hope, but by the warm darkness of complete though quiet despair. The possibility—which Letty's vanity had taken for granted—of Dr. Stedman's attentions being to herself, awoke in her sister's mind no jealousy or dread—indeed no sensation of any kind. In those early days—when she was so ignorantly happy—Edna had thought the matter over in all its bearings, and set it aside as a mistake. For had he really fallen in love, there was no reason why he should not have spoken, nor why afterwards he should not have hunted

Letty out and followed her to the world's end. Edna
thought, if she were a man, she would have done so. She
could imagine no hinderance strong enough to prevent a
man who really loved a woman from seeking her out,
wooing her, and carrying her off triumphant—like one of
the old Paladins—in face of all the world.

Yet all these three months William Stedman had lived
close by them, and given no sign of his existence. Therefore, of course, there was but one conclusion to be drawn.
Letty, she supposed, had come to it likewise, or else had
forgotten the whole matter—Letty could so easily forget!

Still, this summer was a dull time with poor Letty Kenderdine. After the fever, pupils were naturally slow of
returning; the sisters were likely to be very poor this
half year. Edna did not care much for the fact; but she
tried to make things as easy as she could to Letty, whom
want of money always affected keenly with a hundred
small wants and petty humiliations, which her sister, if
unable to sympathize with, felt heartily sorry for. She
taxed her ingenuity to lighten Letty's school-duties, and
out of school to invent inexpensive amusements for her;
but still the dullness remained. Only dullness; certainly
not disappointed love, for Letty spoke more than once of
accepting her latest offer from an Australian sheep-farmer,
once the boy-brother of one of her pupils, whose ardent
admiration had gone so far as to entreat her to come out
to Geelong and marry him. And so Edna, who, in her
simplicity, could not conceive the possibility of liking one
man, and in the remotest degree contemplating marriage
with another, became quite satisfied as to the state of her
sister's affections.

Thus they went on, teaching school daily, and spending
the time as well as they could after school-hours, generally in the arduous duty of making ends meet, until the
leaves which had budded out in that happy, merry spring-
time in the Isle of Wight began to change color, wither,
and fade.

"How fast the year slips by!" said Letty, drearily, one
half-holiday when she sat at the window, with nothing to

do but to look over the long flat of market-gardens, and
wish she was anywhere but where she was. " I declare,
to-day is the last day of the band playing in Kensington
Gardens, and we have never yet been to hear it. It is
your fault, Edna. Why wouldn't you let us go?"

The question was not easy to answer. There was, of
course, the obvious reason that Letty was too beautiful a
person to promenade much in so public a place without
father or brother; but Edna's conscience told her this was
not the only reason why she had so persistently resisted
such a very harmless amusement.

She knew quite well, that if by walking twenty miles
she could, herself unseen, have caught one glimpse of William Stedman — resting her weary, thirsting eyes on his
brown face, which might not be handsome, yet was so
manly, gentle, honest, and good—she would eagerly have
done it. That even the dim remote possibility of seeing
him — his tall, sturdy, erect figure, turning round some
street corner—a common Kensington street—sanctified to
her even those dusty pavements and ugly roads. Sometimes the craving only to know that he was alive—alive
and well—pursuing his duties, which she knew were so
close to his heart, working at his profession, and carrying
out nobly his useful, beneficent life, without the remotest
thought of herself, came upon poor Edna with a force that
was almost maddening in its pain. But, at the same time,
the chance of really seeing him, of meeting face to face,
and being obliged to bow, or to shake hands and speak to
him, in the visible flesh—him of whom she thought night
and day—was to her an apprehension almost amounting
to terror. The mere thought of it often, in her walks,
made her heart stand still a minute, and then go on beating so violently that she scarcely knew where she was or
what she was doing. Therefore she had contrived always to avoid that band promenade, where Kensington
young men might naturally take an afternoon lounge, and
where Julius Stedman had once said he was rather fond
of going.

But this day Letty was so persistent, that, with a kind

of fear lest her secret reason should be betrayed, Edna ceased resistance, and they went.

Only, however, for one or two turns, during which she looked straight before her, and deported herself as grimly as possible towards the fops and fashionable idlers who never failed to stare at the tall beautiful woman and her unobtrusive companion. Only two turns; but even these were one too many. At the second, Fate came, dead front, to meet the sisters.

"There they are! Don't look, Edna; don't let them fancy we see them; but there are the two Stedmans."

Edna's heart gave a wild leap, every thing seemed turning round and round for a minute, then she gathered up her senses, and recovered her strong self-control, which had never failed her yet. Happily, her veil was down; but Letty's careless eyes roved everywhere rather than to her sister's face. Had it been different, still Edna would have been safe. Usually tears and blushes came readily to that sensitive little face, which changed its expression half a dozen times in a minute; but when any thing smote her hard, Edna neither blushed nor wept, but grew perfectly white, and as quiet as a stone. She did so now.

"The Stedmans, is it? You are right, Letty, we will not look. They are not likely to see us. They are passing on."

And they did pass on, their attention being caught by some acquaintance on the other side of the promenade, to whom they stood talking for some time.

That while, the eyes Dr. Stedman did not see—the sad, fond, lingering eyes—had seen him—vividly, distinctly; had noticed that he was a good deal thinner, paler, graver —very unlike his former self; until in talking he chanced to smile, and then Edna recognized it again fully—the face stamped indelibly upon her memory.

Perceiving he was fully occupied, and that there was no possibility of his noticing her, she looked at him once again, with a quiet, sad feeling—"God bless him; no man is any the worse for a woman's loving him"—and turned

As soon as she could she lured Letty out of the crowd
into one of those green alleys that abound in Kensington
Gardens, in sight of the queer old red brick palace, with
its Dutch garden, where, long ago, the courtiers of William and Mary, and the maids of honor of Queen Anne,
and the first two Georges, may have strolled and coquet-
ted and made love—the old, old story! In their long-
effaced footsteps walked the lovely Letty Kenderdine, as
fair as any of them, and talking, perhaps, not greater nonsense than they had talked.

"Well, I must say it was strange," said she. "It only
shows how easily men forget. To pass me by within a
few yards, and never even see me!"

"They were talking to some gentlemen."

"Oh, but people always see those they want to see.
Perhaps I ought to have bowed. You know they could
not come and speak to us unless we bowed first. And
how nice and gentlemanly they both looked, especially
Julius! Really Julius is a very handsome young fellow,
now he is quite well. I suppose he is quite well by this
time."

"He looked so." And Edna felt glad partly for his
own sake, but more for his brother's. That anxiety at
least was over. And then she let her imagination wander
wildly as to what could be the secret trouble which
showed plainly on Dr. Stedman's face, and had altered
him so much. The desperate longing to comfort him, to
take part of his burden, whatever it might be, came upon
her, sad and sore.

So much so, that she never heard footsteps behind, nor
guessed what was going to happen, until Letty called out
in her loud whisper:

"Goodness me! There they are."

And at an angle of the path the two brothers and two
sisters met, face to face, abruptly and unexpectedly, so as
to make non-recognition, or the half-recognition of a formal bow, impossible. They were all evidently taken by
surprise. Involuntarily they stopped and shook hands.
Not without a certain awkwardness in the greeting, prob-

ably caused by the suddenness of their rencontre; but after the first minute it passed off. In spite of all the good
resolutions on both sides, every body seemed unfeignedly
glad to meet.

The two young men turned back with them in the old
familiar way; Julius by Edna, Dr. Stedman by Letty,
until with some slight excuse Julius crossed over to the
latter, and his brother fell behind with Edna. Thus they
went, walking slowly, the whole way up the broad walk
to the Bayswater Gate. The younger brother and sister
began laughing and talking immediately, Julius making
himself agreeable in his old light way, as if it were but
yesterday that he had carried on the same pleasant badinage on the Isle of Wight shore; but the two others were
rather silent.

Dr. Stedman asked Edna a few questions as to her sister's health and her own; if they had had no return of
scarlet-fever in the house, and if their pupils had come
back; to all of which she replied quietly, briefly, and cate-
gorically; then he seemed to have nothing more to say.
And, far in the distance, they heard the faint sound of
the band playing, and one or two straggling groups of
gayly-dressed people passed them, chattering and flirting
—a great contrast to this quiet, silent pair.

Very silent, very quiet outside, but beneath that—?

Many people might call it wrong for an unsought woman—a tender, sweet, reticent maiden—to feel as Edna felt,
walking along beside him who, she now knew, was the
lord of all her life. But there was no wrong in her heart.
She had no hope of being wooed or married by Dr. Stedman; she only loved him. She only felt that it was
heaven to be near him—to catch again the sound of his
voice—to rest again in the protection of his honest good-

—it would have been not hard, but happy to have done it; for he seemed, now she saw him again, just as heretofore—unlike all others, simplest, noblest, best; truest man and most perfect gentleman—one worth living for—worth dying for.

She idealized him a little: women always do that; but William Stedman was a great deal that she believed; and for her idealizing, perhaps it did no harm. Men so loved not seldom grow to be as good as the fond women believe them.

At the Bayswater Gate Dr. Stedman paused.

"This is our best way home. Will you come, Julius?"

"Certainly not; I have not half talked out my talk. Do you turn? Then so shall we—with your permission, Miss Kenderdine."

Letty bowed a smiling assent. After her long fast from flirtation she was all graciousness, even to the "boy" Julius, as she persisted in considering him, though he was exactly her own age. So the two couples strolled back again to the palace, and then across the grass to the little gate which led to Kensington High Street.

"Here we really must take our leave," said William Stedman, decisively. "I have an appointment; and besides, Julius—" he added half a dozen inaudible words, which his brother did not answer, but turned sharply away.

Then Edna came forward, very dignified. This little woman could be dignified when she chose, in spite of her few inches.

"Indeed, Mr. Stedman, we will not trouble you to accompany us any farther. We have a call to make in Kensington. Good-bye."

She held out her hand—first to Julius, and then to his brother.

"Well, that is the coolest dismissal," said the former. "Must it be? Do you really agree to it, Miss Letty?"

But Miss Letty was making elaborate adieux to Dr. Stedman, and did not hear. Besides, she very rarely con-

tradicted Edna. Her easy nature always yielded to the
stronger will; it was least trouble. But when they had
really parted from their cavaliers she was a little cross.

"Why on earth were you so peremptory, Edna? They
wanted to see us home."

"Did they?"

"At least Julius did. And why not? It would have
been rather amusing. If we ever meet them again, and
perhaps we may, for Mr. Stedman says they always take
their constitutional in Kensington Gardens—we ought to
treat them a little more civilly, and let them see us home
if they desire it."

Edna replied not, but the small mouth set itself closely together. No. Letty might say what she liked—fancy what she chose, but this should not be. Dr. Stedman
should never think that either she or her sister were girls
ready to meet the first advances of any idle youth. Love
was no disgrace; it did nobody any harm; but the feeble
pretense of it — flirtation or philandering — was a thing
which this woman, pure and true, yet passionate-hearted,
utterly scorned. If the Stedmans wanted to marry Letty
—either of them—they must come and ask for her as a
man should ask—and is a coward if he dare not ask under
any circumstances.

Letty—always Letty. That the object of their admiration could be any other when Letty was by did not
occur to Edna. And when Letty took her bonnet off, and
shook back her bright fair hair, and looked into the glass
with her eyes glittering with the novel excitement of the
day, Edna thought the universal admiration her sister excited was not wonderful. If Dr. Stedman shared it—if
that was the cause of his silence and evident preoccupa-
tion—well!

Edna stood a minute to face this thought. She was
alone. Letty had gone down stairs, all smiles and excitement; at least, as much excitement as she was capable
of—quite another woman after the afternoon's adventure,
which was such a pleasant break in their dull life. Was
it only that, or did she really care for one or other of the

Stedmans? And if one of them really asked her, would
Letty marry him?

Such a possibility might occur. The man Edna loved
might marry another, and that other her own sister: a
supposition maddening enough to many—nay, most wom-
en. Even to this gentle little woman it gave the same
sudden "stound"—which had come to her several times
lately. She closed her eyes, drew a long hard breath,
tried to stifle the choking in her throat, and to view her
position calmly.

Jealousy, in any of its ordinary forms, did not affect her;
her nature was too single, too entirely free from both vanity and self-consciousness. No wound could come to her
through either of these points—nothing except simple sorrow, the agony of lost love. Besides, she was accustomed
to view things in the plain daylight, without any of those
distorted refractions to which egotistic people are subject.
She saw that in such a case as hers there are but two ways
open to any woman. If she loves a man and he does not
love her, to give him up may be a horrible pang and loss,
but it can not be termed a sacrifice—she resigns what she
never had. But if he does love her and she knows it, she
is bound to marry him, though twenty other women loved
him, and broke their hearts in losing him. He is not theirs,
but hers; and to have her for his wife is his right and her
duty. And in this world are so many contradictory views
of duty and exaggerated notions of rights, so many false
sacrifices and renunciations weak even to wickedness, that
it is but fair sometimes to uphold the *right* of love—love
sole, absolute, and paramount, firmly holding its own, and
submitting to nothing and no one—except the laws of God
and righteousness.

"Yes," Edna whispered to herself as she sat down, feeling strangely weak and yet strong, and looked through the
open window across the market-gardens, and down Love
Lane, where in the August evening more than one pair of
figures—lovers, of course—might be seen slowly strolling.
"Yes, it is all clear enough, plain enough. Possibly we
shall never meet him again—I hope not. But if we do, if

he loves Letty, marries Letty—" she paused—" of course, I never say one word. He only does right, and she does right too—what I should have done myself. If he loved me, and I knew it, I would hold to him in spite of Letty, in spite of the whole world—hold to him till death!"

Involuntarily, her right hand closed over the other hand. Ay, small and fragile as it was, it was a hand that any one could see would hold, faithfully and firm, till death.

Oh that among us poor, wavering women, driven about by every wind of fancy, prejudice, weakness, or folly, there were more such hands! They would keep back many a man from sinking into the gulf of perdition.

CHAPTER XI.

"I've done it! I've tracked them as cleverly as if I were a bee-hunter on the American prairies. I've found their house—such a little one, in such a shabby neighborhood. No wonder they didn't like us to know it. I say, Will, don't you hear?"

"Yes," growled Will, who had just come in from a severe day's work, as his brother had done from a severe day's play. They were eating conjointly their final meal, half tea, half supper, roughly laid out and roughly served, in the dining-room, which was the one well-furnished apartment of the doctor's large, empty house—a good house in a good street, which as a doctor he was obliged to have, and had contrived to make externally comfortable for his patients—when they should come. But beyond this consulting-room all was dreariness — the dreariness of raw newness, which is much worse than that of ancient dilapidation.

William Stedman was wearied and dull, but Julius seemed in high spirits, insisting on talking and being listened to.

"I tell you I have found out where they live, though they were so confoundedly secret about it. It's a tiny house in one of the lanes beyond Kensington. They must

be poor enough—poorer even than they seemed. But
there they certainly live, and I vow I'll go and pay them
a call to-morrow."

"Pshaw! don't make a fool of yourself."

"Make a fool of myself! You're uncommonly civil to-
day! Pray, may I ask in what way would it be making
a fool of myself? I like women's society, and these two
are the very jolliest young women I ever—"

Will jumped up as if he had been shot. "Hold your
tongue! you'd better!" cried he, violently; and then,
catching his brother's look of utter amazement, he suddenly reined himself in, and, with a sort of laugh, begged
Julius's pardon.

"Well you may! Why, what has come over you,
Will? What on earth have I said or done amiss?"

"Nothing—decidedly nothing. Except that you might
speak a little more respectfully of these friends of yours.
And I do think, as I told you before you went, that it was
hardly right, hardly gentlemanly, to hunt them out, when
they so evidently wished to conceal from us where they
lived. Just consider, we know nothing at all, in reality,
concerning them, except their names."

"And themselves, which is a good deal. I flatter myself I know one of them, at least, pretty well. Miss Edna
and I were capital friends, though I wasn't sweet upon
her, as you thought I was. She's a very nice girl, but
she's not to my taste exactly."

Will poured himself out his last cup of weak tea and
answered nothing.

"Come now, be reasonable, old fellow. You're my elder brother, and I don't like to go against you. Why are
you so fierce at me for wishing to keep up our acquaintance—a perfectly harmless, indifferent acquaintance—with
the two Misses Kenderdine?"

"They evidently do not wish it."

"Oh, trust me for that," said Julius, with a laugh. "I
know women's ways rather better than you. They only
wanted to be followed—tracked down, like bee-hunting,
as I said; and very amusing work it is, and rather clever-

ly I've done it. To-morrow I mean to knock boldly at
their door—such a little door, only fit for a little fellow
like me, so you needn't try it—send in my card, and re-
quest permission to pay my respects."

"And what is to come of it?"

"Nothing; at least nothing in particular. Just a little
bit of harmless amusement."

"Amusement!"

"Why should I not have amusement. Nay, don't look
as if you'd eat me up. Only consider what a dull life
we lead, especially at this time of year. We're not bad
enough, or rich enough, to do things jollily. I'd really
like to be a good boy, if I could find out a house to visit
at, a family house with nice girls in it, where I could go
to tea sometimes. I'd do it, I assure you, as soberly and
respectably as if I were my own great-grandmother."

"And that is your intention with regard to these ladies?"

"What other intention could I have? You may think
of marrying, old boy, if you like. You have a profession,
a house, and a settled income of two hundred a year; but
as for me—bah!"

"We can neither of us think of marrying just yet," said
the elder brother, gravely. "It would be an act of insanity—or worse—scoundrelism, to take a young girl and
plunge her into a life of grinding poverty. But even that,
I think, would be lesser scoundrelism than to intrude on
the privacy of two young ladies who have neither parents
nor brothers; to cultivate their acquaintance or friendship, as you choose to call it—but we couldn't be friends,
it isn't in human nature. It would end in making them
think, and other people say, we were their lovers; and
then we must sheer off and leave them."

"Well, and if so? It would have been jolly fun while
it lasted."

Dr. Stedman turned upon his brother with blazing eyes.
"You're joking—you know you are. For me, I may be
a very bad fellow—I don't think much of myself, anyhow;
but I'm not such a scamp as that. And as long as I am

your elder brother, and have the slightest influence over you, I'll hinder you from being one. You will seriously offend me, Julius, if you carry out your plan of visiting these two young ladies."

Will spoke quietly, the almost unnatural quietness of some smothered feeling or passion: with him a feeling was a passion, or it was nothing. He was not a merely intellectual man, or a sentimental man: it needed but to look at him to perceive that in him the full human tide of life ran strongly and deeply — the more deeply because so completely held in restraint. His measured words, his steady step—for he had risen, and was walking up and down the room—indicated faintly what lay concealed below.

But Julius did not notice it. Either he was too preoccupied by his own concerns, or else this was a novel development of his brother which he did not understand. He only said, lightly:

"You are very kind, but I don't consider myself a scamp, not just yet; even though, in spite of my elder brother, I do certainly intend to call upon the Misses Kenderdine to-morrow."

It would have been a pity had Edna seen what Dr. Stedman next did—Dr. Stedman, her calm, gentle, wise hero—exalted by her foolish love into all that a man should be. Nothing could excuse it, though it might be accounted for by the long under-current of mental struggle that must have gone on within him, before that last touch caused it to burst its boundaries, and forced him completely beyond his self-control. It was a wrong thing, and a ridiculous thing to do, but he did it: he seized his brother by the collar and shook him, as a furious big dog shakes a little one, which he must punish, but will not injure; then let him go, and leaned breathless against the wall.

Julius rose up, not furious, but smouldering in the white heat of passion which he so seldom showed.

"You shall repent this," he said. "I don't know whether you're mad or drunk, or what, but you shall repent it. I'll leave you now: you're not fit for civil men's company; but to-morrow—. Good-night."

Julius had the best of it, and knew he had. Sometimes, though not many times, during their lives, the two brothers had quarrelled—most brothers do: and then generally the stronger and better-governed nature had won. But now they seemed to have changed characters, and the lighter and more superficial one carried the day.

"I have been a fool," muttered Will, as his brother deliberately lit a chamber candle, and passed him by, unobservant, or else regardless, of the hand which was half extended—the old affectionate, brotherly hand. Will drew it back immediately.

"Good-night," said Julius again, very stiffly, and walked out of the room.

Bitterly humbled and shamed, with the bitterest, perhaps the only shame an honest man can ever feel—the reproaches of his own conscience—Will sat down, wrapping his arms on the table, and laying his head upon them in an attitude of complete dejection. There he remained nearly motionless, for a long time. The last faint glimmering of an August sunset crept into the room and crept out again, leaving behind a dull twilight, almost darkness. Then the lamp-lighter's quick step was heard through the open window, as he went down the dreary emptiness of a London evening street, and flashed upon it gleam after gleam of lighted gas-lamps, till at last he reached the one opposite Dr. Stedman's window; it suddenly brightened up the room, throwing fantastic patterns through the window-curtains on the opposite wall.

Will Stedman sprung up as if he had been asleep and the light had suddenly wakened him.

"What a fool I have been!" he said aloud. "What a—" Forgive him, gentle souls of gentle women, if he used stronger language than I care to record. He was only a man, and he was hard bestead. "I wonder what Julius thought of me! what any one would think! Who would believe I could have done such a contemptible thing? How she would despise me!"

She? So the man had succumbed at last. Passion had taken hold of him: that passion which, seizing one like

William Stedman, completely masters him — turns his whole nature either to sweetness or bitterness. How had this come about, and for what woman? For that is the great test, the one fearful risk of a man's life. A woman will sometimes idealize a very inferior man, until her love for him, and her patience with him, exalt him into something better than he originally was, and her into little short of an angel; but a man almost invariably drops to the level of the woman he is in love with. He can not raise her, but she can almost unlimitedly deteriorate him. Why this should be, Heaven knows, but so it constantly is. We have but to look around us with ordinary observation in order to see that a man's destiny, more than even a woman's, depends far less upon the good or ill fortune of his wooing, than upon the sort of woman with whom he falls in love.

That William Stedman was a man to choose strongly, firmly, and irrevocably, no one who knew him, if ever so little, could doubt. That, having chosen, his character would be modified to a momentous extent by the object of his love, and that, once gaining him, she would have almost unlimited influence over him—was a fact also patent, for it belonged to common human nature. Not that he was a weak man, or a sensualist, to be led by an iron chain hid under passion's roses—his thirty years of brave and virtuous life furnished a sufficient denial to both suppositions. But his affections were very strong, and hitherto had been wholly undivided. He had no intimate friend, and not one relative living, except the brother whom he had guarded and guided all his days, in a way less brotherly than fatherly. Still, Julius had often been a great anxiety to him—more anxiety than pleasure; and besides, there comes a time in a man's life—in all lives—when ties, not only of instinct and duty, but of personal election, are necessary for happiness; when, in short, no tie satisfies, except *the* one which God himself made to be the root of all.

Was it so with William Stedman—this good brother; this eager, active worker in the world, who, as yet, did more for it than it had ever done for him, though he lived

in hopes that if he fought on steadily there was a good
time coming?' Had fate suddenly met him in his busy
life, caught him round a corner, grappled with him and
bound him, throwing him into the reckless bitterness, the
angry, dissatisfied craving of a man who feels the key-note
wanting in his existence—who misses the soft, sweet harmony that would resolve all its discords into peace—the
quiet blessedness which nothing ever gives to a man's life
except a woman's love?

William Stedman's good angel standing behind him that
night might well have wept over him, so unlovely and
unlovable he seemed. But angelic wisdom would have
known also that it was only the upboiling of the chaos
out of which was soon to arise a perfect world.

He paced his dining-room—his well-furnished but ugly
and dreary dining-room—till he was thoroughly wearied;
and he had had a long day of hospital work besides; yet
still the restless spirit was not half taken out of him. Then
he went and listened on the staircase, but from Julius's
room came no sound.

"What do I want with him, or he with me? Probably
he is fast asleep, and has forgotten it all. Nothing ever
makes much impression on him for long. Why should I
sacrifice myself? He will be just as happy in any other
house as in mine; and, besides, he might come here often.
He would, if this house were made pretty and pleasant—
as a woman could make it. They are as poor as we are—
thank God for that! Yet what a difference there used to
be between their parlor and ours! How neat her work-
basket was! and how she used to stick little bits of flowers here and there about the room!"

While he thought, the man's hard features softened.

"*She* wouldn't let me be savage with Julius. She always had a kind word to say for him, poor fellow! She
would be a good sister to him, I know. He liked her, too,
and I was such a fool as to think that— Almost as great
a fool as I was for a day or two over the beauty of the
other one. Pshaw! mere flesh and blood—bones and epi-
dermis. But *my* darling; my little bright, active, loving

darling! she is all spiritual: makes me believe in spirit
without the flesh. No death could kill *her*, or the love
that lives in her. Oh, my God, if I had it for mine!"

A great convulsion came over his face, and his thoughts
(which were altogether silent — he **was** not a person to
stamp about and soliloquize) came to an abrupt stop—then
ran rampant in a wild riot. At last he gathered them up
together, and formed them into a resolution—strong and
clear.

"I *will* have her; at least I'll try my best to get her.
I am driven to it, whether or no. As for prudence—hang
prudence! And with regard to honor—well, perhaps it's
as honorable to speak out at once as to hold my tongue
for another year or two, and let Julius go philandering
after them, vexing and fretting her, and setting people
talking besides; while if she were engaged to me—openly
and fairly mine—nobody could say one word. Only let
any one dare, that's all!"

He clenched his fist and struck it with such force against
the table that he actually hurt himself, and then laughed
at his own exceeding silliness.

"I'll take a walk and think the matter over. I shall
get quiet then. But I must send the household to bed.
How late it is! She would not have been so forgetful of
other people." And after shouting down the stairs to
the old man and woman who formed his sole establishment
—one to attend upon patients, and the other to see to the
comfortless comforts of the two young bachelors—Dr.
Stedman closed his hall-door with a bang, and set off at a
quick pace—anywhere.

His feet carried him to a place where he had very often
walked this summer, but never in daylight; mostly, as
now, taking it on his way home from night visits in that
poor neighborhood which lay close by, whence, no doubt,
the scarlet-fever came. Not a wholesome spot, especially
in late summer and autumn, when the air was heavy with
decaying vegetation. Yet to the end of his days William
Stedman thought there was something **pleasant** in the
faint moist odor, half perfume, of jasmine, clematis, and

the like, and half composed of scents much less sweet, which came through the brilliant harvest moonlight, as he walked along under black shadowing trees and stirless hedges, past the Misses Kenderdine's door.

He knew it well enough—had discovered it long ago —though he had allowed his brother to take such a world of pains to find it; but he walked rapidly past it, and not till he was some distance off did he turn round to watch it, as men in love will stand and watch the casket that holds their jewel, to the end of time.

For he was in love—deeply, desperately—as rarely happens to a man twice in a lifetime. Perhaps all the deeper because, like Romeo with his Rosaline, there had previously appeared and vanished the phantom of a mock sun. It sometimes flashed upon him, this deep-hearted, high-minded, and somewhat exacting man, who in midst of all his passion never let his reason go—what a different kind of love his would have been had it been placed on mere outside beauty—like Letty Kenderdine's!

"My little darling! my bright, active, unselfish little darling! you are not plain to me. You are all sweet, all lovely!" and he opened his arms and closed them again over his breast as if he still felt her there, as on the stormy night when he carried her home insensible—that night when he vowed in his heart that no other woman but herself would he ever marry.

Let us look at him tenderly—this man who had no mother or sister, none of those holy influences which are often almost as blessed as that of a wife, if rightly and wisely and unselfishly used. But he had, as he said, nothing; and he felt his nature hardening and corrupting, and a kind of hopeless cynicism stealing over him.

"Oh, save me!" he cried, almost aloud, for the corner where he stood was as desolate as if he had been in a wilderness. "Save me from myself! Make a man of me! You could if you only knew it—if you only knew how bad I am, and how I want you to make me good, my little darling!"

And then and there he took his resolve, leaning on a

railing where many a lover must have leaned before, for it
was all engraved with rough. letters in twos and .twos,
encircled in rings or true-lovers' knots. Ah, to .think
what has become of the owners of those initials now!
How many broken troth-plights, and death-partings, and
marriages more fatal than deaths! Yet still then and
there William Stedman resigned himself to the common
lot, and made up his mind that he would risk his. all on a
brief yes or no from a woman's lips.

The poor old railing has long been broken down, and
there is a range of handsome houses, in which you can pay
morning calls and go to evening parties. on the quiet spot
where the lovers used to linger. But I think more than
one person still living remembers it tenderly, and thanks
God that William Stedman had strength and courage to
take his destiny, and another's also, into his own hands,
after the fashion of those four lines which every honest man would do well to repeat to himself when he goes
a-wooing : .

> "He either fears his fate too much,
>   Or his deserts are small,
> Who dares not put it to the touch,
>   And win or lose it all."

After that decision the doctor walked home with steadier
feet and a bolder heart. He let himself in at his own door
with a feeling that, come what would, he was master there
—master of himself, and, in measure, of his fortunes; as a
man always is who has courage to look his difficulties in
the face, and push his way through them with a firm,
steadfast hand.

To that singleness of purpose — to the consciousness
that, in acting as he had determined to act, there was in
his heart no mean intent, no thought which a good man
need wish to hide, or. a good woman blush to look at—he
trusted the success of his suit. And if it failed—why,
he was not the first man to whom such a thing had happened.

Though when he imagined the possibility—nay, probability, for his humility made him think it very probable—

of his love being rejected, he felt as a man would not willingly feel twice in a lifetime.

Dr. Stedman was no coward; and yet when he lit his lamp, took out his desk, and fairly sat down to it, his hand shook like a leaf.

The letter consisted only of a few lines—he *could* not write more. Some men take refuge in pen and paper, and revel therein; their thoughts and feelings flow out—and generally evaporate also—in the most charming sentences, which, even under the deepest emotion, it is a relief to them to write, and a pride in having written. But William Stedman was of another sort. To express his feelings at all was very difficult to him—to write them, and see them written, staring back at him in terrible black and white, was impossible. Therefore this letter, the first love-letter he ever wrote, was of the very briefest and most formal kind:

"DEAR MADAM,—Will you do me the honor to read this in private and alone?

"My brother has just told me he has discovered where you live, and means to call upon you. May I be allowed to do so first? I have but one reason for this, and one apology for the presumption of proposing it; that I consider neither my brother nor myself have any right to intrude upon you as mere acquaintances. And besides, a mere acquaintance I could never willingly be to you.

"You and I know one another pretty well: we shall never know one another any better unless I dare to ask you one question—Could you, after any amount of patient waiting on my part, and for the sake of a love of which I can not speak—consent to be my wife?

"To-morrow is Saturday. If, during the day, only one line comes to me by post, I will be with you on Sunday. If I may not come—but then I know you will answer me quickly; you would not keep in needless torture any creature living. Yours faithfully,

"WILLIAM STEDMAN.

"Miss EDNA KENDERDINE."

Yes, that was the name—her name.   He wrote it firmly
enough.   The die was cast, and now he must meet either
fortune; and he thought he could.   He did not even re-
read his letter, or speculate upon whether or not it was a
good letter, or the sort of letter to effect its end; for, even
in the midst of his delirium of passion, he had sense enough
to see that a woman who, in so momentous a crisis, could
lay weight upon accidental forms of phrase or mistakes of
expression, was not a woman to be much desired.   One
doubt alone he had—would she show her sister the letter?
and if so, what would Letty say, and how might she influence Edna with regard to him?

But shortly he cast this perplexity also aside.   A woman
who, in such a case, could be influenced by sister or friend
—or even parent—who could not ask herself the simple
question, " Do I love him, or do I not love him ?" and answer it herself, without referring the decision to any human being—such a woman might be good enough in her
way, but she was not Edna Kenderdine—not the woman
whom a man like William Stedman would ever care to
marry.

Saying this to himself, and staying himself therewith a
little—ay, even in the full tide and torrent of his passion
—he closed and sealed his letter; then, with a vague dread
of trusting himself with it till the morning, he went out
again into the dark streets, and posted it with his own
hand.

CHAPTER XII.

THE postman was by no means a daily visitor at the
Misses Kenderdine's door.   It is a fact—amusing or melancholy, according as one takes it—that society in the
aggregate does not very much run after resident governesses or poor school-mistresses; that they are not likely
to be inundated with correspondence or haunted with invitations.   Of course, under no circumstances are young,
good, and lady-like women quite without friends or acquaintances; such loneliness would argue a degree of un-

lovingness, or unlovableness, of which certainly no one
could accuse the Misses Kenderdine. But this is a busy
and a self-engrossed world; it has quite enough to do with
its own affairs; and it likes to get the full value for all it
bestows. The sisters, who had so little to give it, had not
been troubled with any overplus of its affection. Still
there were, in different parts of the country, a few house-
holds who liked and remembered the Kenderdines; and
even at Kensington there were some houses where they
occasionally visited, or went to one of those evening parties which in London middle-class society take the place
of the countrified, old-fashioned "going out to tea."

They were expecting one of these invitations; so the
postman's red coat gleaming against the green hedge of
Love Lane attracted Letty's attention, and his knock roused
her to jump up and take in the letter. Edna allowed her
to go. She herself had not felt well all the day; the
morning school had been an unusual burden to her, and,
now it was over, she took refuge in her favorite American
rocking-chair—a present from an old pupil—and rocked
and rocked, as if in that soothing motion the uneasy feeling in mind and body—half-weariness, half-restlessness—
would pass away. Though she knew all the while it
would not; that there it was, and she must bear it, as
many another woman had borne it before her—the dull
heart-ache, the hopeless want. These sorrows do come,
and they conquer even the bravest sometimes. May He
who ordained love to be the crown of life have pity on all
those to whom it comes only as a crown of thorns, or who
have to endure the blankness of its absence—the agony
of its loss! Both can be endured, and comfort will come
at length, but the torture is terrible while it lasts. Edna
endured it but in a small measure, and for a short time;
yet the pang was sharp enough to make her, till the end
of her days, feel unutterable pity and tenderness over
those whom the world smiles over as "disappointed in
love"—those from whose lives God has seen fit to omit
life's first and best blessing; or else, though this is a lesser
grief, to give it and take it away.

She was sitting listlessly rocking, not thinking much
about any thing, when Letty re-entered with the letter.
"It is for you, dear. What a funny hand!—a lawyer's
hand, I should say. Who can be writing to you, Edna?"

"I don't know," said Edna, indifferently, and then, catching a glimpse of the letter, checked herself, with a startled
consciousness that she did know, or at any rate guess;
that locked up in her desk in a hidden corner she had a
small fragment of the very same handwriting—a most unimportant fragment — memoranda about trains, etc., for
their railway journey; but still there it was, kept like a
treasure, secreted like a sin.

"Miss Edna Kenderdine," read Letty, detaining the letter and examining it. "Then it must be from a stranger.
A friend would know, of course, that you were Miss Kenderdine. Shall I open it for you, dear?"

"No," said Edna, and an unaccountable impulse made
her snatch it and turn away with it—turn away from her
sister, her dear sister, from whom she had not a secret in
the world. At the first sentence she started, glanced at
the signature, and then put the letter in her pocket, flush-
ing scarlet.

Letty looked amazed. "What is the matter with you?
Is it a love-letter? Do say!"

"It begins like a business letter, and the writer wishes
me to read it in private and alone," said Edna, forcing her
white lips—she felt, with a terrified consciousness, how
very white she must be turning now—to utter the exact,
formal truth.

"Oh, very well," replied Letty, a little vexed, but too
sweet-tempered to retain vexation long.

She sat down composedly and finished her dinner—lingering a good while over the pudding—Letty liked pud-
dings and all good things; while Edna sat, with the letter
in her pocket, as quiet and almost as silent as if she were
made of marble, for a quarter of an hour. Then Letty
rose.

"Now I'll go into the kitchen, for I want to iron out
my muslin dress. In the mean time you can read in peace

your wonderful letter. You'll tell me about it afterwards, Edna, dear."

Touched by her sister's gentleness Edna returned a smiling "Thank you," and tried to look as usual while the dinner was being cleared away. But her head was whirling and her pulse beating fast—so fast that when she at last took the letter out and opened it the lines swam before her eyes. She had only strength enough to creep noiselessly up to her room at the top of the house, shut herself in, and lock the door.

There let her be. We will not look at her, nor inquire into what she felt or did. Women, at least, can understand.

Letty's muslin dress had, happily, a good many frills and flounces, and took a long time in ironing. Not that Letty grumbled at that: she had great pleasure in her clothes, and was the last person to treat them lightly or disrespectfully, or to complain of any trouble they cost her. This dress especially always engrossed so much of her attention and affection, that it is doubtful whether she once let her mind stray from it to such commonplace facts as business letters. And when it was done, she was good-natured enough to recollect that while she had the things about she might as well iron Edna's dress. She went up stairs to fetch it, when, to her surprise, she found the door locked.

"I will come presently," answered a very low voice from within.

"But your dress, Edna. I want to iron out your new muslin dress."

"Thank you, dear. Never mind. I will be down presently."

"It *was* a love-letter, then!" pondered Letty to herself as she descended. "I am sure it was. But who in the wide world can have fallen in love with Edna? Poor Edna!"

"Poor Edna!" Rich Edna! rich in the utmost wealth that Heaven can give to mortal woman! Oh, when there is so much sadness in this world—so much despised love

—unrequited love—unworthy love—surely the one bliss of love deserved and love returned ought to outweigh all else, and stand firm and sure, whatever outside cares may lay siege to it. They can not touch the citadel where the two hearts—the one double heart—has intrenched itself, safe and at rest—forever.

Edna's "love"—hopelessly and dearly beloved—had become her lover. He wished to make her his wife. Her solitary days were done: she stood on the threshold of a new life—in a new world. Never, until through the gate of death she should enter on the world everlasting, would there come to her such another hour as that first hour after she read William Stedman's letter.

Half an hour after—to so long a space extended her "presently"—Edna Kenderdine crept down stairs, and then crept on, still quietly, into her sister's arms.

"Kiss me, Letty! There are only we two."

In a few words—strangely few it seemed, and as if the whole thing were quite natural and known beforehand—Edna told her happy secret, and the sisters embraced one another and wept together, the harmless tears that women are sure to shed, and are not women at all if they do not shed, on these occasions.

At first Letty was considerably surprised—perhaps a little more than surprised—but she had the good taste and good feeling not to say overmuch on this head, and not to refer, even in the most passing way, to certain remarks of her own during the last two days, which must have been, to say the least, rather annoying to remember. But if Letty was a little disappointed and humiliated—and it was scarcely in human nature that she should not be—after having so confidently placed herself and Dr. Stedman in the position of the Irish ballad couplet:

"Did ye ever hear of Captain Baxter,
Whom Miss Biddy refused afore he axed her?"

her vanity was too innocent, and her nature too easy, to bear offense long. After the first surprise was over, her congratulations were given with sufficient warmth and sincerity.

"Well, Edna dear, you know I always liked him, and I dare say I shall find him a very good brother-in-law; and really it will be rather convenient to have a man in the family. But to think that after all the offers I have had, you should be the first to get married, or, anyhow, engaged. Who would ever have expected such a thing!"

"Who would, indeed!" said Edna, in all simplicity, and with a sense almost of contrition for the fact.

"Well, never mind!" answered Letty, consolingly; "I am sure I hope you will be very happy; and as for me" —she paused and sighed—"I should not wonder if I were left an old maid after all, in spite of my appearance."

Which catastrophe, so dolefully prognosticated, would have awakened a smile yesterday; but to-day Edna could not smile. Though her joy was only an hour old, it was so intense, so perfect, that it seemed to absorb the whole of life, as if she knew not how she had ever lived without it. Thinking of her sister who had it not—who did not even comprehend what it was—she felt so sorry that she could have wept over her.

But Letty's next words dispelled this tender regret.

"Still, Edna, if I were you, I would not be in any hurry to give the young man his answer. And in the mean time we will make some inquiries as to what sort of a practice he has—whether he is likely to be in a position to marry soon—and so on. Certainly it is by no means so good a match as I myself should have expected to make; but then you are different—I mean your ideas of things are much humbler than mine. Didn't somebody once say you had quite a genius for poverty?"

"*He* said it," and Edna hung her head, blushing; then lifted it up with a bright, proud, peaceful smile—"yes, he said it one day on the shore. He knew me even then, and understood me, thank God."

And there came before her a vision of her life to come —not an easy one; not that of a woman who slips into marriage to "better herself," as servants say—to attain ease, and luxury, and position, and all the benefits which "a good marriage" is supposed to confer. Hers would

be a life in which every energy would be tested, every
power put to use—which would exact unlimited patience,
self-denial, courage, strength; the life, in short, of a woman who does not care to be a man's toy and ornament, but
desires rather to be his helpmeet—supplying all he needs,
as he supplies all she needs, teaching her through the ne-
cessities of every day how to fulfill the perfect law of love
—self-sacrifice.

Edna knew she should have a hard life. Though Dr.
Stedman was still tolerably ignorant about their circumstances, he had taken good care to inform her every thing
about his own. She was well aware that he was poor—
proud also — perhaps on account of the poverty. She
guessed, with her quick-sighted love, that his temper was
not the sweetest in the world—though she could find excuses for that. But she believed in him—she honored
him, for she had never seen any thing in him that was not
worthy of honor; and, last little fact of all, which included
all the rest, she loved him.

Letty watched her a minute—with that happy smile on
her face. "Well, Edna dear, if you are satisfied, so am I.
It is, of course, your own affair entirely. I would only advise you to take time."

"Certainly I shall. It is sure to be a long engagement."

Letty shook her head pathetically. "Ah! if there is
one thing more than another which I should object to, it
is a long engagement. It wears a girl to death, and cuts
off all her chances elsewhere. And suppose, in the mean
time, she should receive a better offer?"

Edna dropped her sister's hand. "Letty, we had better
talk no more. If we talked to everlasting I could never
make you understand."

She spoke sharply, almost angrily; and then, seeing no
anger, only mild amazement on Letty's beautiful face, she
repented. With the yearning that every woman must
have at this crisis in her life to fall on some other woman's neck and ask for a little love—a little sympathy on
the new strange path she had just entered—she turned
back again to her sister, who kissed her once more.

"Really now, I did not mean to vex you, Edna. Of course you know your own mind—you always did; and had your own way, too, in every thing—I'll tell him so, and frighten him."

Edna smiled.

"And what does he say to you? Do show me your love-letter—I always showed you all mine!"

But this was a different thing quite. Edna closed her little hand fiercely over it—her one possession, foretaste of her infinite wealth to come. It was hers—all her own, and the whole world should neither pry into it, nor steal it, nor share it.

"Well, never mind. You always were a queer girl," said Letty, patiently. "But at least you'll tell me when he is coming here. This is Saturday—I suppose he will want to come to tea on Sunday?"

And so the misty, beautiful, wondrous dream condensed itself into a living commonplace reality. There was a note written, which consisted of the brief word "come," naming the day and hour. This was sent by their servant, who looked much astonished, and hoped nobody was ill and wanting the doctor; and then the two sisters sat down side by side, for even Letty was silent a while.

At last, however, she could hold her tongue no longer, but began talking in her smoothly-flowing inconsequent way.

"I wonder what sort of a house he lives in, and whether it is well furnished. Of course we can't go and see—it would not be proper; but I will try and find out. And this house of ours—I suppose it will have to be given up. No man would like his wife to go on keeping school. He would never let her work if he could help it: in such a common way too. Ah, Edna, you are the lucky woman, after all! I wish I had somebody to work for me."

"Do you?" said Edna, absently.

"Oh, how nice it must be! To have nothing to do all day long, and every thing pretty about one, and perhaps a carriage to ride in, and no trouble at all. Heigh-ho! I wish I were married too, though it shouldn't be to any

HALF JOY, HALF SORROW.

body like Dr. Stedman.   But, my dear, since it is to be,
and you are fond of him, and, as I have said, you are your
own mistress, and must please yourself, do just tell me
what you think about things.   In the first place, what
ought your wedding-dress to be?"

   "Hush," Edna whispered.   "Please don't talk any more.
I can't bear it."   And then she threw herself into her sis-

ter's arms, and cried passionately — half for joy, half for sorrow. So the day ended—the day of days which closed up forever one portion of the sisters' lives: a day, to Letty, scarcely different from any other, but to Edna like that first day which marked the creation of a new world.

She scarcely slept all night; still, she rose and went to church as usual. She was neither afraid nor ashamed. She knew the Great Searcher of hearts would not punish her because in every thanksgiving was a thought of *him*, and every prayer was a prayer for two. She walked home with her sister through the green lane — Letty vaguely wondering what church Dr. Stedman attended—she hoped he did go to church regularly somewhere, for nothing made a man look so respectable, especially if he were a doctor. Edna had a sweet composure of mien—a gentle dignity such as had never been seen in her before; inasmuch as more than one stray acquaintance told her "how well she was looking." At which she felt so glad.

But during the afternoon—the long still Sunday afternoon — with the warm jasmine-scented air creeping in through the half-closed Venetian blinds, some of her nervousness returned, her quick restless movements, her little abruptnesses of speech. She went about from room to room, but could not sit long anywhere.

Letty watched her with a condescending interest, rather trying to bear. "It's natural, dear, quite natural. I used to feel the same myself when one of them was coming. Dear me! what a long time ago it seems since anybody came to see me! But even one's sister's lover is better than none. I hope you will settle with Dr. Stedman to come every Sunday. And he might sometimes bring his brother with him, for it will be desperately dull for me, you know. Well, I declare! Punctuality's very self! For it is just five minutes to six, and I am sure I see a gentleman striding down Love Lane. I'll run down stairs and open the door; shall I, Edna?"

Edna assented, but she could not utter a word more. She stood at her window—the window where she was fond of sitting, and had sat so many an hour, and dreamed

H

COMING.

so many a maiden-dream. She watched him coming, a tall figure, strong and active, walking firmly, without pauses or hesitation, and though sometimes turning the head round to glance — Edna guessed whither! There he was, the ruler of her life, her friend, her lover, some day to be her husband. He was coming to assume his rights, to assert his sovereignty. A momentary vague terror smote her, a fear as to the unknown future, a tender regret for the peaceful, maidenly, solitary days left behind, and then her heart recognized its master and went forth to meet him; not gleefully, with timbrels and dances, but veiled and gentle, grave and meek; contented and ready to obey him, "Even as Sarah obeyed Abraham, calling him lord."

Edna long remembered, in years when it was a comfort to have it to remember, how exceedingly good Letty was that day; how she went down herself to welcome Dr. Stedman, and behaved to him—as he told Edna afterwards —in a way so womanly, friendly, and sisterly that it took away all his awkwardness; and by the time another little light footstep was heard on the stairs he was found sitting—as quietly as if he had sat there every Sunday for years — in the great arm-chair by the window, with his face pale indeed, but radiant with the light of happiness, the one only happiness which ever gives that look, turned towards the opening door.

It opened, and Edna came in.

I have said this little woman was not beautiful, not even pretty; but there was a lovesomeness about her — her neat, small, airy figure, her harmonious movements, and her dainty hands—which often grew into absolute loveliness—at least would, in the eyes of any man who had the sense to love her, and prize her at her worth. Woman as she was—all woman—she was

> "Yet a spirit too, and bright,
> And something of an angel light."

And as this man—this big, tall, and, it might once have been, rather rough man—looked at her, standing in the door-way in her lilac muslin dress, his whole soul came into his eyes. Though there was in him a mingled expression of dread, as if expecting that while he gazed her wings would grow, and she would fly away from him.

He rose, and advanced a step forward; then he and the lilac angel shook hands — humanly — in a most commonplace fashion. After which Letty, with astonishing tact, discovered the immediate necessity of "seeing about tea," and disappeared.

There are those who despise small rooms and homely furniture — to whom Love is nothing except he comes dressed in fine clothes, and inhabiting splendid drawing-rooms. Of course, under such circumstances, when Poverty enters in at the door, the said Love will surely fly out at the window. He has been far too much accustomed to think of himself and his own ease. Undeniably it is very pleasant to be rich, to inhabit handsome houses, and be dressed in elegant clothes; and there is a kind of love so purely external, selfish, and self-seeking, that it can not exist unless it has also these things. But the true love is something far, far beyond. And Edna, when William Stedman took her in his arms—just herself and nothing more —in her common muslin gown, with no attractive surroundings, for the parlor was small and humble as well could be—asking her if she could love him, and if she were afraid to be a poor man's wife — Edna knew what that true love was.

They sat long talking, and he told her every thing, including a little confession which perhaps every man would not have made; but this man was so conscientiously honest that he could not have been happy without making it—that his first passing fancy had been for her beautiful sister.

"And I like her still—I shall always like her," added he with an earnest simplicity that made Edna smile, and assured her more than ever of the love that was far deeper than all telling. "And—before you get anxious about it, I wish to say one thing—Letty shall never leave you, if you do not wish it, and I will always be good to her. Who could help it? She is so charming to look at—so sweet-tempered—so kindly. I like her exceedingly; but as for loving—"

Edna gave one shy inquiring glance into the passionate face; then, in the strange familiarity—sacred as sweet—which one little hour had brought about between them, she laid her head upon his shoulder, saying, gently,

"I am not afraid. I know you will never love any body but me."

And when at last Letty came in, after a most lengthy and benevolent rattling of the door-handle, William Stedman went up to her and kissed her like a brother.

"It is all settled, and you are to live with us. We never mean to part with you—except to somebody better than ourselves."

Thus quietly, in his brief, masculine way, he cleared off the only weight on Edna's mind—in the only way in which it could be done. And as she looked up to him with grateful eyes, loving him all the dearer because of the tenderness he showed to her own flesh and blood, he inly vowed that he would never let her know how, in resigning his first great happiness of a married home all to themselves, he had made a very great sacrifice.

Letty thanked him, not with overmuch emotion, for she was so used to be first considered, that she took it quite naturally. Then, with a little commonplace quizzing—not ill-meant but rather inappropriate—she sat down in Edna's place to pour out tea and enjoy the distinction of entertaining "the man of the family."

When the meal was ended, Dr. Stedman, in the aforesaid capacity, which he accepted in a cheery and contented manner, proposed that they should at once enter upon the question of ways and means.

"Which means being married, I suppose?" laughed Letty.

"Yes," he answered, with a deep blush, and then dashed at the subject abruptly and desperately. "I do not wish to wait—not a day after I get a hospital appointment which I have been long trying for, and have now a good chance of. With that and my profession we could live. And Julius, he will have enough to live upon too."

"Will he live with you? Then how can I?" asked Letty, bridling up with a sudden fit of propriety.

"No, not with us," was the answer, strong, decisive, almost angry. "As *she* knows," glancing at Edna, "there is two hundred a year which, if necessary, he can have—part or whole; but I will not have him living with me. Two men in one house would never do;" and then he told, cursorily, the "slight difference"—so he called it—which he had had with his brother, and how he had not seen him since, Julius having gone next morning on a painting expedition.

Edna looked grave, but Letty listened with considerable amusement. "And so Julius—I may say 'Julius,' as he will be my half-brother-in-law, you know—wanted to come and see us, and you prevented him? And if this quarrel had not happened you would not have written? Perhaps you would never have made up your mind to ask Edna at all?"

The silly woman had hit upon something like a truth, or near enough thereto to vex the man a little.

"I assure you, Miss Letty—but excuse my explaining. Your sister knows all."

Yes, Edna did know—all the pride—all the pain—the struggle between duty and passion—the difficulty of determining right from wrong—honor from cowardliness—

rashness from fearless faith. Many a man has gone through
the like before his marriage—the woman neither understanding it nor pitying it; but Edna did both. She laid
her little hand on his—

"No need to explain, I am quite satisfied."

"And Julius?" persisted Letty, who was beginning to
find second-hand felicity a little uninteresting. "Does he
know of all this between Edna and you?"

"No; but when he returns on Monday I shall tell him."

"And what will he say?"

"I think he will say, as a brother should—'It's all right.
Be happy in your own way.'"

"But if he does not?" said Edna, tremulously.

William Stedman looked vexed. Perhaps he knew his
brother better than she did, or was less accustomed than
she was to think of others.

"I do not contemplate any such impertinent interference
on his part. But if so, it can make no difference to me.
When a man of my age chooses his wife, no other man,
not even his own brother, has a right to say a word. Julius had better not; I would not stand it."

He spoke loudly, like a man not used to talk with or to
listen to women; a man who, right or wrong, liked to have
his own way. Truly he was far from perfect, this chosen
of Edna's heart. Yet he had a heart too, and a conscience,
and both these would have understood her momentary
start—the slight shadow which troubled her happy face.
But though the happiness lessened the peace remained,
and the love which had created both.

"I think," she said, very gently, "that Julius is too generous to make us unhappy. He may be vexed at first, having had you all his life—and only you—like Letty and me
here. But perhaps he is not quite so good as my Letty."

And thinking of her gentle sister, and contrasting their
ways with the fierce ways of these two men—lover and
brother, with whom her lot was to be bound up for life—
Edna trembled a little; but the next minute she despised
herself for her cowardice. What was love worth if it
could not bear a little pain? In the darkening twilight

she loosened not, but rather strengthened, her clasp of William Stedman's hand; and as he went on talking, principally to Letty, and about common things, the size and arrangements of his house, and his means of furnishing it, his good angel might have heard that the man's voice grew softer and sweeter every minute. Already there was stealing into him that influence, mysterious as holy, which, without any assertion on their part—any parade of rights or complaints of wrong—makes all women—Christian women—if they so choose it, the queens of the world. Already the future queen had entered into her kingdom.

He was still talking, being left respectfully by these inexperienced maidens to take the man's part of explaining and deciding every thing, when there came a knock to the door, so sudden and startling, in that quiet Sunday evening, that the little house seemed actually to reel.

"Probably some one for me," said Dr. Stedman. " I left word at home where I might be found if wanted; a doctor is always liable to be summoned, you know. It is not an easy life for him or for his household," added he, with a slightly shy and yet happy smile.

"Oh," cried Letty, "I wouldn't marry a doctor upon any account, as I always said to Edna"—whose conscious blush showed how completely the good advice had been thrown away.

But just this minute the front-door was opened, and the voice of a man, hurried and eager, was heard inquiring for the Misses Kinderdine; also, in not too gentle tones, whether Dr. Stedman was here?

"It is Julius," said Letty. But what happened next is serious enough to require another chapter.

CHAPTER XIII.

JULIUS STEDMAN entered the parlor in a rather excited state. Not with wine—that was a temptation impossible to the pure-living, refined young artist; but his excitement was of a kind peculiar to the artistic and nervous temper-

ament, and might easily have been mistaken for that of
drink. His face was flushed, his motions abrupt, his speech
unnaturally loud and fast, and as he stood shading his eyes
from the sudden dazzle of the lamp-light, even his appearance spoke against him; for his dress was dusty, his long
hair disorderly, and his whole exterior very far below that
standard of personal elegance—nay, dandyism—which was
a strong characteristic of Julius Stedman.

He bowed to Letty, who was the first to advance towards him.

"I am ashamed, Miss Kenderdine, of intruding at this
unseemly hour; but my brother—ah, there you are! I
have found you out at last;" and he darted over to the
doctor's chair. "You're a pretty fellow, Will; a nice elder brother!—a proper person to lecture a younger one,
and teach him the way he should go—a good, honest, generous, candid—"

"Julius!" cried Will, catching him by the arm, and
speaking almost in a whisper, "command yourself. You
forget these ladies."

"Not at all!" And there was no abatement in the
shrill, furious voice. "I have the highest respect for
these ladies. And out of my respect, as soon as I came
home (unexpectedly of course, like a fool that I was, to
make it up with you), and found where you were gone, I
came after you—I came, just to tell them the plain truth.
Miss Kenderdine, this brother of mine, who comes sneak-
ing here on the sly—"

"Julius!" Not a whisper now, but thundered out in
violent passion; then controlling himself, Will added, "Julius, you are under an entire and ridiculous mistake. Either leave this house with me instantly, or sit down and
listen to my explanation."

"Listen!—explanation!" repeated Julius, and looked
bewildered from one to the other of the three whom he
had found sitting together so familiarly and happily in
the pleasant little parlor.

"Yes," said Will, laying his hand firmly and kindly on
his brother's shoulder, "I will explain every thing: there

is no reason now why I should not. I objected to your visiting here, because you had no right to come; and your coming was an injury to these ladies, and would have exposed them to all kinds of unpleasant remarks. But with me it is different. I came here to-day—and it is my first visit, I assure you—with a distinct right, and in a recognized character. Julius, I am going to give you a sister."

"A sister!" The young man turned frightfully pale, and his eyes sought—which face was it?—Letty's. Then, as with the strength of despair, he forced himself to speak.

"Tell me—tell me quick! This is so sudden!"

"Not sudden in reality—it only seems so," said William, smiling; "and you like her very much—you know she will make you a good sister. Shake hands with him, Edna."

"Edna—is it Edna?" And then, either out of his own natural impulsiveness, or in the reaction from a still stronger excitement, Julius darted forward, and instead of shaking hands, kissed her warmly. "I beg your pardon; but I can't help it. Oh, you dear little woman—so it's you, is it?—you that have all but brought about a quarrel between Will and me—the first we ever had in our lives."

"And the last, I trust," said Will, cheerily, submitting to have his hand almost shaken off.

"Never mind—never mind, now, old fellow. All's well that ends well. I give you joy. I'm quite content. She will be the best little sister in all the world. Shake hands again, Edna—let's shake hands all round."

But when he came to Letty, he stopped point-blank.

Letty extended her long fingers in a dignified manner, and smiled her benign smile—alike to all—upon the flushed, passionate young face.

"I suppose, Mr. Stedman, this makes you and me a sort of half-brother-and-sister-in-law. I am quite willing. I hope we shall always be very good friends — just like brother and sister, indeed."

"Thank you," was the answer, and the young man's excited mood sank into quietness, nay, into more than quietness—sadness. But this was nothing uncommon with Julius Stedman, who, after one of his fits of high spirits, generally fell into a corresponding fit of gravity and melancholy.

This, or perhaps his mere presence as an extraneous element in what had been such a peaceful trio—for, in these early days of betrothal, sometimes an easy negative third rather adds to than takes away from the new-found and still unfamiliar happiness—made the evening not quite so pleasant as before. In vain Will, with most creditable persistency, maintained conversation, and Edna by a great effort shook off her shyness, and, taking her place as hostess, presided at supper—endeavoring to be especially attentive to Julius, and give him a foretaste of the good sister she intended to be. For in the midst of all her own joy her heart warmed to him—this moody, variable, affectionate, lovable fellow, who seemed, as so many young men do, like a goodly ship with little ballast, the success of whose whole voyage depended upon what kind of hand should take the helm. Besides, though she knew it was womanish and ridiculous, she could not help having a sort of pity for any body who had lived with William Stedman for so long, and would not now live with him much longer. She could afford to be exceedingly kind and forgiving to poor Julius.

Still the cloud did not pass away, and in spite of every body's faint efforts to disperse it—except Letty's, who was not acute enough to see any thing, and went talking on in the most charmingly unconscious and inappropriate way —the awkwardness so spread itself, that it was quite a relief when the little quartette broke up. Dr. Stedman proposed leaving, and then stood with Edna at the window, talking for ever so long between themselves; while Letty, with a nod and a wink, went into the passage, beckoning Julius to follow her.

"We're terribly in the way—we two," said she, laughing. "I am afraid, on future Sundays, we shall have to retire to the kitchen—that is, if you persist in coming to take care of your brother when he goes a-courting. But it will be very dull for you with only stupid me."

"Only you!" said Julius, gazing at her as she stood

leaning against the lobby wall, seeming to illumine the whole place, poor and small as it was, with her wonderful beauty. "Only you!"

And Letty looked down, not unconscious of his admiration, and perhaps feeling just sufficiently ill-used by fate as to think herself justified in appropriating and enjoying it — that is, if she ever thought at all; or thought ten minutes in advance of the present moment.

"I suppose those two are very happy," said Julius, at length, with a glance in the direction of the silent parlor.

"Oh, of course. Every body is very happy at first— that is—I suppose so. Not that I know from experience."

Julius regarded her with piercing eyes, and then laughed, half carelessly, half cynically.

"Oh, you and I are old stagers, I suppose. We will not reveal the secrets of the prison-house. Probably, being in love is like being in prison."

"Eh?" said Letty, puzzled, and then added, confidentially: "I don't like to hear you mention prisons. I hope your brother is not in debt—so many young men are nowadays. Is he in sufficiently good circumstances to warrant his marriage? Not that I would say a word against it. Of course my sister knows her own mind, and acts as she thinks right; she always did. But will they not be very poor? And it is such a dreadful thing to be poor."

"A cursed thing!" And there was a gleam, almost a glare, in those wild, bright eyes of Julius Stedman, as he fixed them on the beautiful creature before him. A creature whom some fortunate man—say an Eastern sultan, or a Western duke—might have eagerly bought, the one with a ring, the other with a given number of piastres, and carried off to be robed in silks and hung with diamonds— laden with every gift possible, except that which, perhaps, after all, she might not care for, or only as it was accompanied by these other things—his heart. "Yes, poverty is a dreadful thing. There I quite agree with you, Miss Kenderdine."

"You might as well call me Letty, and so get our relations clear at once," said Letty, coquettishly.

"Thank you, thank you, Letty," and he seized her hand.

"I mean—our brother and sisterly relations," said Letty, drawing back, upon which Julius apologized, and also drew back immediately.

"As you were saying," observed he, after a pause, during which the low murmur of talking within came maddeningly to his ears, "those two, our brother and sister, regarded by our wiser eyes, are—simply a pair of fools. My brother's certain income, since you so prudently ask it, is only two hundred a year. Besides that he may make another two hundred by his profession, which comes to four hundred altogether. And four hundred a year is, of course, to a woman, downright poverty. I myself think Will is insane to dream of marrying."

"What did you say, my boy?" cried Will, coming behind him, with a radiant light on his face, though it looked thin and worn still, "insane, am I? Why, it's Julius, and not I that deserves a lunatic asylum. He has been in love, off and on, ever since he was fifteen, and never found any body good enough to please him for a month together. Wait, man! Wait till you have found the right woman, and have won her, too!"

"Ah, wait," said Edna, softly, as in a pretty demure sisterly fashion she put both her hands into those of her future brother, and then took them away to remove some stray dust that disfigured his coat-sleeve; "wait till that good time comes. And she will be so happy, and so very fond of you."

"Bless you, my little sister," said Julius, in a choked voice, as he suddenly bent down and put his lips to Edna's hand. "No, he's not mad, he's a lucky fellow, that scamp there. And he has had a comfortless life of late, I know that; and I have not helped to make it more comfortable. Perhaps we shall both be the better, we jolly young bachelors, for having a woman to keep us in order. Though you'll find me a tough customer, I warn you of that, Miss Edna."

"Never mind. I'll take you just as you are, and make the best of you."

With which light jest the two sisters sent the two brothers out under the narrow jasmine-scented door-way —out into the brilliant harvest moonlight, so dazzling white that it smote one almost with a sense of chill.

Will put his arm through his brother's, and they walked on a considerable way before either spoke. At last Julius took the initiative.

"Well, old fellow, this is a pretty go! Catch a weasel asleep! I certainly have been that unfortunate animal. I had no more idea that any game of this sort was afoot than—than the man in the moon, who perhaps has more to do with such things than we suspect. Of course, love is only a fit of temporary or permanent insanity. By-the-by, what a precious fool I was near making of myself to-night!"

"How?"

"Oh, in several ways; but it doesn't matter now. I've come out safe and scot-free. And pray, how long is it since you made up your mind to marry that little thing?"

Will winced.

"I beg your pardon, but she is such a little thing; though, I own, the best little woman imaginable; and has such neat pretty ways about a house—even such a shabby house as theirs looks cozy with her in it. How jolly comfortable she'll make us—I mean you; for, of course, I shall have to turn out."

Will said nothing—neither yes nor no. He felt upon him that cowardice, purely masculine, which always shrinks from doing any thing unpleasant. He wished he had had Edna beside him, to put, as plainly as his own common sense put it, the fact that a man has no right to lay upon his wife more burdens than she can bear; and that with his changeful, moody ways, his erratic habits, and his general Bohemian tendencies, Julius was, with all his lovableness, about the last inmate likely either to be happy himself, or to make others happy, in a married home. That is, unless the home were his very own, and the mistress of it had over him the influence which was the only influence that would keep Julius safe—that of a passionately-loved and loving wife.

All this Will thought, but could not explain. Therefore his only refuge was silence.

"Yes, it's all right," said Julius, somewhat coldly; "and quite natural too. I don't blame you. You have done a deal for me, Will: more than any brother, or many a father, would have done. I'll never forget it. And I dare say I shall be able to shift for myself somehow."

"There will be plenty of time, my dear fellow," answered Will, in rather a husky voice. "I shall not be married until I get something quite certain to start with —probably that appointment which you know I have been after so long. And then I shall be able to pay over to you, in whole or part, for as long as you require it, the other half of grandfather's money."

"Will, you don't mean that?"

"Yes, I do. In truth, she was so sore about you, and especially your being 'turned out,' as she called it, that she would not have had me without my promising that arrangement, which will make our marriage, whenever it does take place, none the worse for any body."

"But—"

"It's no use arguing with a woman, especially one who won't talk—only act. Edna is quite determined. Indeed I may say I have purchased her at the alarming sacrifice of two hundred a year, payable quarterly—"

"Will!" cried Julius, stopping suddenly, and looking his brother full in the face. The moonlight showed his own, which was full of emotion. "You're a pretty pair, you and she—six of one and half a dozen of the other. I see it all now. Give her my love. No; I'll take it to her myself. For me, I've been a selfish, luxurious rascal all my life; but I'll turn over a new leaf, hang me if I won't! I'll take an oath against light kid gloves, and rings, and operas. I'll dress like an old-clothesman, and feed like a day-laborer. And I'll work—by George, won't I work!"

"That's right, lad," said the elder brother, cheerily. "And you'll find it all the better when, some day, you have to work for two. Meantime, instead of the 'family house' you wanted to visit at, you'll have a brother's home always to come to. And she will make it so bright, as you say. Besides, Letty will be there," continued Will, dashing at this fact with a desperate haste, uncertain how it might be taken.

Julius did start, very uneasily. "Is she to live with you?"

"Yes; there was no other way. As must be obvious enough, Letty is not the person to be left to live alone."

"No," said Julius, concisely.

"I doubt whether she will like living with us, for we shall have a hard struggle to make ends meet, at any rate for the first few years; and she is not well fitted for poverty—Letty, I mean."

Julius was silent.

"But in that case, if she got tired of us, she could easily return to her old life as a resident governess, which she often regrets still—unless, in the mean time, some young fellow snaps her up, which is far from improbable. Her sister says she has had lovers without end, as was to be expected; but none of them were good enough for her. Edna hopes, when she does marry, it will be some nice, good fellow, with plenty of patience and heaps of money. Letty would never be happy unless she lived in clover and cotton-wool. Poor Letty! It's well for me that my Edna is different."

William Stedman must have been strangely blind—perhaps that little word " my " produced the blindness, and carried his thoughts involuntarily away—not to have noticed how dumb grew his talkative brother; how he walked on fiercely and fast, swinging his cane, and slashing at the hedges in a nervous, excitable way, as they threaded the narrow lanes, which were so pretty twenty years ago, but are now vanishing fast, in the streets, and squares, and "gardens" of Campden Hill. At last Julius said, with that sudden change from earnestness to frivolity which was too common in him to cause Will any surprise—

"Nevertheless, it's odd that you, and not I, should be the fool or the madman—for you certainly are both—to commit matrimony. Catch me giving up my freedom, my jolly, idle life, to tie myself to any woman's apron-strings! You'd better think twice of it: eh, old fellow? Edna's a good girl—I don't deny that; and likes you—I suppose; she'd be an ass if she didn't. But is there a girl alive who would go on caring for a man unless he had lots of money—could give her all she wanted? and they're always wanting something. All alike, all alike; and a precious lot they are, too. So—

> 'I'd be a bachelor born in a bower,'"

carolled the young fellow, startling the green lanes and a solitary policeman with the then popular tune of " I'd be a butterfly," and inventing a doggerel parody to it, which was, to say the least, rather inappropriate that quiet Sunday night.

"You are not yourself, Ju," said William. "You have got overtired. Didn't you say you had walked fifteen miles to-day? That was far too much. I shall have to keep a sharp look-out after you, even when we have a separate establishment."

And the elder brother, out of his deep heaven of peace, looked tenderly upon the foolish fellow who did not understand what peace was, who was making a mock of it, and trying, like so many other skeptics, driven into skepticism less by nature than circumstances, to believe that to be non-existent which was only non-beheld.

Then the two Stedmans, with their bachelor latch-key, entered their dull, dark, close house, which breathed the very atmosphere of dreariness and disorder. Julius went up to bed almost immediately; but William sat long in his empty dining-room, peopling it with wondrous visions, brightening it with hearth-light and lamp-light, and, above all, the perpetual light of a woman's smile — the smile which happy love brings to a woman's lips, never to be wholly lost from them until they are set in that last, loveliest peace upon which the coffin-lid closes—which seems to say even to mourning husband or children, "Be content—I am loving you still—with God."

William Stedman had to-day seen, beyond a doubt, this love in his betrothed's face; and he felt by that in his own heart that it would be his until death.

He knew, as well as his brother did, that he should be poor enough, probably for years; that, with most men, to marry upon his prospects would be the height of madness. But then they were men who had not learned, like himself, the calm self-denial which disarms poverty of half its dangers, half its dread, because holding as its best things the things which money can neither give nor take away; being far too proud for the ordinary petty pride of being afraid to seem what one is, if that happens to be a little inferior to one's neighbors. True, he had never starved, never been in debt; for neither alternative often happens to an unmarried man who has ordinary health, honesty, and brains—at least, if it does, he has usually only himself to blame. But William Stedman had been poor, very poor; he had known how hard it is to go on wearing a threadbare coat because you have not five pounds to spare for a new one; how harder still to crave for many an accidental luxury which you know you have no right to indulge in. And perhaps, hardest of all, to associate with people who, in all but money, are fairly your equals; and who never suspect, or never pause to think, how your every penny is as momentous as their pounds. In short, he had learned, in the many wholesome but painful ways that early poverty teaches, the best lesson that any young man can learn—to control and deny himself.

Therefore, fitter than most men was he to enter upon that "holy estate," which, perhaps, derives its very holiness from the fact that it requires from both man and woman infinite and never-ending self-denial—teaching, as nothing else can teach, that complete absorption of self into another, which is the key-stone and summit of true happiness.

Possibly William Stedman did not say all these things to himself, for he was not much given to preaching or to self-examination—in truth, he never had time for it; but he felt them in a dim, nebulous way; he "took stock of

himself," so to speak, as to whether he was fit for the life
which lay before him—fit to be trusted with the happiness
of a sweet, fond, ignorant, innocent woman; whether he
had strength for her sake to go on with hard work and
little pleasure, to place his enjoyments in inward rather
than outward things, and to renounce very much that to
most young men—Julius, for instance—would be what he
to himself had jestingly termed, like the linen-drapers' ad-
vertisements, an "alarming sacrifice."

He was not afraid, for he knew Edna was not. He
knew that whatever he had to give up in the world without would be made up by the world within. That this
little woman would come in on his cheerless, untidy hearth
like a good fairy, reducing chaos to order, and charming
away gloom and dullness by her bright, sweet ways. Besides that, he felt that with her direct simplicity, her un-
worldly tone of thought, her divine instinct for right and
truth, she would come and sit in his heart like a conscience
—a blessing as well as a delight, making him better as
well as happier, and happier just because he was better.

"God has been very kind to me—far kinder than I deserved," said the young man to himself, thinking, in his
happiness, more than he often found time to think, of the
Source whence all happiness flows. And his heart melted
within him; and the long pent-up storm of headlong passion, and frantic pride, and bitter self-distrust which had
raged within him for weeks and months, and had come to
a climax two days ago, when he felt himself driven mad
by the sound of a voice and the touch of a little ignorant
hand—all this calmed itself down into a most blessed
quiet, like a summer evening after a thunder-shower, when
every thing is so perfumy, fresh, and green, and the flowers are lifting up their heads, and the birds sing doubly
loud and clear, even though the large-leaved trees are still
dropping—as more than one great, heavy drop fell, in this
sacred solitude, from William Stedman's eyes.

They came from a sudden thought which darted across
him — the thought, not of Edna, but of his mother. He
scarcely remembered her—he was only seven years old

when she died; but he knew she was a very good woman; and he had kept up all his life this faint, shadowy remembrance with a sort of silent idolatry which had begun then in his childish yet tenaciously faithful heart.

He wondered whether she had any knowledge of what had happened to him to-day, and whether she would have been satisfied with the wife he had chosen; and he thought, the next time he saw Edna, he would tell her all these his childish recollections, and take her instead of pearls and diamonds, which she altogether refused to accept from him, the simple guard-ring which had belonged to his mother.

CHAPTER XIV.

IT was now fully ten months since William Stedman and Edna Kenderdine had plighted that promise which, when made deliberately, wisely, and justifiably on both sides, should be held as inviolable as the subsequent vow before the altar — that is, if the love, which is its only righteous foundation, lasts. Otherwise, the best wisdom is that which Edna sometimes gave in answer to Letty's murmurings of the misery of long engagements, and the advantage of keeping "free." "When he wishes to be free, he is free. The moment he ceases to love me, let him go!"

But this contingency did not seem likely to happen. Though the promise had been made conditionally—that is, he had told her, in his deep humility, that when she found out all the bad things in him, she might break it·at any time, and he should not blame her—still she found out all the bad things, and she did not break it. Perhaps he too discovered certain little earthly specks in his angel's white wings, just enough to keep her from flying away from him, and survived the discovery. For two people, who expect to find one another all perfection, must be taught such wholesome lessons; and doubtless these lovers had to learn them. But they had the sense to keep both their

experience and their mode of acquiring it strictly to themselves.

"You two never quarrel," Letty would say sometimes,
half puzzled, half vexed. "I thought lovers always quarrelled. I am sure I squabbled continually with all mine."

At which Edna smiled, and only smiled. Her sister's
unconscious plurals precluded all argument. As well reason with the Grand Turk on the Christian law of marriage
as talk to poor Letty of the mysterious law of love.

And yet she was most kind, most good-natured—an ever
welcome and convenient third in the various week-day
walks, and meetings for "sight-seeing," which Dr. Stedman
contrived to steal out of his busy life, and add to those
blessed Sundays which he spent with his betrothed, heal-
ing thereby all the cares and worries of the seven days
past. And he was so good to Letty; he took such pains
that she should never be forgotten in any pleasure which
could be given her, that she liked Will very much. But
still she moaned sometimes—Letty rather enjoyed moan-
ing—over the probable length of Edna's engagement, and
the misfortune of her marrying a poor man.

"For talk as you like, my dear," she sometimes oracu-
larly said, "I am certain you would be a deal happier in
an elegant house, with a carriage to drive in, and plenty
of good society. And—don't look so indignant—I dare
say he would love you better—men always do, you know
—if you were a little better dressed."

But Edna only smiled, and smoothed out her pretty cot-
tons and muslins as carefully as if they were silks and sat-
ins. Perhaps Heaven had mercifully given her a temperament that did not much care for luxuries, except those of
Heaven's providing, common and free as air and sunshine
—such as cleanliness, order, simplicity, and harmony. And
then she was so happy, for God had sent her heart's desire.
She sang over her daily work like an April thrush in a
thorn-tree, building its nest through rain and shine. Letty complained bitterly of the delay which made school-
keeping still necessary; Dr. Stedman openly grumbled at
the school and all belonging to it; and often behaved ex-

ceedingly badly, and very like a man; but Edna was as
gay as a lark, and never swerved from her firm determination not to be married till a small certainty made the marriage prudent as regarded them all. She declared she
would work steadily on, like a brave independent little
woman as she was, till the very day of her marriage.

"For," she said once, with her sweet, earnest face lifted
up to the clouded one of her lover, "I see no pleasure, and
no dignity either, in idleness. If you had not loved me I
should have been a working-woman to the end of my days,
and have worked cheerily too. When you can work for
me, I'll work no more. But if you ever needed it, and I
could do it, I would fall to work again, and you should not
hinder me! I'd begin once more to teach my little butch-
ers and bakers and candlestick-makers, and think myself
honored in the duty."

And then the strong man would catch her in his arms,
and thank God he had chosen a woman who, in the count-
less troubles that man's lot is heir to, would neither be
selfish nor cowardly, a burden nor a snare; but, under her
soft meekness, would carry about with her a spirit fearless
as his own.

After much delay the long-hoped-for hospital appointment was given—and given to some one else. William
told this news to Edna one dark night coming through
the green lanes home from church—told it briefly, almost
sharply; which showed how deep was his disappointment.
She only pressed his arm, and said:

"Never mind. We are young still. It is said to be
good to bear the yoke in one's youth."

"Yes, if it is not so heavy as to make one humpbacked
for life," answered Dr. Stedman, with a laugh, tuneless and
hard; then, stopping under the next gas-lamp, he saw
Edna was crying—his poor Edna, whose life was no easier
than his own! In the next dark place they came to, he
turned and clasped her to his heart, with all the bitterness
melted out of it, but with a passion of yearning that even
she could not understand. After that they spoke of the
lost hospital appointment no more.

Then, too, Julius fell into a very unsatisfactory state, physical and moral, which, even if Will had not confided it to her, Edna was too sharp-eyed not to see. He looked wretchedly ill, was often moody and out of temper; took vehement fits of work, and corresponding fits of despondent idleness. Whether it was that the home he was soon to quit lost even its small attractions for him, or from some other nameless fancy, but Julius became more erratic than ever: in his comings and goings entirely unreliable, save on those Sundays when, whether invited or not, he always presented himself with his brother at the Misses Kenderdine's door.

There might have been a pleasanter guest; for sometimes he sat whole evenings, like a cloud of gloom, by the cheerful fireside; or else startled the whole party by his unnatural flow of spirits. They bore with him — every body always did bear with Julius. And these lovers had a quality not universal among people in their circumstances — their own happiness made them very patient with those who had none. Besides, Julius was not always a dead weight upon Edna and Will; with astonishing tact he always contrived, early or late, to escape to the kitchen-fire, which, the servant being absent at church, was faithfully presided over by Letty's favorite cat, large and lovely as herself—and by Letty. There he and Letty shared each other's companionship for hours.

What resulted was sure to result, even if the two elders, for once in their lives sufficiently so self-engrossed as to be oblivious of others, had seen what they did not see until too late to prevent—that is, supposing they had any right to prevent it.

Letty too—she should not, at this point, be blamed too severely. She was like many another woman, not wicked, only weak. It was very pleasant to her to be adored, and it would be to nine out of ten of the women who read about her in these pages—girls who are taught from earliest maidenhood that the grand aim of life is to be loved rather than to love. She did not at all dislike — who would? — after her dull week's work, to have, for some

hours every Sunday, those passionate eyes following her
about wherever she moved, that eager breath hanging on
every word she uttered, whether silly or wise; those looks,
which said as plainly as words could say—sometimes
joking, sometimes earnestly, when he glanced at the lovers
—"Never mind them, *I* live only for you." Only looks.
Julius never committed himself—never said a syllable
which, to use Letty's phrase afterwards, could be "taken
hold of." As for flirting, of course she was well used to
"that sort of thing;" but this was admiration of a novel
kind—persistent, permanent, and yet kept so safely within limits, and under the shadow of their approaching re-
lationship, or connection, or whatever they chose to call
it—that if at any time during the winter and spring Letty
had been asked the direct question, which she never was
asked — "Is Julius Stedman making love to you?" she
would have answered, without any falsehood—that is, not
in *her* notion of falsehood—"Oh dear, no! not the least in
the world."

And yet all the while she was maddening him with her
beauty, bewildering him with her caprices—sometimes
warm, sometimes cold; having little quarrels, and making
it up again; assuming the tenderest "sisterly" confidence,
and then sliding off again into perfect coldness and unap-
proachable civility. Doing it all half consciously, half un-
consciously; aware of her power, and liking to exercise it
up to a certain extent—an extent that gave herself no inconvenience. But once, when the thrushes were singing
on the budding trees of Kensington Gardens, as they
walked there of evenings—and again, on the first day of
the Royal Academy, when Julius took them all in great
pride to see his first well-hung picture, and Letty looked
so beaming and beautiful that every body turned to stare
at her—then, seeing certain alarming symptoms in Julius,
she drew in her horns, and was exceedingly cold and cautious for a day or two. "For," she reasoned to herself,
and long afterwards repeated the reasons to Edna, "what
was I to do with the young man? He hadn't a half-
penny."

Quite right, Letty Kenderdine—not a half-penny!—only
a man's heart, or worse, a man's soul, to be lost or won,
according as a woman chooses. But that, in these days,
and with many people, is quite immaterial.

It was a day rather momentous—that first Monday in
May—when Julius learned his picture was hung. Will
had decided with Edna that they must all go to see it,
and the sisters had a wild struggle after sudden spring
bonnets, to be assumed at a few hours' notice; "for," said
Letty, "we can't go at all unless we go respectable." And
possibly William Stedman thought a little beyond respectability the happy face circled with white daisies under a
round-brimmed straw bonnet — such as was the fashion
then—which smiled beside him, so delighted in the brief
holiday with him. For Letty—Letty always looked beautiful. She was a picture in herself. But, as fate so often
balances things, she did not care half so much about the
pictures as Edna did; nor, handsome as it was, did her
face look half so beaming as that one from whence William Stedman learned to see mysteries of loveliness which
had never come upon his darkened mind before. There
was in him just enough of the poetic nature to wish he
had more of it, and to be tenderly reverential towards the
beloved woman who had it, and whom he thought so infinitely superior to himself. While she, who knew herself
to have so many faults, to be at times so fierce and hasty,
passionate and unwise, held a different opinion.

They examined the pictures, none of which Edna liked
better than Julius's own—the landscape about which she
had heard so much—painted as Julius dared to paint, and,
in that anti-Pre-Raphaelite time, was greatly despised for
painting—from absolute nature, instead of nature diluted
through faded Old Masters—Claudes, Poussins, and Salvator
Rosas—each a degree farther off from reality than the last.

"Yes," said Julius, a gleam of hope lighting up his melancholy eyes, as they followed a stray sunbeam which
kindled in deeper beauty his beautiful work; "this year I
think I have not wasted my time. Perhaps I may end in
being an artist, after all."

"Were you thinking of being any thing else?" asked Edna, surprised.

Julius blushed slightly. "Oh, I think of so many things. A painter never makes money, and I want money—terribly. But let us look at the pictures, Letty." She was hanging on his arm, piloted carefully through the crowd. "You were admiring that portrait's velvet gown—here is another well-painted bit of velvet for you, and a bit of sentiment too—a girl taking a thorn out of a boy's finger. What a mildly determined air she has! she won't let him go, though he winces at the pain—just like a man, and just like a woman. The old story. She is beginning to hurt him even at seven years old."

"She ought to hurt him, nor be afraid of hurting him, if she can take the thorn away," said Edna, gently.

"Listen, Will! Now you see what lies before you! Bravo! Who wouldn't rather be a bachelor, if all men's wives are to be ready with needle and penknife to wound their spouses—of course, entirely for their good. Heighho! What say you, Letty?"

"I beg your pardon; what were you talking about?" replied Letty, whose attention had been wholly distracted by a charming bonnet which she was most anxious Edna should see and imitate. But Edna was absorbed in a picture which she never saw after that day, and never even knew whose it was; but it fastened itself upon her memory, to be revived, even after many years, like invisible color, which some magic touch makes fresh as ever.

It was called "In another Man's Garden," and was simply a suburban cottage-door, painted with the intense realism then altogether pooh-poohed and despised. Thereat—also modern and real, down to coat, hat, and stick—stood a young man, bidding the cheery morning adieu to his wife and child before going to business—a happy, intensely happy little group, safely shut inside the rose-trellised walls. While outside, leaning against the gate, was a solitary figure—a broken-down, dust-stained, shabby man—gazing with mournful yearning into "another man's garden."

I

Edna looked at her betrothed, then at the picture; and
her eyes filled with tears. She could not help it. She
understood it all so well. So—out of his deep content—
did he.

"Poor fellow!" said William, as if he were speaking of
a real person.

"Oh, that's me!" cried Julius, with a short laugh. "I
thought you would recognize the likeness. The painter
is a friend of mine. He asked me to sit, and thought I
looked the character to perfection. Do I, Letty?"

"What, the gentlemanly young man in the garden?"

"No; the blackguard outside. That was the character I personated. I got quite used to my battered old hat,
and stockingless shoes, and coat all rags and tatters."

"Did you really put on these things? Oh, how nasty
of you!" said Letty, turning away in great disgust.

The artist laughed again, more bitterly than before.
"Then if I ever appear as a returned convict, or a repent-
ant prodigal, it's of no use my coming to you, Letty?"

"Julius! how can you talk of things so very shocking?
It makes me quite miserable."

Here Letty gave—and Edna caught, startling her into
uneasy suspicion—one of those sidelong, downcast looks,
which might well delude a man into that mad passion
which, for the rest of the afternoon, gleamed in every feature of Julius Stedman's face, as he followed her like her
shadow, and seemed only to live upon her smile.

"Something will surely happen; and oh, I wonder—I
wonder what—" thought Edna, very anxiously; longing
for the next Sunday, when she would have a quiet hour
to lay all her anxieties upon the wise, tender, manly heart
which was her comfort in all her troubles now.

But as yet there was no chance of a quiet word with
William, for the four came home to Kensington ignominiously in an omnibus, to Letty's unconcealed dismay.

"Ah," sighed she, "how nice it would be if Dr. Stedman
kept his brougham, like so many London doctors—I do so
like a carriage!" At which Will laughed, but Julius looked
dark and sad for the whole journey.

It was a recognized rule that the Stedmans should only be received on a Sunday, so the four young people parted at the Misses Kenderdine's gate, and Edna and Letty sat down to their late tea, very tired both of them—one a little cross, and the other just a little weary-hearted.

Edna could bear her own burdens—their own burdens, she and William together; but she thought, if an added weight were to come, and such a serious anxiety as a love-affair or marriage engagement between Letty and Julius must inevitably be, however it might end, her cares would be heavy indeed; for neither of these two were the sort of people capable of bearing their own troubles, to say nothing of lightening other people's.

As she looked at Letty, so handsome and so helpless, and thought of Julius, who had turned from the door in one of his sad, sullen fits, painful and yet pathetic as those of a naughty child, Edna felt her courage give way, and her heart sink with that strange foreboding of evil which comes sometimes, we know not how or why. Without saying a word to Letty—it would have been neither delicate nor wise—she pondered over the whole question, till at last, utterly bewildered, it settled itself into her one grand refuge for all distresses—"I will tell it to William next Sunday." And, comforting as this thought was, it brought also a vague longing for the time when their life would be all Sundays, when they would be continually together. With it came a fear—the fear that will come with deep love—lest something should come between them. Only, to their faith and constancy, nothing could come but death; and that she did not fear, for it would only be falling, as David wished to fall, into the hands of God—the same God who had already made them so happy.

"Yes, we have been happy—very happy, and I am very, very thankful!" thought poor Edna, and her serenity returned—the unchangeable peace of those who have the blessedness of being able to recognize their blessings.

Tired as she was, she took out her work and was sitting —let us boldly confess it—mending a large basketful of stockings, when there came a knock at the front door.

Letty started up from the sofa. "That's William's knock—I know it is. Oh, what can have happened!"

"Nothing to be frightened at," said William, who was in the room almost as soon as she spoke. Good news, not ill, were written on his face. "I beg your pardon. I could not help coming." He shut the door behind him, and then, regardless of her sister's presence, clasped Edna tight in his arms. "It has come at last—come at last, thank God!" And in an ecstasy of joy which betrayed how sharp had been the unacknowledged suffering, he kissed again and again his betrothed wife—then went over and kissed Letty, and bade her wish him joy.

Presently, when he was sufficiently calm for a consecutive statement to be got out of him, Dr. Stedman told the great news—strangely little it would seem to some people, yet to these two was enough to uplift them into perfect felicity.

It was one of those bits of "good luck"—he called it nothing more, and always protested he had done nothing to win it—which occasionally turn the tide of a man's fortune by giving him, at the outset of his career, that slight impetus of help without which a fair start is nearly impracticable. A great lady, and good as great, who had been interested in Dr. Stedman's incessant labors among the poor, had offered him a permanent appointment as physician to a charitable institution which she had founded and principally supported. His salary was to be £300, and, by-and-by, £400 a year—a solid foundation of annual income; while the work could not interfere with his practice, but would rather give him opportunities for that continual study of his profession which a doctor so much needs, and which, at the begining of his career, he finds so difficult to obtain. Thus the lady, a far-sighted and generous woman, in securing his services, benefited both sides, and in doing a prudent did also a kindly deed.

"I wish she knew all the happiness she has given us!" said Edna, trembling and agitated; while Letty, as was her wont under all novel and exciting circumstances, began to cry. In fact, they all shed an honest tear or two, and then they sat down together—Edna close by William, holding Letty's hand on the other side—to try and realize the sudden bliss—this unexpected change in all their affairs.

"Does Julius know?" asked Edna, anxiously.

"No—the letter came after he had gone out. You know he almost always does go out of evenings. But it will be a brighter home for him to come to when you are there—and Letty."

William said this in all simplicity, as Edna at once perceived; and his evident unconsciousness of the idea which had lately entered her mind shook Edna's faith in her own quickness of perception. If William were quite at ease concerning his brother, why should she perplex herself or perplex him by speaking of this matter of Julius and Letty? So, for the present, she let it slip by; and when Letty benevolently quitted the room, and left her alone with her lover, she forgot every thing, as lovers do.

Forgive them, if so be there is any need of forgiveness. Life is so short, so changeful, so full of infinite chances of grief and loss, who would grudge to any body a little love, a little happiness? These two were ready to take both the sweet and the bitter, the evil and the good, believing that both come alike by the Father's will. Yet who can wonder that, as they sat together, knowing they were going to be married—not exactly "to-morrow," as Dr. Stedman had ingeniously suggested, but within a few weeks —and that, come weal or woe, they would never more be parted, it was surely pardonable if, for a while, they forgot every body but themselves.

"And you are not afraid to begin life with me—to be a poor man's wife? for it will be that, Edna. I can't dress you any better than this"—touching tenderly her gray merino gown; "and the carriage Letty wants, it may be years before I can give it you, if ever. Oh, my love, am I harming you? In marrying you now at once, while I have still only just enough for us to live upon, am I doing you any wrong?"

"Wrong!" she cried, as she clung round his neck for
a minute, and then drew back, looking at him with the
brightest face—the most radiant, and yet half-indignant
eyes. "Wrong! you are showing me the utmost love,
and paying me the chiefest honor that a man can give to
a woman. You are taking me at your life's beginning,
that we may begin it together. That is the right thing.
Don't be afraid, William. I'll help you—I know I can, for
I am not a coward, and I have *you*. Oh! if men were
more like you, had your courage, your faith, there would
not be so many broken-hearted women in the world."

"And there would not be so many bad, ruined men, I
think, if women were more like my Edna."

So talked these two—foolishly, no doubt, and with a
vicarious self-laudation which is very much the habit of
lovers. And yet there was truth at the bottom of it—a
truth which, day by day, as she and Letty busied themselves every spare hour in those innocent wedding prepara-
tions which every honest heart, either of friend or stranger,
can not help taking pleasure in, forced itself deeper and
deeper upon Edna's heart. No worldly show was there
—no hiding with splendid outside formalities the hollow-
ness within: she was going to be, as William said, a poor
man's wife; and expensive clothes and extravagant out-
lay of any sort would be merely ridiculous; but Edna prepared herself for her great change with all the happy-
heartedness that a bride should have, a bride who knows
that down to the lowest depth of her soul is not a feeling
that need be hidden, not a thought that God and her husband may not see.

One little thing made her sorry. Julius did not come
to see her; indeed, he had taken himself off on an artistic
tour in Wales, to be "out of the way," he alleged; but
he wrote, after a few days' delay, an affectionate congrat-
ulatory letter, and asked her to seek out for him bachelor
lodgings as close as possible to their own house, where
he meant to be exceedingly jolly, and inflict himself upon
them several times a week. And he sent her, as a wedding present, a lovely portrait of Letty, composed out of

the many studies he had made of her face, which he said, briefly, "he knew by heart." At which remark Letty blushed a little, and pouted a little, saying it was "impertinent;" but was exceedingly gratified to look at her own exquisite portrait, and hear every body admire it and say how very like it was.

So fled the time, long, and yet how short—dwindling first into weeks and then into days, until the last breaking-up day came, and the two young school-mistresses, not without a few sincere tears, sent away their little pupils forever. After that there was only one more Sunday left for the Stedmans to come to tea in the old way, which for nearly a year had gone on now, and brought with it so much of peace and pleasure. No more now of those "courting days," which are said by some to be the happiest, by others the most miserable of their lives. Probably the real truth lies between both these facts, and that the happiness or misery is according as the lovers create it for themselves. Life is not all joy—neither God nor man can make it so; but it may be made all love. And love, that infinite and endless blessing, had been held out from heaven to these two, Edna and William; they had had eyes to see it, strength to grasp it, faith to cling to it. They had cause to be glad and thankful, and so they were.

CHAPTER XV.

DR. STEDMAN came alone to spend his last Sunday with his bride and her sister. Julius had returned home and promised to come, but changed his mind and disappeared for the day.

"He is so constantly changing his mind and plans, that I hardly know what to make of him. I do wish he had a wife of his own," said the elder brother, with a sigh. "But a sister will be better than nothing: you must be very good to him, Edna."

"I will," said Edna, in her quiet way. And then they all spent together — contentedly, yet half solemnly—the last Sunday of so many Sundays, the last which would ever see them as they were. It hardly seemed real—this great change—and it had come about so naturally that they felt none of the agitation and excitement which a marriage brings. No one made any unnecessary fuss; and even when Letty took Dr. Stedman up stairs to see the bridal finery—the white muslin dresses and white bonnets gloriously displayed—he only said, "Very pretty," and came down looking happy, indeed, but rather grave.

Indeed they were all three a little subdued, and, arrangements being now completed—for the wedding was fixed for Tuesday—they had little or nothing to talk about. Tea over, they were sinking into a rather sombre silence, when, to their amazement, Julius appeared.

The sisters had never seen him since the day of the Exhibition, and the welcome they gave him was hearty and warm. He received it with eager happiness.

"Yes; I thought I would come, if only to have a last look at Edna Kenderdine. Though I know I am frightfully in the way: not wanted—never shall be wanted—anywhere—by any body!"

"Oh, Julius!" said Edna, reproachfully; then, without more words, she busied herself in getting him tea, and all those creature comforts which a man sorely needs, especially when he comes in worn and worried—as Julius did. After the first flush of excitement had faded, she saw, and was shocked to see, how great was the change in him during these few weeks. He had grown exceedingly thin, and had at times a restless, hunted look, as of a man pursued by one relentless idea which he vainly tries to master, but which conquers him against his will. He was quieted a little, however, during the tea and talk, and recovered his old self—so charming, brotherly, and kind.

William Stedman looked on, pleased and smiling, but he said nothing. Nor did Letty, which was a still more remarkable fact; and when Julius, having accomplished his usual aim by asserting volubly, to every body's great amusement, that he must retire to the kitchen, as his sole

purpose in paying this final visit was to take a farewell
sketch of it and the cat, disappeared, Letty drew herself
up with dignity, and, instead of accompanying him, went
up stairs. Whence, however, she was soon heard to descend, Letty being one of those people who prefer any
body's company to their own.

"I hope she will be kind to him, even though he has
neglected you and her a little of late," said William, innocently. "I do trust they will get on well together—
our brother and sister. They ought, for there is such a
deal of good in poor Julius. He shows it, by being so
very fond of you. He told me last night, when I was
urging him to end his nonsensical flirtations and get honestly engaged to some nice girl, that he would, if only I
could find him such a girl as my Edna."

Edna laughed.

"Do you know he once made me half jealous—I mean
when I began to want you myself, and fancied he did the
same. Now, little Conscience, if it had been so, what
ought I to have done? Given you up to my brother, eh?"

Edna's light laugh ceased. She thought a minute, and
then said, seriously, "No; if you loved me, and I loved
you, you ought to have married me in spite of all the
world."

So talked they—half merry, half grave—recalling their
past, or planning their future, and then scarcely talking at
all—content with the simple fact of being together.

Meantime, in the kitchen there was also comparative
silence. Not the talking and laughing which generally
went on between Letty and Julius, who always ridiculed
the extreme soberness of "the folks in love." Just a low
murmur of conversation sometimes, and then long pauses
—so long that even the betrothed pair in the next room
noticed it at last.

"I wonder if the sketch is finished. Shall we go and
see, William?"

"Not yet—please not just yet. I must leave early this
evening, and you will not let me come to-morrow. But
after to-morrow you will never get rid of me."

I 2

"Never, all my life! I am so" — sorry, a coquette would have said; but Edna, wholly true, had not a spark of coquetry in her, first or last. She said ".glad."

"Thank you, my blessing of blessings!" And then they talked no more.

But when at length Edna, with a certain uneasy feeling that she could not get rid of, though she kept it strictly to herself, wondering at the long stillness, went to see, she found Julius sitting all by himself over the fire, which, out of its dull, burnt-out hollow, threw occasional sparks of flame, giving a ghostly look to the neat kitchen, as neat and pretty almost as a parlor, which Julius used to say was "the finest room in the house." He was so absorbed that, till Edna touched him on the shoulder, he did not notice her entrance.

"Where is the sketch, Julius?" asked Will.

"And where is my sister?"

"Gone up stairs. Hey, Will! is that you, man? I'm going home."

"Not this minute; not before supper," pleaded Edna.

"Supper! I've had mine. I've 'supped full of horrors,' like Macbeth. Now, 'to bed—to bed—to bed!' Edna, couldn't you give a poor fellow something to make him sleep—forever?"

"Ju," said Will, "what is the matter with you? You're half asleep now, I think; wake up, man!"

"I will," cried Julius, springing to his feet with a violent gesture. "I have been asleep; but I'm awake now. Give me my hat; I'll take a walk and come back to my senses, and to supper likewise, if you please, Miss Edna."

But he never appeared. Letty came down stairs flushed and uncomfortable-looking, and to William's jesting question if she and Julius had been quarrelling, gave an answer so sharp that Dr. Stedman said no more. Silently, uneasily, ended the last evening of so many merry evenings which they had spent in that little house, every corner of which Edna felt she should love to the end of her days.

Yet, as she stood at the door on the solemn dark night —for it had been raining heavily, and there was not a

star visible — even
though her hand
was clasped in her
lover's, and his safe
arm round her, a
weight of foreboding sadness gathered over her.

"Oh, William,
if trouble should
come!"

"We will bear it,
whatever it is, together."

And when he
said that, and drew
her closer, and she
felt the beating of
his warm, living,
loving heart, so
tender and so true,
she knew that she
could bear it.

After Dr. Stedman was gone, Let-

FOREBODINGS.

ty called Edna into the kitchen—Letty still flushed, and
full of the excitement of a secret.

"Don't be running off the very minute you have sent
your lover away. You might have some little sympathy
with other people's love-affairs—mine, for instance."

"Oh, Letty!"

"Yes, you need not look so shocked. It has just come
to that. I knew it would. I have been afraid of it for
ever so long. Very provoking. A wretched business altogether. How could the poor fellow be such a goose!
though I suppose he couldn't help it."

And Letty tried to look grave, while a furtive, gratified
smile twinkled round the corners of her mouth.

"But you could have helped it, if it is as I suspect,"

cried Edna, greatly distressed. "How could you let him
do it? For of course it is Julius—poor Julius!"

Letty nodded. "I promised not to tell any body, and
of course I won't. You will notice, I have never mentioned his name, and I never told you of it, though I have
suspected it for months. Poor fellow, he is desperately
fond of me."

"Oh, Letty!"

Edna could not say another word. She saw, as in an
ominous vision, Julius's face, as he snatched up his hat
and rushed from the house—a wild, fierce, maddened face
—full of that overwhelming passion, a compound of the
senses and the imagination, which sometimes seizes upon
a young man: whom, having played at love throughout
his first fantastic youth, it takes hold of at last in terrible
earnest, either making or marring him for the rest of his
life. For Julius was one of those weak, loving natures
who must cling to somebody, be in love with somebody.
And he had fallen in love with Letty, the very last person, any third party would say, whom he ought to choose.
But third parties are not infallible, and Edna snatched at
a fragment of comfort and hope.

"Surely, Letty, you like Julius?"

"Like him? Oh yes; very much—in a sisterly way. I
told him so. I promised to be the best sister possible to
him, as I always have been, I am sure. But as to marrying him, that is quite another thing. Why he has not a
halfpenny but what he earns, and he will never earn much
—geniuses never do. He will be poor all his life. And,
oh dear me, Edna," shrugging her shoulders with a trick
she had learned at her Paris *pension*, "you know I have
had quite enough of poverty."

"But you might wait."

"Wait—till my appearance was all gone. He is an artist, and has an eye for that, I know," said Letty, with the
pathetic intuition which sometimes dawned through all
her silliness, of favor being deceitful, and beauty vain—
"Wait till I got old and ugly, and couldn't enjoy good-
fortune when it came? Oh no, Edna! that would never

do. Better even for the young man himself that I won't marry him. And yet he is frantically in love with me—he is, indeed. I had no idea there was so much earnestness in him about any thing till now. Would you believe, he almost frightened me."

And Letty, sitting at the kitchen - fire, meditatively warmed her lovely foot, glancing round half triumphantly, half pensively at her sister, whose heart slowly, slowly sank, heavy as lead. For vainly she sought in those beautiful eyes some trace of the feeling—call it love, nay, passion, if you will—which, however sad, however unfortunate, when earnestly and honestly felt, ennobles any woman; while that other side of it—the weak pleasure of conquest, the petty egotistical vanity of being loved—only deteriorates and degrades.

THE TWO WOMEN.

"Oh, how blind, how careless I have been!" cried Edna, almost in a sob. "And you, Letty, you have been playing with edged tools—you know you have. That poor fellow! And you guessed it all, yet you let it go on. How could you! But it is not quite too late. Perhaps you don't · know your own mind—perhaps you really love him?"

Letty laughed. "How should I know? Certainly not in your sort of love. I'm very fond of him, and I told him so, as a sister. For any thing else—but it's no use thinking of that, as you must see; for us to be engaged, Julius and me, would, in our circumstances, be ridiculous —perfectly ridiculous."

Edna answered, with a strange harshness, which she repented afterwards, or would have done but that Letty did not seem to perceive it at all, "I think you are right. It would be even worse than ridiculous. When Julius is my brother, I shall warn him that the most fatal thing he could do would be to marry my sister Letty."

"Yes," said Letty, composedly misapprehending, "I considered that point also. Two brothers marrying two sisters rarely get on together. And then there would be the difficulty of the money-matters; for Julius said he only wished me to be engaged to him; he would never think of marrying me till he had an income of his own, and was quite independent of his brother. And I couldn't wait— I really couldn't, you know. So it is a great deal better as it is. Of course he will get over it; men always do," added Letty, looking as if she were comfortably persuaded to the contrary. "After all, it has been a little excitement. One isn't quite an old woman yet, I see."

And then, scarcely observing Edna's dead silence, Letty unbound her great golden sheaves of hair, and, while she brushed and combed them, chattered unceasingly of Julius —all he had said, all he had done; his frantic pleadings, his bitter despair; till Edna—thinking of the heart that would bleed for every wound of Julius's, the heart whose every emotion she kept sacredly to herself, and always would have done, whether she had loved him or not—Edna started up in a passion of wrath, and grief, and shame.

"Letty, hold your tongue! I won't hear you! the last time you talked like this I was a girl, and I did not understand it—did not mind it. Now I do. I say you have done a wicked thing. Every woman who thinks a man loves her, and lets him go on loving her till he asks her to marry him, and then gives him No—a cold, prudent, heartless No — does a wicked thing. I am ashamed of you, though you are my own sister. I am bitterly ashamed of you."

Letty opened her eyes in the utmost astonishment. She did not get angry; it would have been almost a comfort if she had done so; but she sulked a little, and then melted into tears.

"I couldn't help it, and you have no right to scold me. It was partly your fault; you should not have left us so much together, or you should have spoken to me beforehand. I always listen to what you say, Edna. You are very, very unkind; but now you are happy and going to be married, it does not matter what becomes of me."

And so, with that strange tyranny of weakness to which the strongest often mournfully succumb, she softened her sister's heart towards her, and, despite her common sense, her conscience, her bitter, bitter grief for Julius and Julius's brother, Edna kissed Letty, and scolded her, as she called it, no more.

Instead she talked to her, seriously and tenderly, of things concerning which she had often talked before, till she gave it up as hopeless. But now her reasoning was not, as then, out of theories which Letty had always set aside as "romantic," "impossible." She spoke of what she knew—out of her own blessed experience—of the sacredness of love, given or received; the wickedness of trifling with it; the awful responsibility it was—things once dimly dreamed of by Edna Kenderdine, but now seen by William Stedman's bride, with a fatal vividness and a passionate intensity of belief that made her fearless either of ridicule or contradiction: determined to speak out, whether listened to or not.

Letty did listen—as she said, she generally listened to

Edna—at the time; and this time, either through the excitement of the evening or because she was really touched
by Julius's devotion, she listened with an expression of
earnestness which made Edna almost believe she understood it all.

"What you say may be very true, Edna—I am sure I
hope it is—only you seem to fancy love is the only thing
in life. Now I think there are many other things."

"So there are; but love is the first, the best, the root
and crown of all the rest. And more for men even than
women. If that goes wrong with them every thing goes
wrong. Oh, Letty, take care!"

"Nonsense! what must I take care of? It isn't my
fault that men fall in love with me."

"No; but it is your fault if you treat them in such a
way that they never believe in love again—that they despise it and despise you."

"Will Julius despise me, do you suppose? I hope not!"

"Then behave to him so that, whatever you make him
suffer, he may still respect you. I don't know what has
been—how far you have gone on with him; but oh, Letty,
from this time be very careful how you treat him!"

"Bless us!" said Letty, half crossly, half laughing, "how
seriously you do take it! I might be going to murder the
young man."

"You do murder him, in reality, when you trifle with
him—play fast and loose, warm and cold, as I have seen
you do with some people. Don't do it with him—it will
be the ruin of him. Oh, Letty!"—and she grasped her
sister's hand in an agony of entreaty—"for my sake, for
William's sake, take care!"

"What on earth am I to take care of? As if Julius
were the first man that ever was crossed in love. He
must just get over it."

"Yes; but how? We women don't understand. We
can but break our hearts; but they—they turn wicked.
If Julius does, I shall blame you."

Letty looked uneasy.

"I am very sorry. I am sure I did not mean any harm,

and I hope none will come, for it would be extremely unpleasant. But what am I to do? It is the most uncomfortable thing. Oh! I wish I had never been brought into it. I wish you were not going to marry William Stedman, or that somebody was going to marry me—some suitable man, with plenty of money, who would take me quite away out of all these troubles."

"Then you do not care—not one atom—for Julius."

"Oh yes, I do—I like him very much. I dare say I shall never get any one to be so fond of me again. I would take him to-morrow if he had a tolerable income, or a chance of getting on in the world. But he has none; and, as I told you, I can't wait—so he must go."

"Clearly," said Edna, setting her firm little mouth together, not without a curl of contempt in it, and rising to light her candle and go to bed.

"Oh, stop a minute—do help me! Tell me how I am to manage it all. What do you mean by my treating Julius so as to do him no harm, and to make him respect me?"

Edna paused to think. Unto her, in her brimming happiness of contented love, Julius's lot seemed bitter to an almost exaggerated degree. She mourned for him from the very depth of her heart, yet she could not, she dared not, urge Letty to accept him. She knew that "love bidden is love forbidden;" and that far safer for Julius would be a short, sharp blow, and over, than the torturing suspense of uncertainty and indecision.

"I hardly know what to advise, except that you must meet him as seldom as possible. I will manage that. But when you do meet, though you need not be unkind to him—still you must never let him doubt your mind. You must not waver; you must keep firm, Letty—as firm as a rock."

And then the impossibility of firmness to that weak, vain, pleasure-loving nature, which always did the easiest thing at the time, without much regard to consequences, forced itself upon Edna with a mournful foreboding. Yet, for a little while, Letty's evident sincerity gave her hope.

"I will do every thing you tell me; I will, indeed," said

she, her ever-ready tears flowing down apace. "Poor Julius! I am so sorry for him—so sorry if this makes you and William unhappy. For, of course, you will tell William, though I wish you wouldn't."

Nevertheless, Letty's looks betrayed a sort of satisfaction that William was obliged to be told.

"Yes, I shall tell William. Oh, my poor William!" sighed Edna to herself, knowing how keen would be the pain to that tender heart, in whom the best love of all only made all other affections the stronger. "Letty, we can't help what is past, but you *must* do what is right now; you must make William respect you, ay, and Julius too, even though you refuse him. I don't know it of myself—thank God! nobody ever loved me but William— still, I am sure it is quite possible for a good woman to turn her rejected lover into her truest friend—that is, if he had nothing to blame her for except rejecting him. But we will talk no more now. Let us go to bed, sister. Oh, my sister! my only sister!"

Worn out with all the emotion of the day, Edna threw her arms round Letty's neck, and they clung together— like sisters, in whom no difference of character could break the tie of blood—at least not yet. And then they went to sleep in peace together.

All next day—the day before the wedding—Letty went about the house with a very sad and serious face, though it brightened up occasionally—especially at sight of any thing in the shape of clothes. And when she tried on her own dress—a costume so tasteful and becoming, that she looked fit to be brides-maid to a queen instead of to that dainty, white-robed, yet plain little woman, who was to William Stedman all his heart's desire — Letty's spirits rose amazingly.

"I wonder if there will be any body to look at us; it is a shame to waste all these pretty things upon the parson and the clerk, and old Mr. Marchmont"—a city merchant, whose house had been Edna's only situation as resident governess, and who, in default of nearer friends, had claimed the pleasure of giving her away.

"Except Julius—if Julius comes," said Edna, gravely.

Letty looked a little conscience-smitten. "He is sure to come—he told me he should. He did not wish William to find out any thing, and, besides, it would be his last look of me. He means to go abroad—to Switzerland, I think. Poor fellow! I am really very sorry for him," added Letty, as she glanced in the glass, and could not— who could?—help smiling complacently at the charming image reflected there.

But Edna said nothing, and shortly afterwards went out of the room.

Strange! she could not have believed it of any body else, yet any one who knew her unselfish nature might have believed it of her; but Edna, even on her marriage-eve, thought less of herself and her own feelings than of poor Julius. Do what she would, she could not get him out of her mind. The contrast between him and the rest —William and she going off together on a marriage-tour to their old haunts in the Isle of Wight; Letty taken to a cheerful visit in the Marchmonts' luxurious home, where, among those wealthy, but rather dull city people, she, with her beauty and her familiarity with "high families," was very popular; and forlorn Julius left alone to bear his grief how he might—all this smote Edna with exceeding pain. She was one of those who find it hard to be happy when others are not; who would have leaned over the edge of paradise itself to drop bitter tears upon the poor souls in purgatory. And when, towards evening— the last day of her maiden life—she left Letty, still busy about some trifling adornment, and started on a quiet, solitary stroll, to consider what was to be done, and how and when she should tell the sad secret to William, she felt so unhappy that she could hardly believe to-morrow was her wedding-day.

Nevertheless, she walked on, trying to compose herself by walking, when she heard footsteps behind her, light, quick, and hurried, and, turning round, saw Julius.

She looked in his face, and he in hers, and both understood that each knew all. She put out her hand to him,

JULIUS AND EDNA.

he grasped it hard, and then turned away. They walked along side by side for some distance before either spoke. When Julius did, his voice was hollow and unnatural.

"I have been hanging about here all day. You know why; she would be sure to tell you. She promised not, but of course she did. Women always do."

"Yes, she told me."

"Well, I don't blame her. Perhaps, if I had told you

myself before now, I might have been saved all this. You knew her mind?"

"No," said Edna, firmly, afraid lest his eager questioning might betray her into any admission that might lead him astray, "I could have told you nothing, for I had not a suspicion of such a thing till last night—I mean, till just lately."

"You did suspect, then? *You* thought she cared for me?" said Julius, eagerly. "You must have seen I cared for her? More fool I! But it's over now. Women are all alike—all alike."

"Julius," said Edna, appealingly, and her soft eyes brimmed over. For he was so changed, even in those few hours—so haggard and wild-looking, with neglected dress and excited manner.

"I beg your pardon; no, you are different. I know Will has found his good angel, as he deserved. I deserved nothing—and got it. Edna, you once told me to wait till my time came. It has come, from the minute I first saw her beautiful face through the lodging-house window. It was a madness—quite a madness. If ever the devil comes to a man as an angel of light—as the Bible says he does come, you know—he came to me in the shape of your sister Letty."

"Hush!" said Edna, putting her arm through his, and drawing him on, for his loud voice and violent manner had caught the notice of a stray passer-by. "Come with me: I am going a walk, and you can tell me every thing."

"Every thing?"

"Yes, every thing," said Edna, with firmness, for he was so past all self-control that it became necessary. "You need not mind speaking to me—I never chatter to any body. Besides, to-morrow I shall be your own sister—William's wife."

"William's wife! Oh, happy, happy Will! But you'll promise not to tell him, not till after to-morrow? And you'll see how I'll behave. He shall guess nothing, for it would vex him so. Dear old Will! I'm right glad he is happy. Lucky, lucky Will!"

Edna could not speak for crying. Her tears seemed to calm her companion in some degree. He pressed her hand.

"Are you so very sorry for me, you good little woman? Then you think there is no hope?"

Edna shook her head in a silent negative. She dared not do otherwise. For, knowing her sister as she did—and seeing Julius now in the new light in which his passion had shown him—the expression she had used last night of "playing with edged tools." but faintly expressed the danger of any trifling. Foolish Letty!—she might as safely emulate the juggler's tricks of swallowing fire, or tossing up and catching gleaming daggers, as attempt, with her weak, womanish, uncomprehending nature, her small caprices and coquettish arts, to deal with such a man as Julius Stedman. Well might she say she was "frightened of him." Edna almost was. Never before had she witnessed the desperate agony of thwarted love, as shown in one who was capable, by fits, of self-repression —but of self-government had none. What passed between her and Julius for the next three minutes Edna hid in the deepest, darkest recesses of her pitying heart; she never betrayed it, not even to William.

At length she said, softly, "Tell me how it happened. How came you to care for Letty, or to fancy Letty cared for you?"

"Fancy! It was no fancy. You know better than that. She must have told you? No? Then I'll not tell. I'll not be such an ungentlemanly wretch as to tell. I was mistaken—that's all. But, Edna—I'm not a conceited ass, I hope. And when a girl lets you talk to her, sit by her, hold her hand, kiss her—"

Edna started, and then Julius also drew back in bitter shame.

"I was a coward to say it; but no matter. It was no harm: only 'sisterly.' She told me so. No blame to her, of course. Only, Edna, mind this, if a girl wants to send a young fellow to hell, body and soul, bid her treat him 'as a sister.'"

Edna walked on, sadly silent. Mad as his words were, there was truth at the bottom of them, though much might be said on the other side. For Julius implied, though he did not actually own, how this passion had come upon him —fierce as retributive justice—when he was first amusing himself, as he had often done before, with that tender philandering, half love, half friendship, saying nothing, yet implying every thing, by which so many a young man has broken the heart, and blighted the life of a young, foolish, innocent girl, who would only have laid to his charge the pathetic lament of Ophelia — when Hamlet says, "*I did love you dearly once ;*" and she answers, "*Indeed, my lord, you made me believe so.*"

Yet two wrongs can never make a right: Letty was inexcusable. And the worst of it was, she would never be conscious that she needed excusing. But the mischief was done. Here was this young man, to whom a strong, real passion for a good woman, however hopeless, would have been salutary—might have shaken him out of his frivolities and follies, and awakened him to that new and holier life which elevates a man, less by possession than by striving after the nobleness which deserves to possess —but, trifled with by such a girl as Letty, he would sink lower and lower—whither? For there are no depths of depravity to which a man may not fall, from whose heart and lips come the bitter cry which startled Edna many a time during their miserable walk—"They are all alike— all alike. I will never believe in any woman more."

"But," she said at last, "you will believe in men. By-and-by you will come and talk to William. He will help you. Why," she said, trying at last playfulness, when all serious arguments failed, "you are not the first man who was refused and got over it, married somebody else, and lived happy ever afterwards. Even Shakspeare says, ' Men have died, and worms have eaten them, but not for love.' "

Julius laughed angrily. "No; I shall not die. You may tell Will that, if he cares about it."

"You know he does. It would break his heart—both our hearts—if you broke yours. But you will not. You

will yet find a far sweeter woman, a far more suitable
wife, than my sister Letty."

. "Suitable? Yes, that was the word she used. It was
not a 'suitable' marriage—that is, I could not give her a
carriage and pair, and a house in Belgravia. Nor, indeed,
could I marry her at all just yet. I could only love her,
and she did not care for that. Edna "—and he turned
fiercely round—"Edna, I'd honor the meanest milliner-girl
to whom I came with only a wedding-ring, or perhaps with
no ring at all, and said, 'Love me' (if she did love, and
some of them do, poor things!), more than your fine lady
who will accept any body, no matter who, so that she is
well married. But it isn't marriage at all; it's—"

"Be silent," interrupted Edna, in her clear, firm voice,
severely sweet as Milton makes that of his angels. "You
are speaking of what you do not understand. You only
see half a truth. Because one side of a thing is wicked,
does it make the other good? There are people like
what you say—who marry in unholiness, or who love,
omitting marriage, in equal unholiness; but there are others who love with all their hearts, and marry because they
love, like William and me. Come to us; we will take
care of you. We will not let you 'go wrong.'"

"You can't help it."

"No; but *you* can. Julius, a man may be grievously
injured by a woman; but if he lets himself be ruined by
her, he is one of two things—either a coward or a fool.
You are neither; you are a man. Be a man, and bear it."

He turned towards her, the sweet woman, so loved, so
happy; who out of all her happiness could spare thought
and sympathy for others — for his miserable self. She
stood, looking up at him with her pale, tear-stained, eager
face, through which, in midst of all her grief, gleamed that
hopeful courage which women often possess so much more
than men, given to them, perhaps, that they may the better
help men. The strong spiritual attraction mastered Julius in spite of himself.

"You are an angel!" he said, in a broken voice. "I
think, if any thing could save *me* from going to the devil,

it would be my sister Edna. Tell Letty—no, tell her nothing. Tell William—"

"What?" asked Edna, seeing he hesitated.

"Every thing; I had rather he knew it. Tell him"— with a feeble smile—"tell him to-morrow afternoon. And then say, he need not vex himself, for I shall go to Switzerland to-morrow night—to work hard and trouble nobody. And, mind you, nobody need trouble themselves about me, since I shall come to no harm for three months —I promise you that."

"And afterwards?"

"God knows!"

"Yes," Edna answered, reverently. "God does know. And He never tries any one of us more than we can bear. Now, walk with me to the end of the lane. Then go straight home."

Julius obeyed, without the slightest resistance, and with the gentleness of a child.

Next morning, quite early—for they were to start at once, there being no wedding breakfast—with Letty looking charming as brides-maid, though a little nervous and agitated, but not unbecomingly so; with Julius as best man, very handsome, well dressed, and agreeable, but, on the whole, more absorbed in attention to the bride than to the brides-maid, which fact much surprised Letty's warm admirer, old Mr. Marchmont—next morning, William and Edna were married.

CHAPTER XVI.

A dark wet November night—or evening ; but it looked like night, for the houses were all shuttered up, and there was no light except the gas-lamps, and the one red doctor's lamp, to break the dreariness of the long, monotonous, shopless street, where every house was so exactly like another—outside at least. Within—what an immeasurable difference !

What is it makes a house bright? pleasant to go to—to

K

stay in—even to think about, so that even if fate totally annihilates it we recall tenderly for years its atmosphere of peace, cheerfulness, loving-kindness—nay, its outside features—down to the very pictures on the walls, the pattern of the papering, the position of the furniture? While other houses—we shiver at the remembrance of them, and the dreary days we spent in them—days of dullness, misery, or strife—these houses we would not revisit for the world!

Why? If a house with fair possibilities of home comfort is thoroughly comfortless—if there is within it a reckless impossibility of getting things done in the right way or at the right time—or if, on the contrary, it is conducted with a terrible regularity, so that an uninvited guest or an extempore meal sends a shock throughout the whole abode—if the servants-never keep their places long—and the gentlemen of the family are prone to be "out of evenings"—who is to blame?

Almost invariably the women of the family. The men make or mar its outside fortunes; but its internal comfort lies in the women's hands alone. And until women feel this—recognize at once their power and their duties—it is idle for them to chatter about their rights. Men may be bad enough out-of-doors; but their influence is limited and external. It is women who are in reality either the salvation or the destruction of a household.

Dr. Stedman's household had done with its bachelor freedom, and passed into feminine sway — a sway more complete than in most; and yet there are many professional men who, like a doctor, are so engrossed by outside toil that they are obliged to leave every thing else to their wives. Well for them if, like William Stedman, they have married a woman who is fit not only to obey, but to rule. Especially so when, as in this case, there are few appliances of wealth to aid her—no skilled servants, no well-appointed and well-furnished establishment; but one which requires, in every point, not only the mistress's head, but her eye, and often her hand.

Thus, in the drawing-room, where Edna sat sewing, always sewing, and, for a wonder, Letty was sewing too,

MRS. WILLIAM STEDMAN.

there was a combination of old things and new; the furnishing being accomplished by means of devices which would have shocked a respectable — and expensive — upholsterer. Yet the general effect was neat and pretty; an ordinary eye would have discovered no deficiencies, and a good heart, even if discovering them, would have been touched by, rather than have laughed at, these pathetic incongruities.

The mistress was not unlike her house; carefully, though any thing but richly, dressed; still she was dressed for dinner, with her soft hair all smooth, and her laces dropping daintily over the little busy hands. Some people said—and not untruly—that Edna had grown a deal prettier since her marriage. Yet she was worn and thin, as if she had a rather anxious life; but there was no anxiety in her eyes at this moment—nothing but perfect content—perfect rest.

She listened—patiently, though with a far-away look, as if she only heard half of it—to Letty's incessant stream of rather fretful talk about the inconveniences of the establishment.

"I am sure I am quite glad to do all I can, and be of
use in the house; but there seems no end to all we have
to do, Edna. It's much harder work than keeping school,
I think."

"Perhaps," said Edna, smiling; for there was some
truth in Letty's complainings. Dr. Stedman, in his bachelor helplessness, had been compelled to marry first and
"settle" afterwards; and the settling cost more trouble—
and money also—than they had calculated on. Happily,
there was Edna's share in the good-will of the school—
Letty's being conscientiously invested for herself; still, as
William, like the sisters, held strongly to the only safe
rule for poor people—of never buying what he could not
at once pay for — the difficulties of furnishing were not
small; and it required all Edna's cleverness to reduce extraneous expenses, and make sixpence go as far as sixpence honestly would. Thus the first few months of their
married life were not easy.

None the more so because Letty shared them. All people make mistakes sometimes; and Edna and William soon
discovered that for a young couple to have the constant
presence of even the least obnoxious "third party" is not
to be desired. Poor Letty! they tried to keep her from
suspecting this, and to make the best of it, till the change
which she already began to talk about and long for—name-
ly, going out again as a governess — should arrive; but
still she helped to make the first six months of her brother and sister's marriage the most difficult portion of their
lives.

Nevertheless they were happy—blessed as two people
must be who love with all their hearts, and trust each
other from the inmost depths of their souls. That their
life was all smooth I do not aver; but it was like what
learned men tell us of the great ocean—the storms only
troubled its surface, and came from extraneous agencies,
such as no life is free from; in its deepest depths was a
perpetual calm.

Calmness, perhaps, was the strongest characteristic of
Edna's face now. She had been a restless little woman

heretofore — easily moved, ready to catch each flitting
shade of pleasure or of pain; now she had learned the
self-control which every human being must learn who has
another human being to care for—bound by the only tie
which entirely takes away the solitude of individuality.
This fact alone made a difference wider than had before
existed between her and Letty, and it made her also very
patient with Letty.

She heard all the grumblings — giving an occasional
gentle reply—till a loud knock thrilled through the silent
house—the master's knock.

"There he is!"

And Edna ran down stairs to open the door to William
—a foolish custom which Letty always condemned—declaring she wouldn't do it to her husband; it spoiled one's
collar and one's hair, and gave far too much trouble! Uncomprehending Letty!

So William's first greeting at his own door was always
his wife's face—bright and gay, with all the worry smoothed out of it and the anxiety banished—he had enough of
both outside.

"All right, my darling?"

"Yes; quite right."

"I'll go up and change my clothes. I have just come
from the hospital. Then we'll have dinner."

A doctor's wife has a hard life, as Edna found. Yet
there was something grand in it, even in its dangers;
something heroic enough to touch her sense of the ideal,
which in this little woman was very strong. Continually
there was much to be done, and as much more to be suffered — silently and without appeal. When Edna first
married, and realized all that her husband went through
daily and hourly, she found it very hard to bear. It was
an agony to her every time he entered a fever-ward, and
was sent for to those dens of misery and crime where a
doctor is often the only messenger of good that ever
comes. But now she bore all quietly. She knew his life
was in God's hands—that he must do his duty, and she
hers, which was to help rather than to hinder him. Yet

often when she saw other wives whose husbands went into
no danger, were exhausted by no hard work, and William
came home, as to-day, utterly worn out, so that the smile
with which he always met her only lasted a moment—the
sinking at her heart returned, the deadly fear or wild out-
cry of prayer that all who love can understand.

But she said nothing; and when she took the foot of
her husband's dinner-table, it was with the cheerful face
that a wife ought to wear, and which does more good
than food or warmth to a weary man.

"Oh, this is such a pleasant room!" said Dr. Stedman,
looking round it with a sense of infinite rest, and comfort,
and relief. "I am glad I have not to go out again. It is
such a wretched night outside. I hope Julius will wait
in Paris, and not be thinking of crossing till the weather
alters. There is his letter, Edna, which came to-day. He
speaks of being in London soon."

This was said looking at his wife, but not overlooking
her sister, who maintained a demure silence.

To Letty William had never spoken one word on the
subject of Julius, nor indeed very many to Edna. He had
heard all, of course, and been deeply moved; but afterwards, with a man's sharp cutting of many Gordian knots
which women wear their lives out in untying, he had disposed of that painful domestic complication by simply
saying:

"What is done can not be undone. We shall not mend
it by talking about it, and we may make it much worse.
Let us say no more, and it will all gradually slip by."

Nor was he cold or hard to Letty; perhaps, man-like,
he was ready to find excuses for a woman—and a woman
so beautiful. Whatever he felt on the subject, he had
only shown his feelings by writing long, and unfailingly
punctual, letters to Julius, with a persistency rather rare
in a man and a brother. And now—with that good common sense of his, which never made unnecessary fuss about
any thing—he just mentioned, in an off-hand way, the fact
of Julius's coming home.

"He comes home rather prosperous too. He has just

sold a large picture to your friend Mr. Marchmont, Letty."

"I am sure I am very glad to hear it," answered Letty, looking down.

"And he sends me back—honest fellow!—his quarter's allowance, saying he can well do without it, better than we; which is partly true, Edna, my dear."

"We'll keep it for him, in case he wants it," said Edna, kindly. "What has he been doing lately?"

"Read, and you will see. He and the Marchmonts seem to get on capitally. He has shown them Paris, and speaks a good deal of them; thinking of them much as you do—worthy, kindly people, with heaps of money and not too much of brains—except, perhaps, your pupil, Miss Lily, who he says is so pretty."

"Lily Marchmont pretty?" cried Letty. "I never heard such nonsense! Why, she is a mere roly-poly dot; as red as a cherry, and as round as a ball. What can Julius be thinking of? Is he falling in love with her? But, indeed, I should be very glad to hear of any thing of the kind," added Letty, with a sudden accession of demureness.

"So should I," replied her brother-in-law, gravely. "Nothing in this world would make me more glad than to see Julius married—happily married. He is the best fellow I know, and would be better still if he had a wife —just such a wife as mine."

And, with eyes overflowing with love, William glanced across the table to the sweet face that was all his sunshine, all his delight. Yet, just as in her case towards him, the joy was not without its attendant pain.

"You are looking pale, my wife; you have been overtiring yourself."

"A little. I was in town to-day. I was obliged to go."

"Those horrid omnibuses! Oh, I wish I could give you a carriage! Do you know, sister Letty, I am seriously thinking of following your constant advice, and starting a brougham, which people say is a *sine qua non* in the success of a doctor commencing practice; it makes such an

excellent impression. Suppose I try it? Only you must
be sure not to tell the mistress. She would be so exceedingly displeased."

He laughed while he spoke, and gave a glance over to
Edna—half joking, half anxious—as if feeling his way, and
seeing how the land lay. Was "the mistress" grown
such an alarming little person, after all?

She smiled, but said not a word. Letty dashed eagerly
into the question.

"I am sure Edna would never be so foolish as to object
to any thing that was for your advantage. Besides, a
carriage would be such a great convenience to us. You
might have it all the day, and we could use it of evenings
instead of a nasty cab, which always spoils one's dresses.
And how grand it would sound—'Dr. Stedman's carriage
stops the way'—at theatres and evening parties!"

"That implies you have both to go to. But I dare say
you would. If I started a brougham, people would think
I had no end of practice, which would create more. The
world always worships the rising sun. Yes, perhaps it
might be an advisable investment," added William, changing from his satirical tone to that of prudent worldliness,
which agreed ill with his honest voice and mien.

"Not so much an investment as a speculation, since at
present we have no money to pay for it," said Edna, gently.

"No more have half the world that rides in carriages.
Yet how content it looks, and how comfortable its carriages are!"

"Very comfortable," said Letty, "and, if carefully lined,
always so clean and nice for one's clothes."

"And consciences," added William, with a light laugh;
"which I see, by her looks, is what Edna is thinking
of— What! another message? Have I got to go out
again to-night?"

And he rose, not looking particularly glad; but when
he opened the letter he showed uncontrollable surprise
and delight.

"Who would have thought it? While I was speaking
about him, Julius was close at hand. Bid the messenger

wait; he shall have an answer in a few minutes. Yes,
Edna, you had better show it to Letty."

For Letty, not wholly unmoved, had come to look over
her sister's shoulder at the few words which explained how
Julius had just come in from Paris, and was at a coffee-
house close by, where he said he would be glad to see his
brother.

"Of course you will go to him at once, dear?"

"Certainly. Poor fellow, how very glad I am!"

And William's eyes were shining, and his fatigue all
vanished. Then, suddenly, his countenance changed.

"I forgot — I really quite forgot for the minute; but,
Edna?—no, I suppose *that* is not to be thought of. Yet
it's hard that I can not fetch my own brother at once to
my house. Of course nobody is to blame. Yet it is very
sad—very annoying."

Dr. Stedman did not often speak so irritably, as well as
sorrowfully. Edna knew not what to say. Letty drew
herself up with a dignified air.

"I assure you, William, if out of consideration for me—"

"No; I'm not considering you at all," was the blunt
answer. "I am considering my brother, Letty. I have
never named this matter to you before, and do not suppose I am blaming you now; you had a right to give
Julius any answer you pleased. Moreover, I have every
reason to believe that he has quite 'got over it,' as you
women say, and would no more mind meeting you than
any other lady of his acquaintance."

"I am sure I am delighted to hear it."

"Only, if you do meet," continued William, pointedly,
"it must be clearly understood that you meet only as
acquaintances."

"Certainly," replied Letty, tossing her head, and retiring
to the other end of the room, while the husband and wife
consulted together in an undertone. At last Edna came
up to her sister.

"Letty, should you object to Julius coming here for a
day or two—that is, if he will come—if William can bring
him back with him? It would make William so happy."

Then for goodness' sake do it! Really nobody hinders you. I don't. I am sure it is very hard for me to be the cause of family dissension. I will set you all free by-and-by. I will go away and be a governess as soon as ever I can." And Letty began to weep.

William was touched. "Come," he said, laying his hand affectionately on her shoulder, "don't be foolish, Letty. Don't let us be making miseries where none exist, or exaggerating any little difficulties that we have. Rather let us try to get through them. If you never cared for Julius, and Julius has ceased to care for you, there can be no possible objection to your meeting, or to his coming here. Shall I say so, and ask him to come?"

Letty brightened up at once. "Do, for I am sure it would be the very best plan. There is plenty of room in the house, you know. Besides, we are rather dull—Edna and I—with you away so much. And Julius used to be so very amusing."

So William departed; and after half an hour of rather anxious expectation, the two sisters welcomed the two brothers, in changed relations certainly, but with all the warmth and cordiality of yore. And then William and Julius stood on the hearth together, the elder with his arm on the younger's shoulder, and regarding him with eyes out of which beamed the old affection—the old admiration.

The brothers had always been strikingly dissimilar, but now the dissimilarity was particularly plain—not so much in face as in the difference which character and circumstances make in outward appearance, which increases rapidly as people grow older. Nothing could be a greater contrast to the hard-working doctor than the fashionable young artist—who laughed and talked so fast, with more than his former brilliancy; greeted every body, complimented every body; admired the house, and paid the tenderest attentions to its mistress.

"You have grown quite a foreigner. I should hardly have known you, Julius," said Edna. "There is scarcely a bit of your own old self left in you."

"Perhaps not, and all the better," answered he; then added, gayly, "but I don't see the least change—indeed, I should not like any change—in my little sister. I hope she means to be as good as ever to me?"

"No fear of that," said William, looking from one to the other in great content, and really almost forgetting Letty, who, on her part, took very little notice of the rest, but remained aloof in stately dignity.

Nor did Julius take any special notice of her, or manifest any agitation at meeting her; in fact, the whole thing passed over so very quickly and quietly that Edna almost smiled to think of what an anxiety it had been to her and William. Glad as she was, it gave her a certain sad feeling of the mutability of all things, and especially of men's love in general—lightly won, lightly lost. Was every man's love so, except her own William's?

"No," she said to herself, as she watched the brilliant Julius, the beautiful Letty — both equally self-controlled and self-satisfied. "No, we need not be in the least afraid. Nothing will happen."

Undoubtedly it was a relief and a great pleasure to spend such a merry evening. Julius gave endless accounts of his continental life, where he seemed to have made good use of his time—in bringing back sketches innumerable, and in making acquaintance with foreign artists of note—of whom he talked a great deal. He spoke also kindly, though with an undertone of sarcasm, of his rich and stupid patron, Mr. Marchmont.

"You saw a good deal of the Marchmonts?" observed Edna.

"Yes, they needed me, and I needed them; so we made it mutually convenient."

"And you call Lily Marchmont pretty?" here broke in Letty, irresistibly. "I never heard of such a thing! Lily Marchmont pretty!"

"Are not all young ladies pretty—just as all young men are estimable — when they are rich?" said Julius, laughing.

Letty drew back and spoke no more.

But as, in the course of conversation, Julius made as much fun of the young lady as he did of her respectable papa, Edna thought there was not much to be hoped for in his praise of Miss Lily Marchmont.

In truth, glad as she was to see him—gladder still to see her husband's happiness in his return—there was something about Julius which inexpressibly pained Edna. No human creature ever stands still; we all either advance or deteriorate, and Julius had not advanced—either in earnestness, or simplicity, or manliness. Externally, his refinement had degenerated into the air of the *petit maître*—the man who placed the happiness of his existence on the set of a collar or the wave of a curl; while his conversation, lively and amusing as it was, flitted from subject to subject with the lightness of a mind which had come to the bitter conclusion that there is nothing in life worth seriously thinking of. He was not unaffectionate, and yet his very affectionateness saddened her; it showed how much there was in him that had never had fair play, and how his best self had been stunted and blighted till it had shot out, by force of circumstances, into a far smaller and more ignoble self than Nature had intended. Of course, a strong character would have controlled circumstances; but who is always strong? Clever and charming as he was, Edna felt something very like actual pity for Julius.

He refused to stay in his brother's house, alleging that his ways were not their ways—they were married, and he was a gay young bachelor—he should scandalize them all; but he commissioned Edna to procure him lodgings close by.

"Such lodgings as I troubled you about once before, only the trouble was all wasted, like other things," said he. And this was the only reference he made, even in the remotest degree, to any thing of the past. Of the future he talked as little. Indeed, he seemed to live wholly the life of the present.—"Let us eat and drink, for to-morrow we die." As for his passionate love for Letty, he seemed to have quite forgotten it. But there is an oblivion which is worse for a man than the sharpest remembrance.

"Yes," said William's wife, as, Julius having left, and

Letty having gone to bed immediately, her husband came and sat beside her at their fireside—"yes, we might have spared ourselves all anxiety about Julius. Oh, William, how seldom does love last long with any body!"

"You did not surely wish this to last, you most unreasonable and contradictory little woman? You must feel it is far better ended?"

"I suppose so. And yet—" Edna was half ashamed to own it, but she was conscious that in the depth of her foolish, faithful heart she should have respected Julius much more if he had not in six little months—ay, it was this very day six months that he had poured out to her compassionate ear all the agony of his passion—so completely "got over" it.

She sat down by her husband's side for the one quiet half hour when the master and mistress of the household were left to themselves, to discuss the affairs of to-day, and arrange for those of to-morrow. Although so short a time married, Edna and William had already dropped into the practical ways of "old married people," whose love demonstrates itself more often by deeds than words—by giving one another pleasure, and saving one another pain; which latter, in their busy and hard life, was not the lightest portion of the duty. Neither ever dwelt much upon any thing that must needs be a sore subject to the other, and so a few more words ended the matter of Julius. It was William's decided opinion that their brother and sister should be left as much as possible to themselves—not thrown together more than could be helped, but still neither watched nor controlled.

"For," said he, "we really have no right to control them, or to interfere with them in the smallest degree. If there is one decision in life which ought to be left exclusively to the two concerned, it is the question of marriage. If I had a dozen sons and daughters"—Edna half smiled, faintly coloring—"I would give them all liberty to choose any body they liked; only taking care to bring them up so that they would choose rightly—in a manner worthy of themselves and of me."

"What an admirable sentiment, and so oracular, it ought to be printed in a book," answered Edna, laughing. William laughed too at his own energetic preaching.

"But now," said he, "I am going to preachify in earnest; and, my darling, it is about a very serious thing, which you must give all your wise little mind to, and tell me what you really think about it. I want to set up a carriage."

He said it a little hesitatingly, between jest and earnest. Edna looked up.

"You don't mean it, William? You are only jesting with me?"

"Not in the least. I mean what I say, as I am rather in the habit of doing," and the dominant hardness which was in his nature, as it is in the nature of every strong man, betrayed itself a little. "I have been thinking of the matter ever so long, and it is an experiment I feel strongly inclined to try."

Edna was silent.

"Something must be done, for my practice is no better than it was two years ago, except for my fixed salary, which, of course, we have need to be thankful for. Still, I want to get on; to make a handsome income; to give you every thing you need."

"That is not very much," said Edna, softly.

"I know it. You are a careful wife, my love. But our lot is somewhat hard."

"We knew it would be hard."

"Yes, but I want to alter things—to make a desperate effort to get on. This is a plan which many young doctors try. Some, indeed, say that nothing can be done without it. It is like setting a tub to catch a whale— baiting with one's last trout for a big salmon, as we used to do in my glorious fishing days of old. Ah, I never go a fishing now. Never shall again, I suppose."

"I wish it was different," said Edna, sadly. "You get no holidays, and I don't know when you will. They are among the pleasant things you have lost through marrying."

"My darling!" But there is no need to particularize William's answer, or what he thought of the loss and the gain. "And now," said he, at last, "let us go back to practical things. This carriage—"

He met somewhat uneasily his wife's fond, grave, questioning eyes.

"Yes, this carriage. Do you really require it? For the sake of your health, I mean? You are often very much worn out, William?"

"But not with walking; I wish I were! I wish I had enough of patients to wear me out. No, Edna, I can not conscientiously say I require a carriage, but I want it, just for the look of the thing. We must meet the world with its own weapons; if it insists upon being a humbug, why, I suppose we must be humbugs too. Don't you see?"

"I am afraid I don't."

Dr. Stedman laughed, not his own joyous, frank laugh, but one more like Julius's. "Oh, you are such an innocent, my darling. Why, many a fashionable doctor, now earning thousands, has started upon nothing, and lived upon credit for the first two or three years. Just make people believe you have a large practice, and you get it. Patients flock to you one after the other, like sheep. That 'sawbones'—in the funny tale by some young fellow named Dickens, which you read last night—who sent his boy about delivering unordered medicines, and had himself fetched out of church every Sunday on imaginary messages, had not a bad notion of the right way of getting on in the world."

"The right way, William?"

"Well, the best way—the cleverest way."

"But—the honest way?"

"I was not talking of honesty."

Edna regarded her husband keenly. Like every married woman, she had to learn that there is much in masculine nature difficult to understand; not necessarily bad, only incomprehensible. As, no doubt, William Stedman had before now found out that his angel was a very woman, full of many little womanish faults that his larger na-

ture required to be patient with. It was good for both
so to be taught humility.

"Don't let us discuss this matter to-night," said Edna,
rather sadly. "Do let it rest."

"No, it can not rest. You do not see—women never
can—that a man, if he has any pluck in him, will not sit
quiet under ill-fortune. He must get on in the world, by
fair means or foul. But this is no 'foul' means. It is
only doing, for the sake of expediency, a thing which,
perhaps, one does not quite like. Yet—"

"But how can you do it at all? Keeping a carriage,
you say, will cost two hundred a year, and we have, altogether, only five hundred a year to live upon."

"Yes, but — in plain English, Edna, we must strain a
point, and do it upon credit."

"Upon credit!"

"I see you don't like that, neither do I; but there is no
other way."

"No way to get on in the world without making people believe we are better off than we really are, in the
chance of becoming what we pretend to be ?".

"You put the matter with an ugly plainness, considering how many people do it, and think nothing of it. Why,
half London lives beyond its income—peers, ministers of
the crown, professional and business men—why not a poor,
struggling doctor?"

"Why not? if he can bend his pride, and reconcile his
conscience to such a life," said Edna, with—ah, let us confess it—a slight thrill of scorn in her clear voice. "Only
I should despise him so much that I should not like his
name to be Doctor William Stedman!"

Will sprung up. He was more than annoyed—angry;
with that sudden wrath which has its origin in sundry inward twinges, that sometimes hint to a man he is not quite
so much in the right as he tries to believe himself to be.
He walked up and down his dining-room, much displeased.

Let us give him his due. He was a very good man,
and a truly good man is, in some things, better than any
woman, because he has so much more temptation to be

otherwise. But the best man alive, who is compelled to knock about in the world, receiving and giving many a hard thump sometimes, finds it not easy to preserve quite unstained that instinctive, ideal sense of right and wrong which seems to be set in every good woman's breast, like a deep, still pool in a virgin forest. Happy the man who can always come to its pure, safe brink, and find heaven, and nothing but heaven, reflected there !

It was not in William Stedman's nature long to bear anger against any one, least of all against his wife. They differed occasionally, as any two human beings must differ, but they never quarrelled ; for the bitterness which turns mere diversity of opinion into personal disputes was to them absolutely unknown. After a time Dr. Stedman stopped in his rapid walk.

"William," said Edna, "come over here and explain what you mean, and I will try to understand it better. You must not be vexed with me for saying what I think."

"Certainly not. I told you, when I married you, that I wanted a thinking, feeling, rational, companionable wife, not a Circassian slave. A man must be either a fool or a tyrant who likes a woman to be his slave."

"And I am afraid I could never have been a slave, even to you," replied Edna, laughing, with her old gayety; "because I should first have despised you, then rebelled against you, and finally I believe I should have run away from you. But I won't do that, William—not just yet !"

She put her arms round his neck, and looked at him with eyes loving enough to have melted a heart of stone. She might be a very fierce little woman still: undoubtedly she was impulsive and irrational sometimes ; but she loved him.

Dr. Stedman sat down again, and began to explain, repeating, though not quite so forcibly as at first, the many advantages of meeting the world on its own ground, and of guiding one's conduct by that intermediate rule between right and wrong — the law of expediency. No doubt all he said was very wise ; but he did not seem to say it with his heart in it, and there was an undertone of sarcasm which pained Edna much.

"I wonder," said she, "whether all the world is a sham and the encourager of shams?"·

"Or the dupe of them? It's a melancholy truth, Edna; but I do believe my only chance of getting a good practice is by pretending to have it already. Then, no doubt, I should soon become a successful physician."

"And if so, would you really enjoy it? Would you not rather despise the success that had been obtained by a lie?"

William started.

"You are awfully severe. Who spoke of telling lies?"

"An acted lie is just the same as a spoken one. And to spend money when you have it not, and do not know when you may have it, is nearly as bad as theft. Oh, William, I can't do it! I can't reconcile my conscience to it. You must act as you choose—I have no right to prevent you. Don't ask me ever to put my foot into your grand carriage, or to enjoy the prosperity that was purchased by a deception—a cheat!"

She spoke vehemently—the tears gushing from her eyes, and then she clung to her husband and begged his pardon.

"I have said it wrongly—violently; I know I have; but still I have said the truth. Oh, please listen to it! I want to be proud of you, William. I am so proud of you—the one man in the world that I am thankful to have for my husband and my—"

Edna stopped. Moved by some strong emotion, she hid her face, and began to tremble exceedingly.

William took her closer to him.

"What is the matter with you? My darling, what is wrong?"

"Nothing is wrong. Oh no! Only, will you listen to me?"

"Yes; say your say."

She repeated it—in quiet words this time, and Dr. Stedman listened also quietly; for he was too wise a man to be unreasonable.

"There, now, you speak like a rational woman," said he, smiling, "and you don't use bad language to your hus-

band, for it was very bad, Edna, my dear. 'Liar' and
'thief' I think you called me, or nearly so."

"Oh, William!"

"Well, I'm not quite that—at present. And, my darling, I own there is some little truth in what you say. I
am afraid I should not care for any success that was not
fairly earned—without need of resorting to a single sham.
And if it did not come—if I failed to make a practice after all, and found myself fathoms deep in debt, like some
poor wretches I know—"

"Still, that is not the question. I was not arguing as
to consequences. Dearest husband, don't do this, I be-
seech you, but only because it is *not right* to do it."

William paused a little—half thoughtful, half amused;
then he said, with a smile—

"Well, then, I won't. But, my little woman, if you
have to trudge on your two poor feet all your life-long,
remember it's not my fault. Now kiss and be friends."

Ay, they were "friends." Neither goddess and wor-
shipper—tyrant and slave—simply and equally friends.

"And now tell me, Edna, what you were going to say
just now when you broke off so abruptly, and got into
such a state of agitation as I never saw before? You
foolish little woman! Why were you so fierce with me?"

"Because I did not want you to do any thing not quite
right, or that you might afterwards be ashamed of, since
you will have to think not only of ourselves, but"—her
voice fell and her hand drooped—"of more than ourselves.
Because next summer, please God, if He keeps me safe
and alive—"

She threw herself on her husband's bosom in a passion
of tears, and he guessed all.

"I was afraid to tell you," Edna said, after a long silence, "you had so much anxiety, and this will add to it.
I know it must. Are *you* afraid? Are you sorry?"

"Sorry!" the young man cried, with all his soul in his
eyes, as he clasped his wife to his heart. "I sorry? Let
us thank God!"

CHAPTER XVII.

It was in sunshiny summer weather—like those days in the Isle of Wight when she was first married, that Edna's little baby came to her. The same evening there came to the tall elm-tree in their little bit of garden a blackbird, who, like Southey's thrush, took up his abode there, and sung—morning, noon, and night—his rich, loud, contented song to the mother, as she lay, a "happy prisoner," with her first-born by her side. In after-days, Edna never heard a blackbird's note without remembering that time, and its ecstasy of restful joy.

What need to write about it? a joy common as daylight—yet ever fresh: to the queen who gives an heir to millions, or the poor toiler in field or mill who brings only a new claimant for the inheritance of labor and poverty. But upon neither does the unknown future look with angry eye—the present is all in all. So it was with Edna. Her eldest son was born amidst considerable straitness of means and many anxieties; his mother made him no costly baby-clothes, nor welcomed him in a grand nursery, with every device of fantastic love: she only took him in her arms and rejoiced over him—as the Hebrew women rejoiced of old—her man-child, her gift from the Lord.

And William Stedman—the young man thrown ignorantly and unthinkingly, as most young men are, into the mystery and responsibility of fatherhood—how did he feel?

Whatever he felt, he said little: he was not in the habit of saying much—except to his wife. Nor, at first, did he take very much notice of the small creature in whom his own face was so funnily reproduced. But he never forgot something repeated to him by his sister-in-law during a certain fearful half hour when his wife lay, half conscious, her life hanging on a thread—"Tell William to be a *real* father to my poor baby."

Many a time, when nobody saw him, Dr. Stedman would creep in and look at his boy, a grave tender look, as if he were pondering on the future—his son's and his own—with infinite humility, yet without dread. More sadly wise than Edna in worldly things, and not having —no man has—that natural instinct for children which makes them a pure joy, and, at first, nothing else: yet it was clear that he too was striving to take up the conjoint burden of parenthood—accepting both its pleasantness and its pain; and so was likely to become worthy—oh, how few men are!—of being a father.

Letty did not understand her sister's felicity at all. She thought the baby would be a great trouble and a great expense, when they had cares enough already. She wondered how people could be so foolish as to marry unless they had every thing nice and comfortable about them— as was far from the case here, especially of late, when double work had fallen upon poor Letty's elegant shoulders. She had more than once declared that if ever a baby was born she would look out for a situation, and relieve her brother-in-law from the burden of her maintenance, and herself from the alarming duties of a maiden aunt. But Letty always talked of things much oftener than she did them; and besides— But it is useless attempting to analyze her motives; probably for the simple

reason that she had no motives at all. As she said one
day to Julius, who all this winter and spring had kept
coming and going, sometimes absenting himself for weeks,
then again appearing every evening at his brother's house,
to sit with Edna and Letty, though he paid the latter no
particular attention — "What did it matter where she
went or what she did ? nobody cared about her—she was
a solitary creature, and therefore quite free."

The evening she gave utterance to this pathetic sentiment Aunt Letty was a very lovely object to behold.
She had taken the baby ; for, though not enthusiastic over
it, she was a woman still, and liked to nurse it and "cud-
dle" it sometimes. As it lay asleep on her shoulder, with
one of its tiny hands clutching her finger, and her other
hand supporting it, she looked not unlike one of Raffaelle's
Madonnas.

"Stop a minute—just as you are; I want to sketch
you," said Julius, rousing himself from a long gaze—*not*
at the baby, for whom, though it was his namesake, Uncle
Julius had testified no exuberant admiration. But still, it
being safely asleep, he continued sitting with Letty in the
drawing-room, as he had got into a habit of doing of evenings, since Edna's disappearance up stairs.

"Dear me, Julius, I should think you were quite tired
of taking my likeness; but Edna will be in raptures if
you draw the baby."

Julius curled his satirical lip—more satirical and less
sweet than it once was, and then said, with a certain com-
punction, "Oh, very well; I'd do much to please Edna,
the dearest little woman that ever was born. How she
puts up with a fellow like me is more than I can tell. I
think—that night I walked our street with Will, and we
did not know but that she might slip away from us before
the morning, I would almost have given my life for poor
Edna's."

The voice was so full of feeling, that Aunt Letty opened her eyes wide to stare at Uncle Julius—only to stare ;
the penetrating, yet loving gleam of sympathy was not in
those large beautiful orbs of hers.

UNCLE AND AUNT.

"Not that my life would have been much of a gift," added Julius. "It is of little value now to me or to any body. Once, perhaps, and under different circumstances, it might have been."

Letty dropped her eyes. It was the first time her rejected lover had made any reference to those "circumstances," though she had sometimes tried, a little coquet-

tishly, to find out whether he remembered them or not.
For it was provoking, to say the least of it, that he should
so quickly have overcome a passion which he had vowed
would be eternal—that he could see her—Letty—in all
her fascinations, weekly, daily, if he so wished, and yet be
as apparently indifferent to her as he was to the many
other young ladies of his acquaintance, whom he was always talking about and criticising, as probably he criti-
cised her to them in return.   The idea rather vexed Letty.

She, and even his own brother, knew little of Julius's
life beyond what they saw when he made his erratic ap-
pearances and disappearances. Now, as of old, all his
brother's friends were his, but only a small proportion of
his friends were also his brother's. Julius cultivated a
class of intimacies which William had never cared much
for, and now cared less—the floating spin-drift of literary,
artistic, and semi-theatrical society—clever men, and not
bad men, at least nobody much knew whether they were
bad or good, and certainly nobody much cared, brains being of far greater use and at a far higher premium than
morals. With this set, lounging about during the day,
and meeting of nights at various well-known symposia
of men—only men, and not their wives, even if they had
any — Julius spent much of his time. But he never
brought these friends to his brother's house, or, indeed,
said much about them, except that they were "such jolly
clever fellows—so excessively amusing."

Amusement was, however, not his whole pursuit. He
sometimes took vehement fits of work, which lasted a day
or·two, perhaps a week or two; then he would throw up
his picture, in whatever stage it was, and devote himself
to every form of ingenious idling. In short, he was slowly drifting into that desultory, useless existence, grasping
at every thing and taking a firm hold of nothing, which,
without any actual vice, is the very opposite of that calm,
pure life—laborious and full of labor's reward—which is
the making of a real man.

And its effects were·already beginning to be painfully
apparent. Sallow checks, restless eyes, hand shaking and

nervous; brightening up towards night, but of mornings, as he confessed, utterly good for nothing except to lounge and smoke, or lie and sleep in thankful torpor—all these signs foreboded fatally for poor Julius. His brother began to doctor him for "dyspepsia;" but Edna, less learned, yet clearer-eyed, detected a something more—a sickness of the soul, far sadder, and more difficult of cure.

He who had no one to think of but himself, who earned a tolerable livelihood which he spent wholly upon himself, was beginning to look older and more anxious than his brother, with all his burdens.

Now, while Letty and Julius were talking lightly down stairs, in Edna's room overhead was a grave silence. William, coming in to spend a quiet hour beside his wife's sofa, had fallen dead asleep through sheer weariness. And Edna was watching him as Letty watched his brother, but with, oh! what a sort of different gaze! The difference which always had been, and would be to the last—eyes that said honestly, "I love you;" and the coquettish, down-dropped glance that inquired selfishly, "I wonder how much you love me?"

Women are often attracted by their opposites in men, and perhaps some woman, bright and wise, with large patience, and courage enough to sustain both herself and him, might have loved deeply and understood thoroughly this Julius Stedman. But Letty—beautiful Letty—was not that sort of woman. Therefore, while he made his last remark about his life being of no value to any body, she only sat and looked at him.

"Yes, mine is a wasted life, Letty. I shall end like that stranded ship on the Isle of Wight shore; you remember it?"

"Nonsense!" said Letty, blushing a little. "Or if it is so, it will be your own fault. You artists are always so miserably poor."

"Some of us do pretty well, though, if we run after titled patrons and high society. Or, if we happen to be especially fascinating, we marry rich wives, and—"

"Perhaps that is what you are thinking of doing?" interrupted Letty, with some acrimony. "Indeed it struck me there was more than met the eye in a hint Mrs. Marchmont gave me to-day, as I dare say Mr. Marchmont has given to you."

"What?" asked Julius, eagerly.

"That, if you liked to change your career, he thought so well of you, and of your extreme cleverness for every thing—business included—that he would take you into their house at once; first as a clerk, and then as a partner."

"'Marchmont and Stedman, indigo-planters!' How grand it would sound! What an enviable position!" said Julius, satirically; though not confessing whether or not the news had come upon him for the first time.

"Very enviable indeed," said Letty, gravely; "and especially with Miss Lily Marchmont to share it."

Julius winced, but turned it off with a laugh.

"Lily Marchmont—poor Lily! A nice creature! if she were only a little taller, and not quite so fat."

"She is getting as thin as a shadow now, at any rate," said Letty, in much annoyance. "But it is no use speaking to you, or trying to get any thing out of you, Julius. Indeed you're not worth thinking about."

"I was not aware you ever did me the honor to think about me at all."

"Oh yes," returned Letty, with an air of sweet simplicity. "Who could help it, when you are always here, and every body is so fond of you, and makes such a fuss over you? Edna told me that if any thing had happened to her, you were to come back and live here again. I was to tell you that she depended upon you to take care of and comfort William."

"Poor Edna—dear Edna—to fancy I could comfort any body! But this is ridiculous!" added he, abruptly. "Here are Edna and Will, both as jolly as possible, and that young rascal besides, to carry down the ugly name of Stedman to remotest ages. Every body is all right—except me—and as to what becomes of me, who cares? Not a soul in this mortal world. But I beg your pardon, and I am wasting your time. Just move your right hand,

The rich merchant's only child had fallen in love with the poor artist, frantically, desperately, and held to him with a persistent passion that, being concealed, came in time to sap the very springs of life. In fact, she was dying —merry, rosy-faced Lily Marchmont—dying literally of a broken heart. How far Julius was to blame nobody could say: he himself declared that he was not — that he had never made love to her, never intended such a thing. And when at last—Lily's secret being discovered—her miserable parents betrayed it to him, and made him this proposal for her sake, he declined it. Whatever he had done, he did the right thing now. He was too honorable to degrade a woman by marrying her for mere pity, when he felt not an atom of love.

"You did right," said Will, with energy. "And all this was going on, and we knew nothing—you kept it so close. What you must have suffered, my poor fellow!"

"Never mind me; there's another I think of much more. Poor little thing! God forgive me all the misery I have caused her!" And could she have seen Julius then, Lily might have felt herself half avenged.

"Does she know about Letty?"

"Yes; I told her — clear and plain. It was the only honest thing to do. But it signifies little now; she is dying; and before she dies she wants her parents to adopt me as a son—to take me into the house of business, either in London or Calcutta—only fancy my going out to Calcutta!—first as a clerk, with a rising salary, and then as a partner. She settled it all, poor girl, and her father came and implored me to accept. But I never thought of it, not for one minute, till they told Letty, and Letty urged me to agree. She has no scruples about poor little Lily."

"And Lily?"

"Lily only thinks of Letty—that is, of me through her. She wants me to be happy with Letty when she is gone. Oh, it's a queer world!"

Will thought so too, as he recalled the merry little girl, whose governess his wife had been, who had now and then come to his house, and whom he knew Edna was fond of